21 0439155

D0229729

£21-00

WITHDRAWN

STRATEGY AND STRUCTURE OF
ENTERPRISE IN A DEVELOPING COUNTRY

To my parents, my husband, my brother Tony, and my three children for their love and support.

Strategy and Structure of Enterprise in a Developing Country

CHI. B. ANYANSI-ARCHIBONG
University of Kansas

Avebury

Aldershot · Brookfield USA · Hong Kong · Singapore · Sydney

Published by
Avebury
Gower Publishing Company Limited
Gower House
Croft Road
Aldershot
Hants GU11 3HR
England

Gower Publishing Company
Old Post Road
Brookfield
Vermont 05036
USA

British Library Cataloguing in Publication Data

Anyansi-Archibong, Chi. B.
  Strategy and structure of enterprise in a developing country.
  1. Management—Nigeria
  I. Title
  658'.009669   HD70.N5

Library of Congress Cataloging-in-Publication Data

Anyansi-Archibong, Chi. B., 1949—
  Strategy and structure of enterprise in a developing country.

  Bibliography: p.
  Includes index.
  1. Industrial management—Nigeria. 2. Industrial management—Social aspects—Nigeria. 3. Nigeria—Colonial influence. 4. Industry and state—Nigeria.
  I. Title.
  HD70.N43A59 1987   658'.009669   87—12020

ISBN 0 566 05471 X

Contents

Figures

Tables

Abbreviations

CMD	Centre for Management Development
ECOWAS	Economic Community of West African States
GDP	gross domestic product
ICON	International Commerce Organization of Nigeria
NAMSET	Nigerian Association of Schools of Management Education and Training
NCMD	Nigerian Council for Management Development
NEPB	Nigerian Enterprises Promotion (Act)
NIDB	National Industrial Development Bank
R&D	research and development
SFEM	Second-tier Foreign Exchange Market
SIM	Sudan Interior Mission
UAC	United African Company

Preface

This book represents a field research effort to study the evolution of strategy and structure of enterprise in a developing economy. The book provides a model of stages of development of a firm which would ultimately serve as a framework for appropriate management technology.

The contents of the book have their origins in an academic exercise involving a three-phase research. The first phase of library research provided evidence for the utmost need of the study. Literature reviews show that between 1962 and 1980 several works were published on the strategy and structure of enterprise in such countries as the United States of America, France, England, Italy, Germany and Japan. A common factor among the above countries is that they are developed. There was no study on a developing country.

In exploring strategy and structure in this African country – Nigeria, the possible effect of culture and the extended family system were closely examined. Also emphasized was the influence of colonization on entrepreneurial management style. The study shows that culture has a major influence on management techniques, that structure does not always follow strategy as studies in developed economies indicate, and that transfer of management technology from the developed to the developing economy could be very dysfunctional. The dynamic, generic model described in the book makes it possible for other developing nations to create the most appropriate management techniques for their economies.

The book is arranged in such a way that the reader will first acquaint him/herself with the type of environment studied prior to the detailed analysis of the findings. The methodology applied and the benefits of the book are also presented in several appendices.

Several people contributed to the successful completion of this work and I would like to extend my immense gratitude to them. To Professors Marilyn Taylor, Howard Baumgartel, V.K. Narayanan, John Garland and Kenneth MacKenzie, all of the University of Kansas, for their assistance and support. My respect and gratitude to Dean J. Tollelson. My appreciation to Dr B.L. Barnes of Harvard Business School, Dr Harry Levinson of the Levinson Institute, Professors S. Paul and M. Saiyadan of the Indian Institute of Management for their time and collaboration in defining the numerous variables covered in the study.

Credit goes to several organizations and directors of institutions for making the necessary data available. These include the set of Nigerian organizations who participated in the field study phase, their chairmen and individuals such as Dr Udo Udo-Aka, Dr Fadehunsi, Dr Oworen and Dr Fasanya of the Center for Management Development (CMI). As much as the names of the firms in the study must remain anonymous, I acknowledge them as the key contributors to the understanding of the solution of enterprise.

I am also indebted to Donna Hutline for transcribing my interviews, and to Alice Fitzgerald and Laverne C. Aikens for typing the manuscripts.

Dr Chi Anyansi-Archibong
August 1987

Foreword

It is doubtful that at the time of its publication anyone, especially the scholarly gentleman who authored the work, expected the effect of strategy and structure to move so directly through multiple generations of scholars. Yet that is exactly the effect of Professor Chandler's classic work. During the 1970s a group of young scholars led by such a worthy master scholar/teacher as Dr Bruce Scott examined the phenomena of strategy and structure in other developed/industrial nations, including Channon in Britain, Dias in France, Pavan in Italy, and Thanheiser in Germany. Not surprisingly these authors found the phenomena similar in these settings.

Yet, there are 150 countries in which to examine the phenomena. And they still await the examination of the phenomena within their boundaries. Perhaps also not surprisingly, only one of the most tenacious would undertake the task. What have been the patterns of development and evolution in business organizations in a developing country, specifically Nigeria? Professor Anyansi-Archibong brings multiple skills to the task and concern for both country, organizations and the people making them up in reporting the phenomena and drawing her conclusions.

The work, like that of Chandler, is a significant one — the result of months spent criss-crossing the country to meet with organizational participants, examine written documentation, and observe participants on site. Indeed, before returning to Nigeria to begin the fieldwork, the author had spent an equal number of months in correspondence to identify appropriate organizations and obtain permission for entry.

And after exit, again, the months were required to write up the results, examine the resulting case studies for similarities and differences, to obtain permissions for release, and finally to put the results in the form that we have herein. As with any task of this nature, the work is monumental and requires the perseverance of a Job.

Perhaps not surprisingly, the author's findings have resulted in two major differences from the earlier work. Part of the explanation of these differences results from the emphasis in seeking data and part from the setting itself.

In the first place, the author was sensitive to the role that family, extended or nuclear, would play in the evolution of an organization that remained in family control. While similar data were present in other settings, in no other setting did the organization exist so strongly controlled by and run for the benefit of the family. Indeed in other settings the time periods to be examined were longer since the organizations in this study trace their establishment only from the Second World War and later.

Second, it is significant that the author finds that government action has a strong effect on the evolution of the firm. Again, data were present in other settings. The effect of the First World War on the DuPont company and the aftermath of the Second World War demographics on Sears are two examples. However, these earlier authors did not see this connection so vividly. This can only be speculated. Even in this study, the author did not originally expect to find such a strong effect. However, in Nigeria two major historical effects, the arrival and departure of the British, and the more recent actions of the government to wean the country's organizations from their dependence on foreign influences have encouraged, nay, impelled the business organizations into strategic diversification. The effect of government action on business is known. In this work its effect is vividly portrayed. Indeed this work is important reading for any government official in a developing country that is considering similar moves.

In addition, scholars will find the work fascinating. Dr Anyansi-Archibong's work clearly portrays her commitment to the tradition and values of clinical work. Business practitioners, in developed countries, will value the portrayal of the family firm with both its richness of human talent and the frailties of its conflicts. Those managing firms in developing countries will resound with empathy to the throes of the evolutionary forces both within and outside of the firms.

We are indebted to this work. But even more clearly it indicates the monumental nature of the original work in this field which inspired it. To Dr Chandler, who provided for us a base on which to challenge yet another generation of scholars, we voice our thanks. To Dr Anyansi-Archibong for daring to step in giant steps, we voice our cheers, our congratulations, and also our thanks.

Marilyn L. Taylor
Associate Professor of Strategic Management
Co-Director, Field Studies Programme
School of Business
University of Kansas
Lawrence, Kansas 66045
August 1987

1 Introduction

This book presents the study of an evolution pattern of enterprise in a Third World country. Since the Third World or developing countries began planning[1] to use industrial enterprise to improve their economic development status, there have been questions about the appropriateness of using management techniques of developed countries in these developing nations.

Many management theorists and authors of cultural studies have perennially addressed the issue of transfer of management techniques developed in one culture to another (Sarpong and Rawls, 1976; Jaiger, 1984; Keesing, 1974; Beckhard, 1969; Hofstede, 1980). However, few, if any, practical steps have been taken to change the situation. The purpose of this study is not to do a complete review of management techniques nor the nature of culture-boundedness. Rather, this study was undertaken to demonstrate the differences in culture and the need to learn more about organizations in other cultures. This understanding is intended to serve as a basis for the development of appropriate management techniques.

To understand the above need, it is necessary to define and describe what is meant by developing country, and by the concept of culture.

Developing country

The term 'developing country', as applied in this study, is used to reflect the economic status of Nigeria's industrial society in relation to that of industrially developed countries such as the United States of America.

It is internationally accepted that those countries with less than 10 per cent of manufacturing contribution to total domestic production are non-industrial developed countries (underdeveloped); those with between 10 and 20 per cent as semi-industrial developed (developing); and those with above 30 per cent are industrialized (developed). If these rough signposts are accepted, it shows from Table 1.1 that Nigeria would be a non-industrial or underdeveloped country if the government-controlled petroleum and mining sector is excluded.

However, in this study, the petroleum and mining sector was included in the manufacturing sector, thereby classifying Nigeria as a semi-industrial or developing country as of the end of 1983. A developing country, therefore, is not industrialized nor modernized according to Kahls' (1968) definition of these terms.[2]

Culture

It is necessary to understand the word 'culture' in order to understand what is meant by 'culture group'. Many management researchers view culture as a set of ideas shared by members of a culture group. However, culture is not an individual characteristic but, rather, denotes the fact that a set of common theories of behaviour or mental programmes are shared by a group of individuals.

In a broader perspective, Schien (1981) has described three levels of culture. These perspectives are

1 basic assumptions and premises;
2 values and ideology;
3 artifacts and creations.

The first level includes such things as the relationship of man to nature, time orientation, beliefs about human nature, the nature of man's relationship to man and man's concept of space and his place in it. These premises are often taken for granted. The middle level includes values and ideology, indicating ideals and goals, as well as paths on how to 'get there'. The third level includes such things as language, technology and social organization. Each successive level is, to an extent, a manifestation of the one before it and all the levels are thus interrelated. From these definitions, one can see that the culture of a group or society is a fairly deep-rooted phenomenon which, in most management situations, must be taken as given.

Also, several other studies have shown evidence of the significant influence of environmental and cultural factors on management

Table 1.1 Nigeria: Percentage of Gross Domestic Product derived from occupational sectors at current prices (1984) 1960–1983

	1960 %	1965 %	1970 %	1975 %	1980 %	1981 %	1982 %	1983 %
Agriculture	63.2	60.1	44.6	26.2	22.9	21.4	20.8	21.5
Mining, Petroleum and Quarrying	1.2	4.9	12.0	23.7	21.5	20.4	18.1	17.5
Manufacturing	4.8	6.2	7.7	7.5	7.2	8.5	8.3	7.1
Electricity, Gas and Water	0.3	0.6	0.6	0.3	0.5	0.6	0.8	0.9
Construction	4.6	5.3	6.3	7.3	9.8	10.6	10.7	11.2
Transport and Communications	3.0	3.5	3.3	3.6	4.2	4.9	5.8	6.2
Wholesale and Retail Trade	9.0	10.2	12.2	17.7	21.9	22.6	23.3	20.5
Housing	2.4	1.5	3.5	4.2	3.9	3.0	3.2	3.6
Government Services	3.9	3.5	5.3	6.5	4.2	4.6	4.9	5.1
Other Services	8.6	4.2	4.5	3.0	3.9	3.4	4.1	5.9
Total Gross Domestic Product	100	100	100	100	100	100	100	100

Source: Prof. Sam Aluko, 'The Progress of Industrialization in Nigeria since Independence', *Daily Times*, 1 October 1984, p. 3.

effectiveness. Thus, for the developing countries to utilize their resources effectively, there is the need to learn more about the evolution of the organizations which have become the machinery for economic development.

Strategy and structure

The concepts of strategy structure and their interrelationships within organizations have been of great interest to both practitioners and researchers. Although there has been no consensus in the definition of strategy and its relations to structure, several authors have put forward

3

definitions and processes of formulation, analysis and evaluation.

Andrews (1980),[3] one of the early proponents of strategic management, defined corporate strategy as:

> the pattern of decision in a company that determines and reveals its objectives, purposes, or goals, produces the principal policies and plans for achieving those goals, and defines the range of businesses the company is to pursue, the kind of economic and human organization it is or intends to be, and the nature of the economic and non-economic contributions it intends to make to its shareholders, employees, customers, and communities.

Andrews distinguished between corporate and business strategy and the fact that strategy is effective over a long period of time, 'affects the company in many different ways, and focuses and commits a significant portion of its resources to the expected outcome'.

It is obvious from the above that the strategy defined by Andrews is the type that is applicable to large corporations. These corporations are mostly diversified and operate in a relatively stable environment.

Chandler (1962)[4] viewed strategy as:

> the determination of the basic long-term goals and objectives of an enterprise, and the adoption of the courses of action and the allocation of resources necessary for carrying out these goals. . . . New courses of action must be devised and resources allocated and reallocated . . . in response to shifting demands changing sources of supply, fluctuating economic conditions, new technological developments, and the actions of competitors.

Chandler went further to indicate that the adoption of a new strategy affects the form (structure) of the organization as a result of the addition of new types of personnel and facilities. Chandler thus defined structure as the design of organization through which the enterprise is administered. The thesis further deduced that structure follows strategy and that the most complex type of structure is the result of the concatenation of several basic strategies.

The deduction in this study is that structure does not always follow strategy. Relative to Chandler's theme that 'changes in strategy which called for changes in structure appear to have been in response to the opportunities and needs created by changing population and changing national income and by technological innovation', the theme in this study is that changes in strategy and structure were in response to the problems and needs created by political changes, economic instability, lack of opportunity for technological innovation and multicultural practices.

For the purpose of this study, strategy is defined as the development of new courses of action (enter new market, create new product, increase or decrease operation, etc.) to be followed by an organization in order to survive in a changing environment. All moves to enter new industry or carry new products are referred to as 'diversification', moves to produce raw materials are referred to as 'backward integration', and moves to expand volume of sales through acquisition or development of new channels of distribution is 'forward integration'.

A basic approach to structure is adopted in this study. Thus, structure is defined as a 'pattern of interaction among a group of participants'.[5] Development of a table of interaction pattern depicts the sender, the receiver and the intensity of participations. Structure is, therefore, relative and there are more appropriate structures for different groups. It is difficult to determine why people interact the way they do thereby creating structure. Nonetheless it can be argued that they do so to satisfy various needs. Therefore, structure in this study is a need-satisfying interaction pattern which changes with the changing needs of participants.

This study obviously cannot solve this problem of shortage or non-existence of appropriate management techniques for the Third World culture, but it is my intent to make some modest contribution towards the creation of a basis for the development of such appropriate management techniques and theories. My interest in this study springs from many reasons — excluding the situation described above — stemming from:

1 The absence of literature on the organizations of the Third World. How can one design a management technique or model without an understanding of both the internal and external environment of such organizations? This need is important because a better understanding of Third World enterprise may help check the inflow of inappropriate technologies (learning, management, manufacturing, etc.). The brief description and statistics on Nigeria as a Third World country in this introductory chapter is followed by a more detailed description of the economic and social processes in Chapter 2, which was developed to help the reader better understand the findings of the study.

2 Another source of interest for the research develops from the observation that family firms in both developed and developing countries are growing and have become strategically important to the economic development and stability of these countries. Because of the family's centrality in any nation's culture, study of the family firm could be considered study of the relationships/conflict between culture and management techniques, especially those techniques borrowed from a non-indigenous (foreign) culture. Some research has been completed on family firms in the USA, but no research has been completed on family firms in a developing

5

country such as Nigeria. This study delves into the processes of these firms and thus addresses the issues of the relationships between the family and the firm's ability to grow from one stage to another.

3 A further source of interest is the increasing application of systematic training programmes by indigenous businesses in Nigeria. A survey by the Nigeria Centre for Management Development shows that there was an over 20 per cent increase by 1982 (over 1980) in the number of Nigerian businesses using management consultancy services in Nigeria and abroad. These services are based on imported management materials.

Other implications of this study are presented in Appendix 1.A. Problem definition and scope are also the subject of this chapter. Three research questions are developed. These questions are selected to effect an integration of some of the factors influencing organizational development and also call for an exploratory research technique. The design and application of the methodology is described in Appendix 1.C.

Chapter 4 discusses the evolution patterns of enterprise in Nigeria, as well as the management characteristics observed at each of the stages of development. Chapter 5 discusses the characteristics of a traditional business strategy and structure and also describes the impact of both government actions and other ecological factors on strategies and structures developed by the firms' studies. Development of diversification strategies is discussed. Factors affecting diversification are presented with emphasis on the impact of external environmental variables.

Chapter 2 presents the development of structures and basic interaction patterns. Chapter 6, using the findings in the study, summarizes the management practices identified including entrepreneurship and family focus interface. Chapter 7 integrates such issues as comparison of Western management theories with such practices described in. Chapter 2; management problems identified and suggestions practices in developing countries are systematically analyzed and presented in Chapter 8.

To understand the historical evolution of organizations' strategy and structures requires more than the exploration of the terms and concepts. It demands presentation and explanation of historical situations within and outside the organization. Such a historical information may be supplied by a general survey of large organizations in Nigeria. Nonetheless this study provides a more detailed history through case studies of some organizations. These cases indicate the causes and trends in strategy and structure of organization. A major impact on the processes identified is the macro-environment and this factor is the subject of discussion in Chapter 3.

Notes

1   Examples of planning objectives include Nigeria's four national development plans. The first four-year plan was designed in 1962, two years after the country's independence from Great Britain. Each of the four 'five-year' plans contained the major objective of industrialization through effective enterprise.

In 1975, 15 West African heads of state met in Lagos, Nigeria, to sign a treaty establishing the Economic Community of West African States (ECOWAS). ECOWAS' main objective was to promote growth through regional interdependence. The signatory countries have undertaken to abolish obstacles to effective trade (goods and services), movement of people; to promote joint agricultural policy, projects in marketing and research and industrial enterprise.

Barbara Harrel-Bond, *ECOWAS — The Economic Community of West African States*, American Universities Field Staff Report, no. 6 (Africa), Hanover, NH, 1979.

2   Definitions:
Industrialization: Comote described a modern society as including such things as a small proportion of workers in agriculture; the application of technology to production; urbanism, a complex, commercial and industrial economy; a relatively open stratification system; an emphasis on education and communications; and rations, secular values. An example of such a society is the United States or other developed Western nations. This is a more elusive term which may occur apart from industrialization.

3   K.R. Andrews, *The Concept of Corporate Strategy*, Richard D. Irwin, Inc., Homewood, I11., 1980, pp. 18—24.

4   A.D. Chandler, *Strategy and Structure. Chapters in the History of the American Industrial Enterprise*, MIT Press, Cambridge MA, 1962, pp. 13—15.

5   K.D. Mackenzie, *Organizational Structures*, AHM Publishers Corporation, Arlington Heights, I11, 1978, pp. 9—11.

Appendix 1.A Research development

Introduction

Several factors influenced the development of this research, and thus the book. My experiences with western managerial literature and a strong grasp of the Nigerian socio-economic status is one of the factors. This study was intended to determine whether findings in several studies done in the United States and other Western European countries on patterns of organizational development also applied in a developing nation. The research problem, purpose, scope and literature review are described in the following paragraphs.

Definition of the research problem

Ever since Rostow's (1960) book on the stages of economic growth, several authors such as Chandler (1962), Wrigley (1970), Scott (1971), have developed themes of ideal types of organizations and of stages of organizational development. However, theories of organizational development go beyond ideal types and, explicit in a number of these theories, is the notion of longer stability periods and shorter evolutionary ones (Greiner, 1972). Other major authors (Burns and Stalker, 1966; Lawrence and Lorsch, 1967; Thompson, 1967; Miles and Snow, 1978) provided empirical support for the existence of clusters of attributes or 'constellations' in organizations which would seem to resemble ideal types. But these authors and others (Galbraith, 1979;

Pfeffer, 1978) have also emphasized the impact of socio-economic factors on organizations' growth patterns. These studies, however, have been carried out mostly in the developed nations of the world and it is therefore questionable whether the application of these findings in developing nations is appropriate.

Of major importance in the Nigerian environment in particular were the findings in the studies by Gilmore (1978) and Sarpong and Rawls (1976). These authors maintain that management training and education programmes in African countries have a very high percentage of foreign consultants who are responsible for developing most of the training and educational courses. These programmes are usually based on Western cultures and assumptions, thereby leaving one to wonder about their effectiveness in a setting such as Nigeria. In spite of the obvious need to further our understanding of companies in developing nations, few or no studies of the evolution patterns of firms have been done in developing countries.

Socio-economic variables such as income level, state of industrial development, technology, education level and culture/norms in general were considered as possible variables for this study. But further interviews suggested the prevalence of privately controlled firms and their contributions to the developing countries' economy. The problem is that these family firms have been understudied. In a developed country such as the United States, there has been a swing in the literature of organizational theory on issues of privately/family owned and/or controlled firms. (Trow, 1961; Levinson, 1971, 1983; Barnes and Hershon, 1976; Longnecker and Shoen, 1978; Filley and Aldage, 1978, 1980; Beckhard and Dyer, 1983; Schien, 1981; Landsberg, 1983; Davis, 1983; Kepner, 1983.) These authors, particularly Levinson and Davis, point out that there are transitional and policy problems specific to private firms and that appropriate resolution of these problems is necessary for the firms' continuing evolution.

In a developing country like Nigeria, the government is offering incentives in terms of loans, tax credits and subsidies to encourage continued growth in the private sector. This effort is in recognition of the contribution of private enterprise to the economy. Of the over one million major businesses in the USA, 94 per cent are privately held and family-dominated, including many of the largest companies. (Barnes and Hershon, 1976; Hollander, 1984). In Nigeria these family controlled firms have always been the major part of the private business sector (Registry of Companies, 1984). Family-controlled firms need to be economically effective for the respective governments to meet their economic objectives. Because a nation's culture has a major influence on managerial characteristics and practices, it is therefore necessary to understand the evolution of the organizations in order

9

to develop appropriate management theories and models for that culture.

With the above background and some correspondence with company executives and consultants in Nigeria, the final research questions were developed. This study specifically addressed the following questions:

1 How do firms evolve in a developing country such as Nigeria? (Are patterns of evolution in a developing nation similar to or different from those found in a developed nation?)
2 How do family 'constellations' influence the firm's pattern of evolution?
3 How do processes of conflict resolution in the privately held firms affect (speed, slow, smooth, etc.) their transition from one stage of evolution to another?

Purpose of research

This study was undertaken because of the existing need to learn more about organizations in developing countries. The theme is to determine the evolution patterns of these organizations in order to provide an appropriate database for the development of better management theories and management education programmes.

Major writers on social change (Rostow, 1960; Hagen, 1962; McClelland and Winter, 1969; McClelland, 1972; and Lauer, 1982) suggest that ideological and cultural factors influence change. These authors also maintain that patterns of change or development differ across societies. Nigeria is a developing country relative to countries such as the USA, the UK and other Western European countries. However, by autumn 1984, most of the management education text books and programmes used in Nigeria were based on data collected from these industrially advanced or the developed countries. In a few educational institutions where case methods of teaching were used, available cases were also those developed on companies in developed countries.

This study therefore yields multiple benefits to several kinds of audiences. These audiences include management training and educational institutions, the government, founders/managers of privately held firms, family members, consultants, and society.

Scope of research

In an effort to determine whether findings from studies in developed countries were applicable to developing countries, the research explores the evolution patterns of privately held and/or controlled firms in Nigeria and compares findings to the evolution stages determined in the economies of developed nations. The study also examines the social and economic environment of Nigeria. These socio-economic factors include some of the demographic variables, the political status and the historical development of the country — pre- and post-colonial era and pre- and post-independence from Great Britain. These environmental factors are the focus of Chapter 3. While examining the general environmental factors, the study also concentrates on the social anthropology of the Nigerian family. This focus is to establish an understanding of the patterns of behaviour exhibited by the privately held firms. Apart from the social anthropology of the family in general, select family firms were examined and methods of conflict resolution explored and compared to the established factors and mechanisms in the developed countries.

In general, the research investigated any relationship between patterns of organizational development, family constellation and other factors influencing the firm's ability to move from one stage of development to another. In conclusion, the research relates the findings of this study to those of past theories and also determines possible future research questions, and frameworks for models and theory development.

Implications of this study

The first set of implications to be discussed is that for management training and educational institutions. There are several management training centres, colleges and universities in Nigeria including the Nigerian Institute of Management, Nigerian Personnel Management Centre, Centre for Management Development, University of Lagos, Nsukka,[1] and many colleges of technology. However, the Centre for Management Development (CMD) was established in 1973 by the federal government 'to define industrial priorities, help in the implementation of the indigenization program by providing citizens with necessary guidelines for buying, establishing and running effective organizations'.[2] CMD was selected for focus because of its functions, especially as a coordinator between the government, its agencies, and private organizations. Before the end of 1978, the Centre extended its services to small-scale industries by establishing the Small Scale Services Division. This division maintains direct contact with the industrialists through the Nigerian Association of Small Scale Industries, which has chapters in each of the nineteen states in the country.

According to Dr Fadehunsi, Director of Management Services at

CMD, the Centre organizes conferences at different locations, using 'tailor-made' programmes for development training. However, a paper published by Dr Udo Udo-Aka, Director General of CMD,[3] concluded that there was a need for immediate and major improvement in the management training programmes. This improvement was intended to create a more effective management training and education for existing and future managers. In Dr Udo-Aka's words,

> Although comments on the quality of management technical skills is favourable, however, the types of subjects in courses have raised eyebrows. Vital courses are conspicuously absent. In almost all Nigerian universities where there are business schools, classes are very large, . . . educators find the lecture method convenient and most practicable . . . . The use of case studies is very rare and when they are used, they are mostly imported cases which most of the time do not quite apply to the Nigerian situation.[4]

The above comment clearly brings out the implications of this study for management training and development programmes. Eight cases were developed from the study and will make some major contributions to a better management education in the country. Also, the writer is developing a note on case writing and its uses. This paper is designed to inspire and encourage the cooperation of Nigerian executives in the development of adequate classroom and training cases.

Apart from the above issue which is specific to Nigeria, other writers have suggested that there is one major weakness often identified by studies on management training and education programmes in Africa. Often, because of the high percentage of foreign management consultants or educators responsible for this training and development, the programmes are more Western-oriented (Gilmore, 1978; Olayemi, 1977; Rake, 1979; Sarpong and Rawls, 1976). These observations suggest that African managers may not be appropriately trained to manage firms developed in their environment. This study therefore contributes to the development of management education by depicting the differences and/or similarities in the evolution pattern and management styles between developed and developing countries.

In specifically academic terms, the study provides a database for further research study. From the information gathered in this project, I expect, with the cooperation of the firms participating in the study, to develop cases appropriate for university classrooms and management development sessions. The Nigerian Association of Schools of Management Education and Training (NAMSET), which was formed in 1978 by the Nigerian Council for Management Development (NCMD), has emphasized the need to bridge the gap between the private businesses and public organizations on one side and the business schools on the other. NAMSET urges business organizations to fund research and cooperate with lecturers (professors) in consulting projects. This study emphasizes similar issues but leans more on the involvement of graduate business students in the development of more indigenous cases for management and training programmes. In general, many international academic institutions and associations will also be exposed to the cultures and organizational evolution processes of a developing country through the medium of indigenous cases.

In the light of the above scarcity and need expressed by both the government and its agencies, this study provides the raw materials for some useful articles and a management book that is based on a field study of Nigerian enterprises.

The government has established plans and programmes to encourage the economic development of the country, especially its industrial sector. It has also realized that it is not just enough to create opportunities for the indigenes to own and control organizations. For this reason the CMD was established one year after the indigenization problem was identified. However, the approach being used by the CMD is limited and does not provide easy access to many who could contribute to the effective management programmes. The objective of CMD, as stated earlier, is to 'educate and help indigenes run the new firm-type organization'. In this effort CMD staff request companies to register for the training sessions. The majority of clients come from public and small-scale firms. There was no explicit effort to encourage large private firms to get involved and these people often turn to private foreign management consultants for their training needs. This process, therefore, brings us back to the issue of possible inappropriate training programmes.

This group of firms, as shown in the statistics in Chapter 1, is representative of over 60 per cent of the country's established companies. If the government is to meet its objectives of improved development, these firms have to be effectively managed. The first step towards the development of adequate management programmes is to determine the problems facing them. This study has taken an initial step toward determination of some of these problems. More field studies are needed to understand the operations of these firms and their interaction with the environment. The understanding of a company's culture and environment is the key to adaptation and innovation, while the existence of these (adaptation and innovation) aid companies' survival and growth. It is necessary to develop closer and more understanding relationships between universities and business organizations in order to expand and build a mutual assistance for each. The planned note on cases developed by the writer is intended to begin developing these relationships.

Founder/manager, family and employees

Major US writers on privately held family business (Davis, 1983; Beckhard, 1983; Hollander, 1984; Levinson, 1984; Barnes and Hershon, 1976) spoke of family firms and their management as that of systems management. These authors suggested that many factors contribute to the difficulties and problems often facing them. Beckhard suggested that the 'fate of family firms goes way beyond its own organization'. It affects the members of the family, the employees, and the community at large. This issue was also echoed by both Barnes and Hershon, and Levinson.

Levinson and the other writers mentioned maintain that a major issue facing the family firm is the attitude and actions of the founder, who is a member of both the family and the firm as separate and intertwined systems. The founder sees both systems as his and would not welcome any challenge or criticism to their management, not even from family or professional managers. In essence, what these authors are saying is that these firms are special and they need to be understood in order for others to consult or work in them.

In Nigeria, this group of private, family owned/managed firms currently dominates the business sector. However, whether the community of management schools recognize the importance of family firms or not, these firms have exclusive management that are yet to be analyzed. Data from this study indicate that unlike the situation in the United States, where research in this area has just begun, no study of this nature exists in Nigeria. This study and future related ones are necessary to make everyone concerned aware of the issues that affect the success or failure of these companies. An understanding of the difficulties or problems in a situation is very important to its solution, especially to the consultant.

Consultant

This study has major implications for both current and future consultants to the family business. The findings aim at bringing out the issues involved, thereby acquainting any potential consultant with the fact that he or she is not only dealing with an economic objectively based firm or organization, but with an emotionally filled set of systems composed of the immediate family, the firm, other relatives, and non-family employees. The study also exposes the consultant to the 'private and tight-lipped nature' of these companies, thereby helping him develop an appropriate approach to effective consultation.

Certainly, the family, the society, and government will benefit from the survival and growth of these firms.

Society

Private enterprises have been recognized to contribute immensely to the economic development of countries. In Nigeria, history has it that there has never been any successful government corporation in the country, irrespective of the fact that this type of corporation and foreign firms had dominated the nation's business sector up until 1972 when the 'indigenization' programme began to make profound changes. Since that time, private and/or family firms have been able to grow economically, provide jobs for the masses, and contribute to the Gross Domestic Product. (In the USA, the 95 per cent of private/family controlled firms employ over 43 per cent of the labour force and contribute over 60 per cent of the GDP.)

Nigerian privately held firms in particular play various roles both at the national and local community levels. Data from this study show that the successes and failures of private firms usually extend to many outside the organization. Evidence exists to show that private firms in their growth strategies tend to locate their factories in their communities, thereby initiating and hastening the development of some necessary infrastructures in the community. In many cases they provide employment to the unskilled labour force usually abundant in these rural areas, thereby reducing the migration into the few cities. They also help reduce poverty by their philanthropic gestures often aimed towards their local communities.

In the field of management this study is expected to make some substantial contribution. In the division of international management, the study will contribute to the development of management techniques by identifying relevant managerial values in developing countries. It will also contribute indigenous properties of the organization for relevant strategic management decisions.

Notes

1 Lagos and Nsukka are cities in Nigeria where the universities are located. Lagos is also the capital of Nigeria and Nsukka is in Anambra state.
2 See appendix 1.B for more functions and structures of the Centre for Management Development.

3   Udo-Aka, Udo, 'Toward the Indigenization of Management Educa-
    tion in Nigeria', Administrative Staff College of Nigeria (ASCON),
    Journal of Management, 1981.
4   The Director General (Dr Udo-Aka) indicated that CMD is making
    efforts to publish some local cases.

Appendix 1.B   Background and functions of the Centre for Management Development (Nigeria)

Source: Centre for Management Development, 1983, Loo Press Ltd, Lagos
ISBN 978-140-014-5

INTRODUCTION

The Centre for Management Development (CMD) is a Federal Government parastatal established in January 1973 to coordinate the activities of, and give proper direction to, institutions engaged in training and retraining of managerial personnel in Nigeria.

The Centre is the operational arm of the Nigerian Council for Management Development (NCMD), its governing Council, whose existence since 1972 was formalised by Act 51 of October 4, 1976.

The Centre's headquarters in Lagos, christened Management Village, Shangisha which is located on the right hand side of Lagos/Ibadan Expressway, before the tollgate, occupies an area of 15.7 hectares.

BRIEF HISTORY OF CMD

The need to establish the Nigerian Council for Management Development and its optional arm, the Centre for Management Development, was first recognized in a meeting of the National Manpower Board which was held on October 20, 1965. The meeting, while deliberating on a report on productivity in industry, observed that a major bottleneck in the effort to raise productivity was the comparatively low quality of management at all levels. The meeting also noted that while a considerable number and variety of facilities for management training were available in the country, the lack of effective coordination and the absence of a central source of information led to wastage and unnecessary duplication of courses. The Manpower Board then directed its secretariat to initiate action on the establishment of an organization that would ensure that courses reflect in frequency, level and types, the needs of the country's economy, and that would devise means to eliminate unnecessary duplication of management courses.

Following consultations with various providers and users of management training, the Nigerian Council for Management Education and Training was established in 1968 to coordinate management training programmes. However, the informal nature of the Council, lack of adequate support for its running and the intervention of the civil war prevented positive development of the Council. It is therefore no surprise that this first experiment in planned coordination of management education and training at the national level did not meet even the most modest expectations.

This initial setback did not obviate the need for adequate supply of well trained and experienced managers nor did it discourage those concerned from making further efforts, in the interest of the nation's fast growing economy, to achieve the objectives for which the Council had been established.

In fact the need for well coordinated management programmes was reemphasized in 1969 by an International Labor Organization (ILO) Report which discovered that although various management training programmes were offered to meet limited needs and interests, there was an appalling lack of coordination in the areas of contents and standards. Some of the organizations offering programmes served only their own staff or limited the coverage of their courses to functional or geographical areas or levels of management. None was paramount in terms of coverage, thoroughness or reputation and none had the staff or resources to offer programmes to more than a limited range of management interests.

The formulation of the Second National Development Plan, 1970–74, provided the Federal Government the opportunity to reaffirm its commitment to the development of adequate executive capacity for the country. The Government therefore decided, as a project under the Plan, to reconstitute the Council which in composition, operational machinery and facilities, would be able to play an effective role in the country's manpower development. It also decided to set up the Centre as the machinery through which the council would achieve its objectives.

On Monday, January 31, 1972, the newly reconstituted Council was inaugurated by the then Federal Commissioner for Economic Development and Reconstruction, Dr. Adebayo Adedeji.

The Chairman of the Council was a well known and well respected Nigerian, Chief Chris Ogunbanjo. On him and the other members of the Council fell the burden of planning the establishment of the Centre and steering both the Council and the Centre through the teething problems of the early days.

With the assumption of office on January 22, 1973, Mr. Solomon Odia as the Director of the Centre, work started in earnest. Staff had to be recruited, departments created and jobs defined; a working organization had to be developed.

Efforts were also being made in respect of the promulgation of a decree which would give the Council and the Centre legal existence.

The efforts were crowned with success when on October 4, 1976 the Federal Military Government issued Act No. 51 formalising the existence of the Council and the Centre.

Under this Act, the Council is required to ensure that the quality and quantity of management training programmes offered by all training institutes including universities and polytechnics are adequate for the growing economy and are of the highest standards.

Membership of the Council was increased from 19 to 26, made up of a Chairman, four persons representing four universities, four persons representing colleges of technology, one person each representing the ministries of education, establishments, industries, labour and economic development, the Director of the Centre for Management Development, one person each representing the Nigerian Employers Consultative Association (NECA), the Industrial Training Fund (ITF), and the Nigerian Association of Chambers of Commerce, Industry, Mines and Agriculture, one representative of labour organizations and four persons with extensive knowledge of and close association with management training, industry and commerce, each chosen on his individual merit. Professor Akin Mabogunje of the Department of Geography, University of Ibadan, was appointed the Chairman of the Council.

On the retirement of the first Director of the Centre in April 1978, Dr. Udo Udo-Aka was appointed to the post. The life of the second Council expired in October 1979.

On July 24, 1981 a reconstituted 20-man Council, chairmanned by Alhaji Fatai O. Lawwal was inaugurated by the Federal Minister of National Planning, Chief (Mrs.) Adenike Ebun Oyagbola. Other members of the Council include:

(a) nine persons with extensive knowledge of and close association with, management training, industry and commerce, each chosen by the Minister on his individual merit and appointed by the President;

(b) two representatives of the Nigerian Employers' Consultative Association;

(c) two representatives of labour organizations;

(d) four representatives of professional management training institutions;

(e) one representative of the Ministry charged with responsibility for matters relating to the Council; and

(f) the Director-General, Centre for Management Development.

FUNCTIONS OF THE COUNCIL

Act 51 of 1976 section 2 assigned the following specific functions to the Council:

(a) to advise the Minister (i.e. Federal Minister of National Planning) on policies, plans and programmes for the enhancement of the number, quality and effective utilization of the managerial manpower resources of the country in all sectors of the economy;

(b) to formulate policies and guidelines for the coordination of management education and training activities throughout the country;

(c) to develop and promote high national standards of management education, entrepreneurial development, and supervisory training;

(d) to keep and maintain a register of training institutions and their training programmes including their subjects, location standards, duration, type and cost;

(e) to assess, from time to time the training programmes offered by the institutions listed in the register mentioned in paragraph (d) above with a view to determining their competence and whether they deserve financial support by the Council;

(f) to provide a forum at which representatives of both the public and private sectors and of management training institutions could exchange information and ideas on trends in management education and training.

CENTRE'S FUNCTIONS

In addition to whatever assignments the Council may give to the Centre from time to time, the Act itself has specified for it certain responsibilities as shown in section 16 as follows:

(a) providing the Council background information and other technical data necessary for the Council's policy-making and coordinating functions;

(b) providing management advisory and consultancy services to Nigerian enterprises;

(c) establishing and maintaining an up-to-date library for management studies;

(d) publishing journals, research papers and books on modern management and supervisory techniques; and

(e) sponsoring, promoting and conducting research into all aspects of management and allied subjects in relation to the Nigerian situation.

The Federal Government also from time to time gives additional functions to the Centre. In 1977, the Federal Executive Council directed the Centre to assist in the development of the small scale industrial sub-sector of the economy through the design and provision of suitable training packages for small scale industrialists and officials of Federal and State agencies which have responsibilities for developing small scale industries in the nation.

In the Fourth National Development Plan 1981—85, the Government again directed the Centre to place greater emphasis on designing programmes aimed at improving the performance of parastatals whose management problems seem to be quite serious.

CENTRE'S ROLE IN MANAGEMENT DEVELOPMENT

As a resource institution and catalyst, the Centre plays vital roles in the development of suitable and adequate managerial resources for the various sectors and subsectors of the Nigerian economy. These are promotional, action, and coordinating roles.

(a) Promotional or Entrepreneurial Role

Within the ambit of this role the Centre encourages organizations in the private and public sectors to undertake new activities and employ more effective measures to improve management practices and performances. This role calls for direct contact with

21

organizations so as to understand their needs and environment in which they operate. It also calls for the rendering of technical, financial and other kinds of support that organizations may seek from the Centre.

In order to play its promotional or entrepreneurial role, the Centre carries out the following activities among others:

(i) identifies individuals, institutions and organizations that need encouragement and determines the nature of such assistance and the best way to render it;

(ii) collects, stores and disseminates relevant information about organizations and resource personnel so as to promote a high degree of mutual inter-dependence and facilitate fast and effective delivery of service;

(iii) organises conferences and seminars to provide avenues for the promotion of new ideas and the exchange of views on topical issues.

(b) Action Role

This consists of under-taking dynamic and change-oriented activities in the areas of training, research and consultancy services. It also involves designing curriculum and training packages, providing relevant training materials, in-plant training and consultancy as well as preparing a management research agenda.

(c) Coordinating Role

This is basically a form of 'indirect' supervisory role which requires the Centre to lay down performance standards, evaluate the programmes of management institutions and liaise with management institutions and institutions of higher learning which engage in management education and development with a view to assisting them in their training, research and consulting assignments.

In furtherance of this role, the Centre carries out the following activities:

(i) paying frequent visits and holding regular discussions with institutions engaged in management development;

(ii) assisting in the training of key personnel;

(iii) forming professional associations among institutions so as to develop ethics of mutual help for solving national problems as well as promoting management as a profession. Some of the associations include Nigerian Association of Management Consultants (NAMCON), Institute of Management Consultants of Nigeria (IMCON), Nigerian Association of Schools of Management Education and Training (NASMET), Nigerian Marketing Association (NIMARK), and Nigerian Association of Small Scale Industrialists (NASSI);

(iv) assisting in the provision of human, material and financial resources. The roles call for strong interaction with national training and research institutions in management as well as direct interface with individual enterprises and development agencies.

ORGANIZATIONAL STRUCTURE

Until 1978, the Centre had a seven-department organizational structure. However, after a review of the Centre's organizational set-up in April 1978, the Federal Government approved a restructuring of the Centre into three Directorate System, each headed by a Director. Each department comprises a number of divisions, some of which are headed by Assistant Directors.

The three departments and their constituent divisions are as follows:

(a) INSTITUTIONAL COORDINATION AND DEVELOPMENT DEPARTMENT:
Comprising Education and Training, Research and Publications and Institutional Liaison and Support Divisions;

(b) MANAGEMENT SERVICES DEPARTMENT:
Comprising Consulting Services, Small Industries Services, and Public Enterprises Divisions;

(c) ADMINISTRATIVE AND TECHNICAL SERVICES DEPARTMENT:
Made up of Administration, Council Secretariat, Technical Services, Library for Management Studies and Budget and Accounts Divisions.

DIRECTOR-GENERAL'S OFFICE

The Director-General is the Chief Executive of CMD. He is responsible for the execution of decisions and directives of the Governing Council. He also has the responsibility for directing and coordinating the Centre's operations. He is assisted by three directors who head the departments.

The Director-General's Office has a number of units including Policy Planning and Monitoring, Public Relations and Information Internal Audit, and Area Offices.

DEPARTMENTAL RESPONSIBILITIES

The Centre's three departments, Institutional Coordination and Development, Management Services, and Administrative and Technical Services, carry out the professional and support activities of the Centre.

INSTITUTIONAL COORDINATION AND DEVELOPMENT ACTIVITIES

Management Research and Publications

Management research and publications are core functional activities of the Centre for Management Development. Act No. 51 of 1976 which gave legal existence to the Nigerian Council for Management Development provided in sections (d) & (e) that among other functions, the Centre should engage in:

* the publication of journals, research papers and books on modern management and supervisory techniques; and

* sponsoring, promoting and conducting research into all aspects of management and allied subjects in relation to the Nigerian situation.

Appendix 1.C   Research methodology

Introduction

The study was multi-site in order to attain some generalizability. Several different sources of data were used and most of the data was in the form of interviews. As far as possible the sources were comparable across sites. The design is expected to yield data which might be tested for significance during analysis, while not losing the nuances and understanding of each firm's environmental context.

Chapter 3 describes the main research setting. Nigeria, one of the fast developing countries in Africa, was selected as the main research site. A summary description of the research site is presented here.

Nigeria lies within the tropics on the west coast of Africa. It is bounded on the west by the Republic of Benin, on the north by Niger Republic, on the east by Republic of Cameroun, and on the south by the Atlantic Ocean. The country (see Figure 1.C.1), which has an area of 924,768 square kilometres, obtains most of its water supply from the Niger and Benue rivers and their tributaries.[1] The country's climate varies from tropical at the coast to sub-tropical further inland.

Nigeria's population (see Table 1.C.1) of about 80 million is multi-ethnic. Among the principal ethnic groups are the Hausas and the Fulanis in the North, the Ibos, Efik and the Ijaws in the East, and the Yorubas and the Edos in the West.

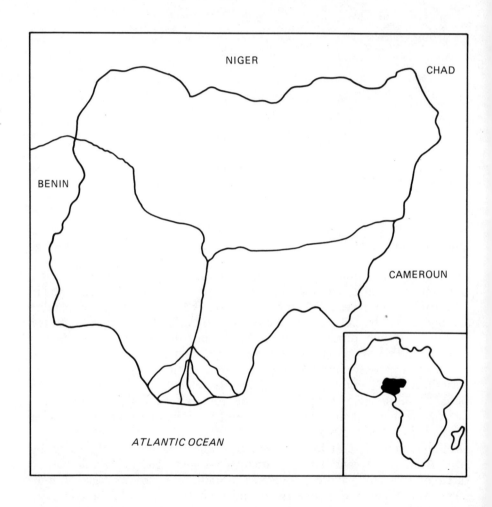

Fig. 1.C.1 Location and map of Nigeria

26

Table 1.C.1 Summary of Nigeria's vital statistics (1983)

Area:	356,000 square miles (924,000 square kilometres)
Population (1980):	84,732,000
Current estimates:	90—100 million
Annual population growth rate:	3.2 per cent
GNP (1980):	US $85,510 million
GNP per capita (1980):	US $1,010
GNP per capita growth rate:	5.3 per cent
Capital:	Lagos
Proposed federal capital:	Abuja
Other commercial centres:	Aba, Calabar, Ibadan, Kaduna, Kano, Jos, Zaria
Principal sea ports:	Lagos, Port Harcourt, Sapele, Burutu, Warrri, Calabar
Official language:	English

Source: World Bank Publications. From INCH Nigerian Company Listings. Lagos, Nigeria.

Research techniques

A qualitative research methodology was used to produce a sequence of transitions among this particular group of organizations. By qualitative research methods I mean the application of in-depth interviews with members of participating organizations, and where appropriate, with knowledgeable individuals outside the firms. Field observations, examination of company records, and review of reports/articles on the organizations in business journals were also applied. Reichardt and Cook (1979) defined qualitative techniques as 'a study which includes methodology, case studies, in-depth interviews, and participant observation. This method subscribes to attributes such as subjectives, close to the data, "insider" perspective, grounded, discovery-oriented, exploratory expansionists, descriptive, inductive, and process-oriented.' Evered and Louis (1981) in their proposition maintained that both qualitative 'inquiry from the inside' and quantitative 'inquiry from the outside' techniques are both necessary and sometimes complementary. These authors defined qualitative technique as being 'characterized by the experimental involvement of the research, the absence of a priori analytical categories, and an intent to understand a particular situation'.

Qualitative techniques have been criticized as being parochial; nonetheless, a qualitative approach appeared under these circumstances to be the best approach for a comparative field study (Becker, 1958, 1970; Webb *et al.*, 1966; Mitroff, 1974; Rowe, 1979; Merton, 1972). In their studies, the above authors and others presented several advantages and criticisms of qualitative research, advising that it is left to the researcher to select an approach that best serves the purposes of the study. For example, Becker and his colleagues note one particular asset of qualitative techniques in their medical school study:

> . . . Such a method afforded us the greatest opportunity to discover what things were of importance to the people we were studying and to follow up the interconnections of those phenomena. It allowed us to revise our model of the organization and the process we were studying by furnishing us with instances of phenomena we had not yet made part of our over-all picture . . .

The method chosen is a grounded theory approach. With its holistic nature and assumption of dynamic reality, it often leads to significant discoveries which may remain uncovered through techniques where the researcher first selected or formulated hypotheses or theories and then gathered data to test their validity. Furthermore, because of the sparsity of existing material regarding this topic, most theories selected or formulated prior to the fieldwork would have had a high chance of being inappropriate to the research problems. Such an approach can force the data to fit the theory. Premature theories may also direct the researcher's attention away from the important characteristics of the evolution processes and the most relevant explanations for the process. Consequently, because of the insufficient amount of knowledge regarding the topic at the time of this study, an exploratory, qualitative evaluation methodology seemed more appropriate than a reductionist approach. Thus, the study applied a research process in which the variables emerged and evolved as the study progressed and the preliminary data were analyzed.

Sample selection

Preliminary firms were selected from a population of 1,000 companies. These firms appeared in one or more of three lists:

1 those classified by the International Commerce Organization of Nigeria (ICON) company handbook;

2   the federal government of Nigeria Register of Companies listing;
3   a listing of 103 firms from the Nigerian Institute of Management.

There was considerable overlap among the lists.

An original aim of the study was to include at least one firm operating in each of the five major industrial sectors in Nigeria. The sectors
were those designated in the 'INCH Industrial Classification'[2] (see
Table 1.C.2). However, the major criteria for selection were that the
firm:

1   was privately held,
2   was privately owned and/or controlled,
3   had been in the family control for at least two generations.

Table 1.C.3 and Figure 1.C.2 present the categorization of the study's
organization population. There were 438 private firms including 247
owned and/or controlled by families. These privately held firms
represent over 53 per cent of the population. In general, private/family
firms as at the end of 1984 dominated the population of firms in
Nigeria, contrary to the late 1950s when government corporations and
public firms prevailed.[3]

The final selection of the sample was based on available information
on the firms and recommendations from individuals[4] acquainted with
the firms' backgrounds. These firms were limited to indigenous
Nigerian companies. This limitation was made in order to observe and
elicit the possible effect of the environment/culture on the firm's
evolution. Without this limitation, some firms, although managed by
Nigerians, would simply be subsidiaries of large foreign corporations
and as such were not expected to be influenced by the socio-economic
factors (family) at certain early stages of development.

An overview of approximately 71 firms was made. Letters of introduction were written and access to further information requested
from 12 firms. A total of eight firms was selected from an in-depth
study as the remaining four firms did not meet the criteria. Table 1.C.4
presents the characteristics of the firms selected while Figure 1.C.3
indicates the dimensions of the families based on 'constellation' —
nuclear and extended kinship. Only one of the participating firms was
owned and controlled by a Muslim family. The other seven controlling
families were of the Christian religion — Catholic and Protestants.

Gaining entry

A pre-test of the research problem was conducted in the United States
with three private/family firms. This exercise was made to familiarize
the researcher with techniques of the research process, especially

Table 1.C.2 Industrial classification of major companies in Nigeria (1983)

	Frequency of companies	%
General services (insurance, banking, printing, transportation)	290	30.34
Manufacturing	105	10.98
Agriculture (farm, food processing)	69	7.21
Wholesale and retail trade	230	24.06
Construction and engineering services	262	27.41
Total:	956	100.00

Source: INCH Classification, 1983

Table 1.C.3 Categorization of companies according to type of ownership

	Frequency of companies	%
Government (federal and state)[1]	93	11.31
Public corporations[2]	137	16.67
Foreign/private joint ownership[3]	135	16.42
Private (all Nigerian indigenes)[4]	191	23.24
Family firms[5.]	247	30.05
Foreign (wholly owned)	19	2.31
Total:	822	100.00

Notes:
1 Companies with federal or state holding majority share (includes companies where government is in joint venture).
2 Companies with more than 50 shareholders.
3 Companies where private individuals are in joint venture — with 40 per cent foreign ownership.
4 Companies with less than 50 shareholders.
5 Closely held firms with only family members as shareholders (all members have blood relationship).

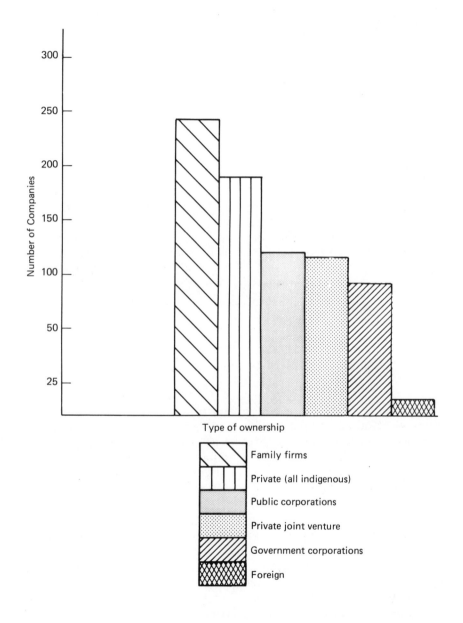

Fig. 1.C.2 Categorization of companies according to type of ownership

Table 1.C.4   Characteristics of firms in this study*

Type of Organization	Group of Companies (Business)	Major Industrial Sectors
Small/Medium	Amadi and Sons Limited Standard Enterprises Employees: 5—150 Assets: $200—500,000 Generation: 2nd —3rd	Timber, real estate, construction, pharmaceutical, hospital supply, soft drinks
Large	Ginano Oko Group Nwoke & Bros Ntiki Group of Cos. Onyeukwu & Sons Francis Employees: 500—3,000 Assets: $50 million—over billion Generation: 2nd—3rd	General merchandise, construction, transportation service, automobile sales, chemical, hospital supplies, agriculture—farm projects, real estate, fisheries, timber milling

*number of employees and assets are approximate.

gaining entry, interview processes and others. The three organizations consisted of one extended kinship and two nuclear families. Access to these organizations was facilitated by their relationships with the University. The General Aviation Company has a long-standing relationship with the school through the school's case writing activities and executive guest speaker programme. The Social Expression industry firm is closely affiliated with the school through its 'foundation' division. One of the current owners of the lumber firm is a member of the school's advisory board and an alumnus of the school. The research study received positive approval from each of these firms. However, it became difficult to get specific appointments for interviews. While interview appointments were being arranged through members of my committee familiar with the companies, I searched for and reviewed newspaper and journal articles, reports, and cases on the companies. Phone calls and memoranda were applied in arranging for interviews and providing a brief explanation of the research (Appendix 1.D

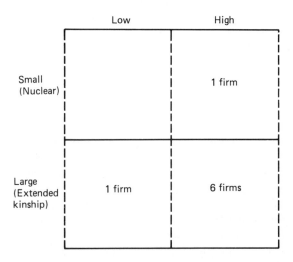

Level of Family Involvement

	Low	High
Small (Nuclear)		1 firm
Large (Extended kinship)	1 firm	6 firms

Fig. 1.C.3 Categories of participating firms' family 'constellation'

presents an example of the approach), and an initial loosely structured questionnaire (Appendix 1.E) was also distributed only to companies participating in the present study.

Data from the three companies suggested that there was some relationship or influence of family forms on the pattern of evolution. For example, in the one extended or large family controlled company, reorganization was taking place at the time of the study. This reorganization was designed to allocate separate business units of the organization to specific successors in the family and had become necessary as a result of growing conflict among the fourth-generation owners.

Fieldwork

Entry processes into the firms located in Nigeria were in some ways similar to the process used in the pre-test. However, because of the private nature of these firms, access was more difficult and sensitive data, such as information on the financial state of the firm, was not always disclosed. Table 1.C.5 presents levels of access and characteristics of the participating firms and Table 1.C.6 presents a listing of the data sources and people interviewed. The method of data collection and means of access in two open-access firms are summarized below. The two firms selected were the Ntiki Group of Companies and Oko Holdings.

Ntiki Group of Companies

Contact was initiated through correspondence between the chairman, the researcher, and a Nigerian university professor who was a close friend of the chairman. I was introduced to the professor through one of his relations. With the receipt of a letter of approval from the chairman, I was made very welcome upon arrival at the firm. I could not start interviewing immediately because most of the management personnel were very busy. However, I was allowed to visit the various sites and facilities owned by the group. I was permitted to interview the general manager on the third day and also to speak with a new employee later the same day. A member of the family and a director of all the companies in the group drove me to see most of the facilities and was very willing to discuss the family relationships within the business during the tour. Part of the interviews were recorded when convenient. Interview sessions with the chairman/managing director were allowed but were constantly interrupted by appointments and telephone calls. The chairman allowed me to sit in the office while waiting, thus offering me opportunities to observe significant business meetings.

Oko Group Holdings

My management contact was on vacation when I arrived in Nigeria. This absence necessitated my making fresh contacts because he had planned to introduce me to the managing director or another executive upon my arrival at the facility. Furthermore, although the company secretary remembered responding to my letters, he was not able to locate them.

Upon introduction to the general manager, I spent a couple of hours explaining my research and my needs from the company. This particular general manager was very difficult, indicating 'that the company was rather too complex for me to study'. He also indicated that he was once a professor of economics in one of the Nigerian universities and

Table 1.C.5 Level of access in the firms

Organization:	Amadi	Open Access Firms				Standard	Limited Access Firms		
		Francis	Ntiki	Nwoke			Oko	Ginano	Onyeukwu
Type:	Small/Medium GOC*	Large GOC	Large GOC	Large GOC	Medium GOC		Large GOC	Large GOC	Large GOC
Permission granted by:	Chairman	Chairman	Chairman	Chairman	Co-Chairman		Group Admin.	Group Secretary	Group Admin.
(Method)	Verbal Informal	Verbal Informal	Written Formal	Informal	Verbal Informal		Verbal	Written Formal	Written Formal
Interview with knowledgable individual outside the firm:	Yes	Yes	Yes	Yes	Yes		Yes	Yes	No
Observation of meetings:	Yes	Yes	Yes	No	No		No	No	No
Personal interview with founders or current owner:	Yes	Yes	Yes	Yes	Yes		No	No	No

*GOC – Group of Companies

Table 1.C.6 List of data sources

Data sources:	Ntiki	Nwoke	Francis	Oko	Amadi	Ginano	Standard	Onyeukwu	Society & Indust. Econ/Environment
Direct interview with:									
—Founder	Yes	Yes	Yes	No	Yes	No	Yes	No	
—Members of family	Yes(2)	Yes(2)	Yes(2)	Yes(2)	Yes(5)	Yes(1)	Yes(3)	Yes(1)	
—Employees	Yes(3)	Yes(2)	Yes(2)	Yes(3)	Yes(2)	Yes(3)	Yes(4)	Yes(2)	
—Outsiders	Yes(4)	Yes(6)	Yes(5)	Yes(3)	Yes(6)	Yes(3)	Yes(5)	Yes(3)	
Interview taped:	Yes(part)	No	Yes(some)	No	No	No	No	Yes	
Questionnaire completion	Reviewed before interview	Reviewed & completed with Res.	Yes(after review)	Reviewed before interview	Reviewed with interviewee	Submitted but reviewed with Res.	Reviewed prior to interview	Submitted two days prior to interview	
Personal observation	Yes	Yes	Yes	Yes(limited)	Yes	Yes(limited)	Yes	Yes	
Site visits	Yes	Yes	Yes	Yes(limited)	Yes	Yes(limited)	Yes	Yes	
Publications:									
ICON Publ.	Motors	No	No	Yes (most cos)	No	Yes (few cos)	No	Yes (most cos)	Yes Company Classes Indust. & Society
Company	None	None	Calendars Commercial Leaflets	Yes – Brochures Pamphlets Calendars	None	Calendars & Comm.	None	Calendar	
Business journal article	Comment on Const. Mag. – ICON Co. Handbook	Article on Co. Yes	–	–	None	–	–	–	Industry Economic Review Review

36

Source	General Industry View	General Industry View	Industry	Industry	Industry Review	London Fin. Times				
Daily newspaper articles	–	–	–	–	–	–	–	On owners political actions	Yes	Yes
Documentary	On 40 yrs of operation Nig.Enterprise Publ.	–	–	–	–	–	–	–	Yes	Yes
Government papers	Industry Analysis	–	'Proposal' for loan	–	–	–	–	Book–Nig. Study of Country, etc.	Yes	Yes
Institutions:										
Nig. Inst. of Management	–	–	Retains membership for consulting & training	–	–	Consulting & training membership	–	Consulting & training membership	Yes List of Cos. & Classif.	Industry Review
National archives	–	–	–	–	on Indust.	–	–	–	Yes–Historical Background of Econ. & Indust. Dev.	–
Center for Management Dev.	–	–	Member	–	–	Member	–	–	Yes–Management Trends in the Society –Govt. Actions	–
Registry of Companies	–	–	–	–	–	–	–	–	Yes–Types of companies, sizes, rate of registration	–
Mins. of Commerce & Industry	–	–	–	–	–	–	–	–	classif. of indus. type. Also historical background.	–

Note: Numerals in brackets indicate number of individuals.

had therefore had experience in student projects. With the above remark, I was able to challenge and convince him to give me access to the information I needed. In the end he offered me some materials and recommended me to relevant personnel conversant with the issues of my research.

In general, initial entry was made possible by third and fourth parties who knew the founder/manager well enough to convince him of the relevance of this study. In most cases it was necessary for the firms that the contact knew the researcher well enough to personally vouch for the confidentiality of the information obtained. A letter of introduction from the university was also necessary to show that the researcher was on an academic quest and was not a government or competitor's agent. Most permissions to speak with the other members of the firm (family and non-family) were usually oral, which meant that these personnel had to confirm the authorization again with the owners. This exercise often delayed the progress of the interviews. However, there was an advantage to these periods of waiting — they invariably offered the researcher an opportunity to observe the daily activities of the businesses. The several times I had to sit in the director's office were useful. In all, gentle persistence led to the degree of data availability achieved.

In the field

Fifty per cent of the interviewees allowed the interviews to be recorded even though notes were also being taken. Both the notes and taped records were reviewed as soon as possible to check for their completeness. All of the taped records were fully transcribed and others listened to two or three times. However, to assure the reliability of the interview data, all factual statements were cross-checked with documents or with data from other interviews. As a rule, the same questions were asked of all those who would be in a position to respond to them. Consequently, it was possible to cross-check a given interview with others. At the end of each day's interview, data were also summarized in a 3x8 matrix (see Appendix 1.F). Mini-cases were also organized by themes or historical happenings and written up as soon as possible, to achieve similar purposes.

The visits to the sites took place over a period of six months. Most of this fieldwork consisted of interviews with owners/founders/successors where applicable (some founders are no longer alive), members of the family within and outside the firms, members of the board of directors, and non-family member employees of the firms. These interviews were supplemented by observation of strategic meetings and other interactions among managers whenever possible. In addition, written documents such as memoranda, business journal articles, annual reports, budgets, and other internal information sources were used as background and complementary information and as collaboration of facts given during the interviews.

Initially the questions were aimed at the founder's background and his contributions to the survival and growth of the firm, the history of the firm and strategic stages in its development, the industry in which the firms operated, the structure of the founder's family and how involved its members were in the management of the firm. Appendix 1.G presents the major interview questions that were ultimately used in the field. The questions were open-ended in structure. The data set were content-analyzed and cases on each of the participating firms developed. The content analysis method has been popular among historians, journalists, and anthropologists (Kaplan and Golden, 1964; Holsti, 1969) in the past. However, this method of analysis is gaining popularity among organizational and policy researchers (Udy, 1959; Schendel and Hofer, 1978).

Notes

1   Source: Nigeria Federal Ministry of Statistics, Lagos, Nigeria, 1984, 'Facts on Nigeria'.
2   INCH Industrial Classification is prepared by the International Commerce Organization of Nigeria, 1983 edition.
3   Federal Ministry — Company Registration and Records Office, Lagos, Nigeria.
4   Interviews with Dr Harry Levinson of the Levinson Institute in Boston; Dr B. Barnes of Harvard Business School; Dr Peter Davis of Wharton Center for Family Business, all in the US. Also interviews with directors and managers at the Nigerian Institute of Management, Center for Management Development and Personnel Management Development Center, all in Lagos, Nigeria.

Appendix 1.D The relationships between patterns of organizational development, socio-economic variables and firms' growth

ABSTRACT OF STUDY

This study of the evolution patterns of organizational development is part of a dissertation research, currently under the director of Professors Marilyn Taylor and V.K. Narayanan of the School of Business and Professor Howard Baumgartel of the Department of Psychology, all of the University of Kansas. The general purpose of the study is to explore the evolution patterns of family owned and/or controlled firms. More specifically, the research will explore the relationships between the evolutionary patterns of the firm, family structure and the firms' continuing growth. It is expected that this study will serve not only as a data base but will provide a better understanding of the various strategies and structures applicable to these organizations as they grow. This understanding will contribute to the design and administration of more effective management programs as well as more effective guidance for firm advisors.

The collection of data for this study and its analysis will be carried out over a period of twelve months. Data will be gathered through in-depth interviews with two or three different individuals from each of the participating firms. Interview data will be complemented by review of available company records and publications as well as articles about the businesses in the business journals. The study uses a research process in which the variables are expected to emerge and evolve as the study progresses and the data are analyzed. I am interested in the patterns that emerge in each firm as it grows or expands, in how the owners manage the business, how and, where possible, why they make decisions at significant points in the organization's development. A more comprehensive list of our areas of interest is presented in the attached Questionnaire [see Appendix 1.E] .

The selected firms appear to provide the setting and the situations needed for this research. At the same time, these firms raise special problems because of their nature. Often the approach in this study takes into account some personal characters or life history of the entrepreneur since these may influence the way the owners/managers made decisions today. Thus, I am also interested in the brief history of the entrepreneur/manager. The main thrust of the research is how the firm got to where they are today. Personal history and important company records will only be used with the consent of the firms.

Because of the unique characteristics of these firms (privately owned and closely run by members of the family), they provide interesting variables to be investigated. For example, how do these firms survive, grow, diversify, etc., on private funding for many decades. This is a multisite, multisource methodology designed to attain generalizability, comparability and statistical significance in reporting findings while at the same time, not losing the nuances and understanding of each firm's environmental context.

Many sociological studies are associated with ethical questions, however, the purpose in this study is not to evaluate the firms' efficiency nor those [sic] of the individuals managing them. Rather, I am interested in the patterns of growth, the strategies that were developed and the processes by which decisions were reached. With this, it should be pointed out that confidentiality about any information obtained will be maintained. Furthermore, officials of the participating firms will have the opportunity to review the report before all or part of it is published.

Thank you for considering our proposal and for your assistance.

Chi B. Anyansi
306 Summerfield Hall
University of Kansas
Lawrence, KS 66045

Appendix 1.E Corporate Development Questionnaire (early version)

SECTION 1

Name of Organization_____

2. Year started_____ 3. Year of Registration/Incorporation_____

4. Type of Business (please indicate):

   Manufacturing____ Service____ Agroallied____

   Retail____ Wholesale____ Other/s_____

5. Legal Form:

   Sole Proprietorship_____ Family/Private Corporation_____

   Partnership_____ Public Corporation_____

6. Current Number of Employees:_____

7. Approximate Volume of Sales/Year_____

8. The following questions relate to the significant changes which have occurred since the start of the business. Please respond to them as precisely as you can.

9. Change in size:

Period	No. of Employees	Vol. of Product	Vol. of Sales	Number of Branches
19___ to 19___				
19___ to 19___				

10. Changes in Method of Production:

Period	Self Produced	Purchased	Labor Intensive	Mechanized
19___ to 19___				
19___ to 19___				

11. Changes in Growth Technique:

Period	Volume Expansion	New Plants	Diversi- fication	Acquisition Real Unrel.
19___ to 19___				
19___ to 19___				

12. Changes in Product Type:

	19 to 19	19 to 19	19 to 19
Number of Different Products			

13. Please list the products sold by the firm:

Manufactured	Purchased

14. Changes in Structure:

Period	Functional Number	Product/ Location	Divisional Number	Centra. Decent.	Others- Indicate
19___ to 19___					
19___ to 19___					

15. Indicate type of structure mostly maintained:

Horizontal_____   Vertical_____

16. Is there a discernible hierarchy of authority? If yes, please indicate period/s and the position/s, below.

17. Are there any major changes in management? If yes, please indicate period/s and the position/s, below.

18. Changes in Methods of Control:

Period	Centralized	Decentralized	Autonomous Units	Other
19___ to 19___				
19___ to 19___				

19. Changes in Methods of Appraisal/Reward and Incentive Plans:

Period	Owner/Manager Decision	Standard Evaluation System	Informal	Other
19___ to 19___				
19___ to 19___				

20. Goals and Objectives: Have there been any major changes in the goals and objectives of the business? If yes, please explain in what ways they have changed.

21. Problems/Issues: Please indicate problems/issues, if any, which the company might have found in its lifetime.

Period	Major Problems
Start:	
First 5 years:	
6–10 years:	
11–15 years:	
16–20 years:	

22. Future Plans: Do you have any specific plans for changes in the following areas:

Volume expansion

Diversification

Divestment

Acquisitions

Management Style

Structure

23. Are there any publications by the company (pamphlets, brochures, annual reports, books, etc.)? If yes, please list the publications and indicate the type of information included in each (example: current status, projections, competition, etc.).

SECTION II

I have earlier emphasized the confidentiality of any information obtained in this study. But we would like to say once more that, because of the personal nature of this section, response is optional and where it is given, that the information will be held in utmost confidentiality.

Thank you.

1. Position: Owner/President_____ Professional Manager_____

    Member of Owner's Family_____ Other_____

2. Marital Status: Single_____ Married_____ Divorced_____

    Widowed_____ Other_____

3. If married, are you in a single career family_____

    dual career_____ nuclear family_____ extended family_____

4. Do you have grown children? Yes_____ No_____

5. If the response to No. 4 is yes, are these children and other members of the family employed in the business?

6. Do these children hold significant positions in the firm?

7. How many generations of family have been/are in the firm?

8. Please explain as precisely as you can how you deal with pressures or strains, if any, arising from internal interests in the business? For example, how do you deal with issues (or divergent views on) positioning family members, rewarding or promoting them, or issues of continuity or dissolution of the business.

Appendix 1.F   Stages in evolution: matrix of interview summary

	Performance/ Incorporation	Formation	Early Expansion	Diversi-fication	Maturity: Decline Reorg.	Comment Future Concern/ Plans
Major Stages in the Firm's Development						
Year						
Major Stages in the Society/Industry Development						
Year						
Major Developments in the family						
Structure at Stages of Firm's development						

Management Characteristics	Major Stages of Development	Formation/ Incorporation	Early Expansion	Diversi- fication	Maturity: Decline Reorg.	Future Plans/ Concerns
Goals						
Short-Term						
Long-Term						
Policies/Strategies:						
Product (Purchased Manufacture?)						
Sales/ Distribution/ Promotion						
Research & Development						
Control:						
Quality						
Finance						
Funding						
Reward System						
Structures:						
Direct/ Manager's Major Tasks						
Levels of Management						
Size (Employees)						

Appendix 1.G Evolution of Firms Study: Corporate Development Questionnaire (later version)

The following questions are open-ended and are designed to allow you to respond in your own style. Please feel free to bring up issues that you feel are important in the history of the firm — technical, family values, beliefs and otherwise. Your participation in this project is voluntary and confidentiality will be maintained throughout the study.

Furthermore, these questions will be personally asked by the researcher who is also available to guide and clear ambiguous questions. Where tape recorders are allowed for the interview sessions, the interviewee should feel free at any time to turn off the recorder. In other words, you are free to indicate when any statement is off the record.

Please respond to the following as precisely as you can.

Company Development:
1. Would you please identify and describe as far as you can remember, major stages/periods in the development of the firm. Where possible, describe the management characteristics, achievements and problems of each identifiable period, for example, company/family objectives and major strategies in operations. I am also interested in the founding (basic) and growth in structural changes.

Are there written materials (documents, magazine articles, charts, handbooks, etc.) on the firm?

2. What is your knowledge of the industry/industries the firm operates? How would you describe this industry/s evolution and performance? At what period of development of this industry did your firm enter? How easy or difficult was it for your firm to enter the industry? How would you describe competition in the industry and what is your company's position and competitive strategies?

3. Family Structure and Relationship with the Company:

Has there been more than one generation of families in this firm? Who is the original founder? Would you please describe as much as you can remember of the profiles of the prominent family members, especially those who have chaired this company or were highly involved in its management. How would you describe the relationship between the family members in relation to the operation of the firms. How would you describe the size/structure of the family as the firm developed.

My next question deals with the process of decision-making, however, I am more interested in the mechanisms or processes of settling divergent views among family executives (views which affect successful operation and continuity of the company).

Are there any plans for succession to the chair in the future? Are daughters and in-laws considered for succession at any point? How would you describe the position of these people in the ownership and management of the firm?

4. Are there other historical events in the life of the company that I should know or be asking? Are there any other individuals in or outside the firm or family that you think I should speak with?

Summary:

In summary, may I take it that the following constitute key points of our discussion:

- issues on history and development
- issues on industrial competition
- issues on family forms, relationships, etc.
- issues on conflict resolution mechanisms.

2 Models of organization strategy and structure

Introduction

This chapter focuses first on literature on stages of organizational development, second, on the social anthropology of the Nigerian private and family-controlled firms, and then on conflict resolution mechanisms.

Stages of organizational development

Major works on stages of organizational development (Chandler, 1962, 1977; Thompson, 1967; Lawrence and Lorsch, 1969; Wrigley, 1970; Scott, 1971; Channon, 1971; Pavan, 1972; Thanheiser, 1972; Dyas, 1972; Greinèr, 1972; Rumelt, 1974; Williamson, 1975; Filley and Aldage, 1978; Churchill and Lewis, 1983; Suziki, 1980; Ouchi, 1981) suggest that many environmental factors have influence on patterns of organizational development. These works were concentrated in the USA, Western Europe and Japan.

Each study examined and reported the strategic and structural development of organization in the selected countries. The models developed in these countries present multidivisional forms as the major strategic and structural forms of organizations by the 1960s and 1970s.

The findings of the studies and models developed in six industrialized countries are described below.

Chandler's historical report of US industrial enterprise[1] showed that, before 1850, very few businesses needed the services of a full-time administrator or required a clearly defined administrative structure. These industrial enterprises were very small relative to those of the 1960s and beyond. These businesses were usually family distinct activities in the agrarian and commercial economy. These merchants were also responsible for buying and selling when it came to marketing and distribution of goods. As the businesses became larger they hired agents to handle their accounts.

Chandler's investigation into the beginnings of business administration and the changing strategy and structure of large industrial enterprise in the USA was his first in the writing of comparative business history. Over 100 of America's largest industrial enterprises were briefly examined in the preliminary study. Information for this preliminary examination was readily obtained from the companies' annual reports, government publications, articles in periodicals, and business biographies. However, using the more detailed information from four of the large corporations, the study deduced five developmental stages of enterprises, as follows:

1 Very small firm (little or no full-time management). Expansion of volume.
2 One function, one area of distribution. Geographic expansion.
3 Departmental structure with headquarters and field units. Vertical integration (new functions).
4 Central office and multi-departmental structure diversification.
5 Multidivisional structure.

Chandler summarized his findings in the following statement:

> Strategic growth resulted from an awareness of the opportunities and needs — created by changing population, income and technology — to employ existing or expanding resources more profitably. A new strategy required a new or at least refashioned structure if the enlarged enterprise was to be operated efficiently. The failure to develop a new internal structure, like the failure to respond to new external opportunities and needs, was the consequence of over concentration on operational activities by the executives responsible for the destiny of their enterprise, or from their inability, because of their enterprise, or from their inability, because of past training and education and present position, to develop an entrepreneurial outlook.[2]

A corollary to the above proposition is that growth without structural adjustment can only lead to economic inefficiency.

In his second work, *The Visible Hand*, Chandler examined the changing processes of production and distribution in the USA and the ways in which they have been managed. In this study, Chandler concluded that the visible hand of management has replaced the invisible hands of market forces 'when and if technology and expanded markets permitted a historically unprecedented high volume of materials through the process of production and distribution'.[3] In this conclusion Chandler also tied the ascendency of the manager (the visible hand) to the general patterns of institutional growth.

Building on Chandler's work, Scott (1971) identified and defined three stages of organizational development.[4] Scott's model focused on managerial characteristics and the systems/culture within the enterprise as contrasted to Chandler's model, which focused mostly on structure. Scott noted that companies go through stages of development as they grow and identified the following three steps:

1   Small company with one or a few functions performed largely by one manager — growth in volume, in geographic coverage, and through vertical integration.
2   Multi-departmental enterprises with specialized managerial departments based upon functions.
3   Multidivisional enterprises with division based largely on product/ market relationships.

Scott also identified type of firm and industry, as well as national environment, as being significant in a firm's growth.

One of the most significant steps in Scott's study was the development of a set of propositions relating the various stages in an analytical way, thus superseding the previous approach[5] which was based upon a more or less arbitrary division of the corporate spectrum into three classes of firms. The development of these productions was a joint undertaking with Malcom Salter (1967)[6] in connection with his work on *Stages of Corporate Development: Implications for Management Control*. The results of the 1971 study also reflect the data resulting from the thesis work of Wrigley (1972) and further comparative study in Western Europe, especially France.

Table 2.1 presents a description of the respective stages in a matrix. Each stage is described in terms of nine characteristics as identified by Scott. Comparing Scott's three-stage model to Chandler's five-stage model, two essential differences can be found:

1   Scott's model classifies and then relates companies not by a single managerial characteristic (structure), but by nine characteristics, including structure;
2   Scott's model reduces emphasis on geographical growth (within the USA).

Table 2.1 Three stages of organizational development — Scott's model

Stage/ Co. characteristics	I	II	III
Product line	1. Single product or single line	1. Single product line	1. Multiple product lines
Distribution	2. One channel or set of channels	2. One set of channels	2. Multiple channels
Organizational structure	3. Little or no formal structure — one-man show	3. Specialization based on function	3. Specialization based on product-market relationship
Product–service transactions	4. N/A	4. Integrated pattern of transactions	4. Not integrated
		A– B– C– Markets	A– B– C– Markets
R & D	5. Not institutionalized, oriented by owner-manager	5. Increasingly institutionalized search for product or process improvements	5. Institutionalized search for new products as well as for improvements
Performance	6. By personal contact and subjective criteria	6. Increasingly impersonal using technical and/or cost criteria	6. Increasingly impersonal using market criteria (return on investment and market share)
Rewards	7. Unsystematic and often paternalistic	7. Increasingly systematic with emphasis on stability and service	7. Increasingly systematic with variability related to performance
Control system	8. Personal control both strategic and operating decisions	8. Personal control of strategic decisions with increasing delegation of operating decisions, based control by decision rules (policies)	8. Delegation of product–market decisions within existing businesses, with indirect control based on analysis of results
Strategic choices	9. Needs of owner vs. needs of firm	9. Degree of integration Market share objective Breadth of product line	9. Entry and exit from industries. Allocation of resources by industry. Rate of growth

Source: B.R. Scott, *Stages of Corporate Development*, Intercollegiate Case Clearing House, Boston MA, 1971.

However, this three-stage model lumped small, functionally organized companies together with large, integrated organizations. This study concludes that 'there is a cluster of managerial characteristics associated with the various stages of development, a cluster which suggests not just a form of organization but a "way of managing" and to a considerable extent a "way of life" within the enterprise'.[7]

Further research on the *Fortune* '500' in the late 1960s indicates that most of these companies are in stage III and that none are in stage I. Wrigley (1970) sub-classified these companies according to how and how much they have diversified. The resulting classes were:

(a) Dominant business: companies that derive 70—95 per cent of sales from a single business or a vertically integrated chain of businesses.

(b) Related business: companies that are diversified into related areas, where no single business accounts for no more than 70 per cent of sales.

(c) Unrelated business: companies that have diversified without necessarily relating new business accounts to no more than 70 per cent of sales.

(d) Single business: defined as one that manufactures and distributes a single product, a line of products with variations in size and style, or a set of closely related products linked by technology or market structure. Wrigley concluded that dominant business companies are managed through a hybrid structure in which top management directly controls the basic business through a functional structure while the remaining businesses are managed through product division. Related and unrelated were managed through divisional structures.

With the trend towards multidivisional forms, Richard Rumelt[8] examined 40 per cent of the *Fortune* '500' (by 1967 over 90 per cent of the *Fortune* '500' were diversified). He traced their evolution in strategy and structure using categories developed by Wrigley. Rumelt's analysis which covered the period 1950—70 confirmed what Wrigley's data had suggested (see Figure 2.1). These suggestions include increasing diversification and a trend away from single and even dominant businesses. They also indicate the decline of the functional organization and the dramatic rise on product division.

Rumelt found that geographic division is also on the decline. The holding company structure was rare. The hybrid called 'functional/subs' is where the principal business is managed by top management in the traditional functional form and the rest as product divisions or subsidiaries. This form is common among dominant businesses.

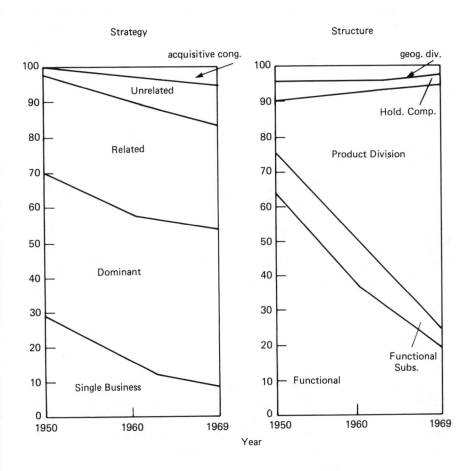

Source: R. Rumelt, *Strategy, Structure and Financial Performance of the Fortune '500', 1950–1970*, unpublished DBA dissertation, Harvard Business School, 1972.

Fig. 2.1   Evolution of strategy and structure of the US *Fortune* '500'

In an attempt to determine whether the above 'relationship was strictly an American phenomenon or whether managerial requirements of diversity among the largest industrial enterprises in the technologically advanced industrial societies of the Western world lead to a converging trend in the adoption of the divisional structure to manage diversification',[9] similar studies coordinated by Scott, were carried out in France, Italy, the UK and Germany. Using Wrigley's classification scheme, Dyas (1972), Pavan (1972), Channon (1971) and Thanheiser (1972) made parallel studies of the evolution of the top 100 firms in France, Italy, the UK and Germany. These studies were planned together with similar methodologies and designed to test a common hypothesis.[10] The findings of the four studies suggested similar trends affecting the respective national populations, thereby providing support for rejecting the hypotheses (see Figures 2.2 and 2.3). However, neither Scott's model nor any of the others cited have been applied in a developing country setting. These four studies also reported that they developed adequate data to trace the evolution of the enterprise, but not economic data which would permit a serious attempt to relate economic performance to strategy and structure. However, this economic linkage was later made by Rumelt using data on large American firms.[11]

Both Pavan and Dyas explicitly reported the dominance of family firms among their samples. These two, together with Channon and Thanheiser, also traced the government roles, war and other economic factors in the evolution of the enterprise.

The general conclusions from the European studies include Pavan's statement that, despite the increased introduction of the multidivisional structure, a large number of diversified firms have continued to use the functional or the holding company structure.[12] Also, where the Italian companies have introduced the multidivisional structure, there remain significant differences in internal characteristics from American multidivisional firms. There appeared to be no use of rewards or punishments for division managers based, at least in part, directly on performance of their division. Division managers were involved in corporate policy determination in a manner which increases the subjectivity of performance measures and resource allocation. Furthermore, top management was concerned to a large extent with daily operations, and greater divisional interdependence dampens internal competition and reduces the ability to discontinue an unprofitable business activity. The unlisted family firms, when diversified, tended not to divisionalize. It is expected that the differences in the degree of diversification and internal characteristics of management between US and Western

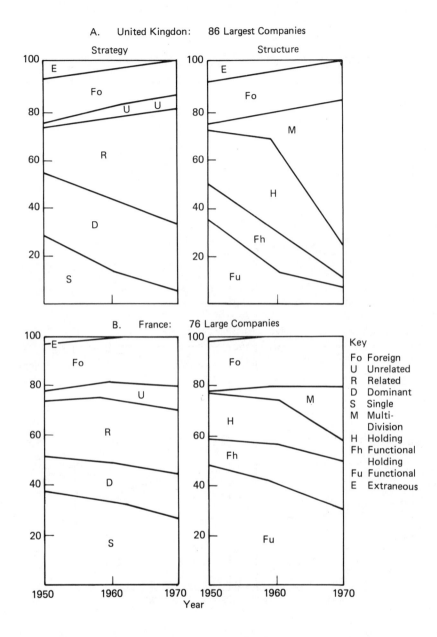

A. United Kingdon: 86 Largest Companies

Strategy

Structure

B. France: 76 Large Companies

Key

Fo Foreign
U Unrelated
R Related
D Dominant
S Single
M Multi-
   Division
H Holding
Fh Functional
   Holding
Fu Functional
E Extraneous

Year

Sources: A — D.F. Channon, *Strategy and Structure of British Enterprise*, 1971.
B — G.F. Dyas, *Strategy and Structure of French Industrial Enterprise*, 1972.

Fig. 2.2 Evolution of strategy and structure in Western European countries (1)

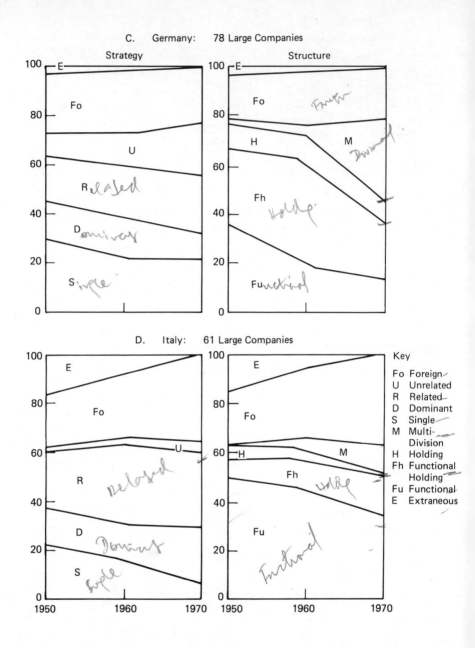

C. Germany: 78 Large Companies

Sources: C — H. Thanheiser, *Strategy and Structure of German Enterprise*, 1972.
D — J. Pavan, *Strategy and Structure of Italian Enterprise*, 1972.

Fig. 2.3 Evolution of strategy and structure in Western European countries (2)

European firms will decrease as industrialization increases in these countries. The above deduction appears to be in line with Selznick's discussion of the value of studying organizational histories. He states:

> Taken as a total experience, each such history is, of course, unique. Nevertheless to the extent that similar situations summon like responses from similar groups, we may expect to find organizational evolutionary patterns.[13]

The Japanese experience

In the Japanese experience, Suziki elected to forego the discussion of the peculiarities of Japanese organizations and management which has dominated academic and journal studies.[14] Applying the same classifications developed by Wrigley and used in the study of Western European nations the author examined the 100 largest Japanese enterprises, tracing the development of diversification in Japan and the emergence of the multidivisional forms of organization.

The period 1950–70 had special meaning within the Japanese context. The year 1950 was the starting-point for the post-war Japanese companies. The year 1970 marks the end of the extraordinarily high rate of growth in the economy. Also by 1970 the majority of the Japanese companies had caught up in size with their British counterparts, hence the existence of 51 Japanese industrial firms in *Fortune* '200'.

The study shows that 48 of the top 100 companies in 1970 were among the top 100 of 1950. These companies featured prominently in iron and steel, metals, textiles and food and drink. New entries came largely from automobiles and parts, and electrical engineering and electronics.

The changing patterns of strategy and structure are shown in Figure 2.4. Like Germany, Japan had more fully diversified companies than Britain in 1950, but the situation in both Britain and Japan became quite similar by 1970. About 65 per cent of the sample firms were fully diversified, and this percentage was higher than in any other European country. The high degree of diversity in the Japanese companies in the 1950s was due to the historic development of large multi-industry firms in the narrow and shallow market existing during Japan's early industrialization and to the lack of adequate technology.

The structural changes which occurred during the two decades were more radical than the shifts in strategy. The multidivisional structure found widespread adoption in Japan, especially during the 1960s. By 1970, 56 companies of the top 100 were organized in this way. In comparison with British or American companies, the divisionalization of Japanese firms remained at a lower level. (By 1970 divisionalization in

Y.   Suziki

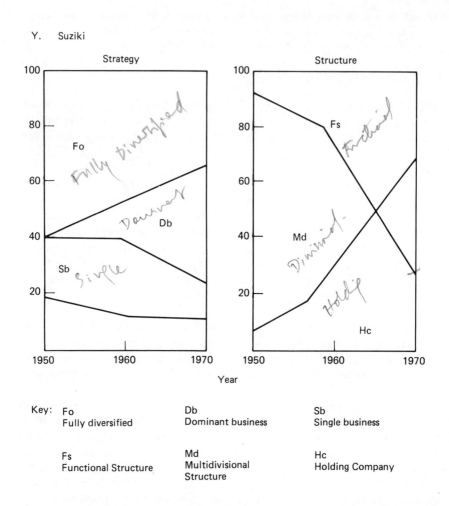

Key: Fo   Db   Sb
      Fully diversified   Dominant business   Single business

      Fs   Md   Hc
      Functional Structure Multidivisional   Holding Company
                            Structure

Source: Y. Suziki, *The Strategy and Structure of Top 100 Japanese Industrial Enterprises*, 1950–1970.

Fig. 2.4   Evolution of strategy and structure of enterprise in Japan

Britain was 72 per cent and in the USA was 78 per cent.) Relative to Germany (40 per cent) and France (40 per cent) Japanese divisionalization was more progressive. The holding structure was almost non-existent in Japan, unlike the western European countries. There were some functional/holding companies such as Nippon Steel and Nissan Motors but the relationship between the parent companies and their subsidiaries was different from that found in the European holding company structure.

Another finding in the evolution of Japanese companies was that there were fewer acquisitive diversifiers compared with the European countries in the two decades. Although multidivisional structure was only a step from functional structure, its adoption was not systematic as in the cases of other new technologies or managerial practices. In some cases the structure was introduced as a step towards rather than an effect of diversification.

Another line of organizational research dealing with organization forms was that carried out by Williamson (1975) and Ouchi (1981). As in the cases of organizational structure and power distribution, Williamson and Ouchi developed a three-fold typology of human resource practices — markets, bureaucracy and clans. These typologies have been used to examine industry structures and organization forms.

Williamson, an economist, focused on simple transactions as the critical concept for understanding both interfirm and intrafirm activities. He argued that ways of controlling transactions will vary according to the kind and amount of uncertainty a firm faces.[15] These uncertainties may be generated by opportunistic behaviour, by dependence on future events, and by bounded rationality. Some combinations of these circumstances favour the use of markets for control of transactions, while others favour bureaucracies.

However, Ouchi, an organization theorist, extended Williamson's argument by explicating the third mechanism, which he calls clans.[16] Clans provide for the control of transactions by means of values that are shared among an interpersonally linked group of people. Shared values tend to generate faith and clans thus obviate the need to consider the equity of every transaction.

The above two studies tend to suggest more of the reasons for some of the transactions among the different forms of firms.

Profiles of family firms

Family constellation and dynamics in Nigeria are strongly related to culture and the level of economic development. Family constellation has been variously phrased and treated by different authors in the past.

Common among the terms used were 'corporate', 'joint', 'extended', 'consanguineal', 'stern', 'nuclear', 'conjugal' and sometimes 'simple'. Literature on the social anthropology of the Nigerian family is scant, and the few works that exist have been written by anthropologists working on social change. Most of these studies — Hagen (1962), McClelland (1976), Lauer (1982) — describe the family system as a broker or agent for character and personality development. This family system was also determined to be a major influence on the type of community and national economic development pattern.

According to Burch and Gendell (1971), typologies used to describe family type or pattern have been traced to the nature of conceptual and operational family forms examined. They concluded that researchers should exercise greater care with definition of the family form than they have employed in the past. Beparta (1964) suggests that two major hypotheses had always been employed in the classification of family types. One refers to the composition of the domestic group and the other to the rights and obligations attached to conjugal and kinship roles. These studies revealed that extended family structure was accompanied by high fertility rates and the nuclear or smaller sized family with low fertility rates. One example of such a study was one by Freedman *et al.* (1969) in which Taiwanese families were classified according to residence patterns — nuclear, stem, and joint. These authors concluded that those who had always lived in nuclear units had lower fertility rates than other couples.

Appendix 2.A presents the taxonomy of the family in Nigeria. However, the family system (extended kinship) in Nigeria is more of a complex set of norms, of usages, of patterns of behaviour between kins with the important element of these relations being the customary rights and duties of relatives to one another. The conceptual framework for distinguishing extended family norms and behaviour from nuclear family norms and behaviour therefore concerns the extension of such rights and obligations attached to conjugal parental and filial roles across the boundaries of the elementary family. Extended kinship refers to families where obligations and rights extend across and beyond the boundaries of immediate family while nuclear represents responsibility or obligation for the immediate small family. In Nigeria, the rights and duties attached to conjugal parental and/or filial roles include the giving and receiving of financial support, education of children, domestic decision-making, and co-existence.

Family firms: definition

The definition of family business is as diverse as the few studies that have been done on it. Researchers have tended to define family enterprises as narrowly as the scope of their studies.

Some authors, through broad use of the terms 'small firms', 'private fims', 'closely held corporations', etc., have applied criteria such as annual sales, size, asset value, geographical location, market share, number of stockholders, type of management and sometimes nature of legal entity in their definitions.

Donnelly (1964) identified his sample of family business[17] as that in which:

1 Family relationship is a factor, among others, in determining management succession;
2 Wives or sons of present or former chief executives are on the Board of Directors;
3 The importance of institutional values of the firm are identified with a family, either in formal company publications or in the informal traditions of the organization;
4 The actions of a family member reflect on, or are thought to reflect on, the reputation of the enterprise, regardless of his formal connection to management;
5 The relatives involved feel obligated to hold the company stock for more than purely financial reasons, especially when losses are involved;
6 The position of the family member in the firm influences his standing in the family;
7 A family member must come to terms with his relationship to the enterprise in determining his own career.

This is perhaps the most inclusive definition in the literature as seen from the subsequent definitions. Dyas defined them as 'companies where a single person or family group had ownership control, defined as effective voting control over the board of directors, irrespective of whether family members were actively involved in management or not'.[18] Dyas also included as family companies those firms in which there is no individual or family voting control 'but where the president or several top managers owned a substantial proportion of the equity (usually over 10%)'.[19] Hershon (1975) included, among other characteristics of small firms, situations where ownership and management are closely related and the culture and traditions of the company and source of managerial talent stem largely from the founding family.

Dr Levinson (1983) identified three types of family firms. These include family traditional, family conflictual and entrepreneurial.

Family traditional is defined as those companies that have been long established (usually over several generations) and that, in business terms, are going along well (with a good reputation for customer service and/or product quality). These companies also have planned continuity in the sense that it is taken for granted by both parents and offspring that the sons (and recently, sometimes daughters) will follow the fathers in the same business. Family conflict exists where 'family cohesion is maintained and there is an effort to sustain a certain kind of tradition, but major conflicts arise, usually out of differences of opinion about the direction in which business ought to go and sometimes these conflicts overpower'.[20]

Entrepreneurial refers to the firm in which 'the entrepreneur who started it continues his leadership or is followed by one or more sons whose leadership efforts are going less well'.[21] Levinson suggests that, in an entrepreneurial situation, family feuds are precipitated, conflicts engendered and family is endemic.

Furthermore, the complexity of family business is more than the simple dichotomy between private/family versus public/professional management issues. Family owned and controlled is best defined as types of relationships that exist among its members. Another definition closer to the above is: 'the fundamental defining characteristic of the family firm is the overlap of family ownership and management group'.[22] In this study, the term privately owned and/or controlled is applied and a company is considered a family firm when it is associated with at least two generations of a family and when this linkage has had significant influence on the company goals, policies, and structure. Such a linkage is indicated when one or more of the following conditions exists:

1 Majority control is held by the founder or members of his family;
2 Strategic decisions are significantly influenced by the founder or his family members and beliefs;
3 Family members may not be actively involved in operations but collectively own majority shares;
4 The firm is privately owned, but has fewer than 50 shareholders.[23]

Table 2.2 indicates the status of each of the eight participating firms relative to these criteria. All the firms met the criteria of majority control held by the founder and members of the family and private ownership. Two of the firms' (Ntiki and Amadi) decisions were significantly influenced by the founder and family beliefs, while only Ginano held control with fewer family members involved in the daily operations of the business.

The ambiguity in the understanding of the definition as well as its nature is partly a result of its uniquely private nature and the difficulty often encountered in the process of studying privately held firms. Their contribution to the societies at large is also often overlooked, because of their association with 'small' and 'entrepreneurial' firms (both being

Table 2.2 Status of companies relative to the criteria for family controlled firms

Companies:	Ntiki Group of Cos.	Nwoke & Sons Ltd.	Francis Group of Cos.	Oko Holdings Limited	Onyeukwu & Sons Limited	Amadi & Sons Limited	Ginano Holdings Limited	Standard Entprs. Limited
Criteria:								
1. Majority control held by the founder or members of his family	+	+	+	+	+	+	+	+
2. Strategic decisions significantly influenced by founder, his family members and the beliefs	+	–	–	–	–	+	–	–
3. Family members may or may not be actively involved in operations but collectively own majority shares	–	–	–	–	–	–	+	–
4. Privately owned but fewer than 50 shareholders	+	+	+	+	+	+	+	+

+ Criteria strongly apply
– Criteria less strongly apply

65

terms which are often also ambiguously defined). However, by the time of this study in the mid-1980s, family controlled businesses had evolved tremendously and could be counted as significant among the giants in both developed and developing nations. In Nigeria there were many growing family controlled firms which were in the second and third generation of ownership (e.g. Odutola Tyres, Inc., Ginano Group of Companies, Ugochukwu and Sons Ltd., Sanusi and Sons Ltd., Oko Holdings Ltd., Akwiwu and Sons Ltd., Chembukawu and Sons Ltd., Isiykwu Rabiu and Sons Ltd., Toyin and Sons Nigeria Ltd., and many others).

Research on relationships between family and organizational transitions and performance (Handwerker, 1970; Barnes and Hershon, 1976) is in its embryonic stage in both developed and developing countries. In the USA, Barnes and Hershon suggest that family and company transition will be more productive when they are simultaneous. These authors identify family rifts or conflicts which often led to company stagnation. They describe the following organizational characteristics at each of the three stages of development: core problem, central function, control systems, reward and motivation, management style, organization structure, and levels of management.

Other authors have suggested that conflicts often arise as a result of complexity in the various roles played by the family members (Katz and Kahn, 1966, 1978; Kanter, 1977; Narayanan, 1975). Levinson (1977) suggested that it was often a better strategy to establish a trust for family members and hire professional managers to run the enterprises in order to save organizations from the results of family rifts. Studies in Africa (Handwerker, 1970; Gilmore, 1978; Saiyadain and Nambudiri, 1981) suggested that managers often hire relatives and members of their tribe, mainly because of pressures from both. The studies also suggest that conflicts arise when the kin employee puts tribal/family codes of behaviour before those of the organization.

Davis's 1982 study depicted family firms' problems as those of an 'Overlap of Family, Ownership and Management Groups'.[24] Davis maintained that 'having membership in two social systems makes it difficult for anyone to be objective'.[25] Hollander (1984), in her systems approach paper, proposed a model of family businesses with three major components — the family, the business, and the environment. This model presented the components as interfaced and affecting one another. Churchill and Lewis (1983), in their five stages of business development, depicted the relationship between business and the owner as the firm grows from survival stage to 'resource' maturity.

Other studies (Beckhard and Dyer, 1983; Landsberg, 1983; Schien, 1981) were concerned with single issues such as managing continuity in the family-owned firms, the role of the founder in creating organizational culture, and the management of human resources in family firms. However, the issue of family firms is even more complex than is generally depicted and complex problems cannot be readily and effectively solved through separation or singling out of inter-related issues.

Conflict resolution mechanisms

Authors on conflict identified levels of conflict and several factors leading to conflict as well as processes for conflict resolution. Pondy (1967) suggested four process approaches to the definition of conflict. These approaches include:

> 1) antecedent conditions (e.g. scarcity of resources, and policy differences) of conflictual behavior; 2) affective states (e.g. stress, tension, hostility); 3) cognitive states of individuals (i.e. their perception of awareness of conflictual situations; and 4) conflictual behavior, ranging from passive resistance to overt aggression.[26]

Conflict, according to Pondy, is a process which begins when one party perceives that the other has frustrated, or is about to frustrate, some concern of his. In this study, the antecedent conditions of conflictual behaviour and actual conflict appeared to dominate in the firms studied. Conflict in this study was defined as divergent views among family members which had potential for spilling over and affecting the management of the organization. Four types of conflicts were identified based on factors which influence conflict. These types included:

1 Goal conflict where the desires for different outcomes were the basis of conflict;
2 Cognitive conflict where ideas or opinions were different;
3 Affective conflict where emotions were incompatible;
4 Behavioural conflict where behaviours of one individual or a group were unacceptable to another.

Neilsen (1976) described the factors of conflict as:

1 Differences in reference groups — for example, differences in race and tribal or religious groups;
2 Distributive justice, that is inequitable allocation of position, salaries;
3 Differences in task orientation and experience — for example, differences in opinion, processes;
4 Competition for scarce resources.

67

It is generally believed that all conflicts are dysfunctional and should be eliminated. On the contrary, several researchers (Coser, 1956; Thomas, 1976; Graves, 1978) show that there are circumstances where some moderate amount of conflict could be healthy for the organization. For example, conflict could lead to new ideas or new mechanisms as a solution to the organizational problems. Stimulation of innovations and change was experienced in some of the participating firms. Also Coser in his 1956 study described this situation as follows: 'Conflict, which aims at a resolution of tension between antagonists, is likely to have stabilizing and integrative functions for the relationship.'[27] This study examined the resolution mechanisms among the firms where conflict existed, with the objective of determining the relationship between the mechanisms and the firm's ability to move from one stage of development to another.

Major authors on conflict (Neilsen, 1976; Miles, 1980; Meyers, 1973) have identified mechanisms for conflict resolution. Common methods among these authors include physical separation of parties, allowing limited interaction, using integrators, using third-party consultants, negotiating without third parties, exchanging members, using multiple level interactions, and persuasion and bargaining/politics. Situational factors influencing the effective application of these methods were also discussed.[28]

This study is designed to deduce the methods applied by the firms studied and then to compare these methods to those listed above.

Most of the literature reviewed in the above three sections — stages of organizational development, privately held or family firms, and conflict — show that most studies were concentrated in the industrialized countries. This situation presents further evidence to the need for this study.

Notes

1 A.D. Chandler, *Strategy and Structure*, MIT Press, Cambridge MA, 1962.
2 Ibid., pp.15—16.
3 A.D. Chandler, *The Visible Hand*, The Belknop Press of Harvard University Press, Cambridge MA, 1977, p.12.
4 B.R. Scott, *Stages of Corporate Development*, Report no.9-37r274 BP998, Harvard University Intercollegiate Clearing House, Boston MA, 1971.
5 The first written formulation of Scott's research was in a proposal for the 1963—64 Business Policy course at IMEDE. Subsequent work led to revisions in 1967, 1968 and 1969.

6   Ref. B. Scott and M. Salter, 1967, *Stages of Corporate Development: Implications for Management Control*, Case Clearing House, Cambridge MA, Harvard Business School.

7   B.R. Scott, op.cit., p.23.

8   R. Rumelt, *Strategy, Structure and Financial Performance of the Fortune '500', 1950–1970*, unpublished DBA dissertation, Harvard Business School, 1972.

9   J.R. Pavan, 'Strategy and Structure: the Italian experience', *Journal of Economics and Business*, December 1974, p.254.

10   The basic hypotheses were: 'there are no patterns or regularities to the way the largest companies have developed over time, and there are no such similarities across industries; two, there are no such similarities or patterns among the major industrial nations of the west', B.R. Scott, 1973.

11   R. Rumelt, *Strategy and Structure and Economic Performance*, Division of Research, Graduate School of Business Administration, Harvard University, Boston MA.

12   R.J. Pavan, *The Strategy and Structure of Italian Enterprise*, unpublished doctoral dissertation, Harvard Business School, June 1972.

13   P. Selznick, *Leadership in Administration*, Harper and Row, New York, 1957, p.103.

14   Y. Suziki, 'The Strategy and Structure of the Top 100 Japanese Industrial Enterprises, 1950–1970', *Strategic Management Journal*, vol.1, pp.265–91, 1980.

15   O. Williamson, *Markets and Hierarchies: Analysis and Antitrust Implications*, Free Press, New York, 1975.

16   W. Ouchi, *Theory Z*, Addison-Wesley, Reading MA, 1981.

17   R.G. Donnelly, 'The Family Business', *Harvard Business Review*, vol.42, July–August 1964.

18   G.P. Dyas, *The Strategy and Structure of French Industrial Enterprise*, unpublished doctoral dissertation, Harvard Business School, 1972, pp.21–3.

19   Ibid., pp.21–3.

20   H. Levinson, 'Consulting with Family Business: what to look for, what to look out for', *Organizational Dynamics*, pp.71–80, 1983.

21   Ibid., pp.73–4.

22   P. Davis, *The Influence of Life Style on Father–Son Work Relationships in Family Companies*, unpublished doctoral dissertation, Harvard Business School, 1982, pp.14–16.

23   According to Federal Ministry of Commerce and Industries in Nigeria (1984), there are four major categories of private firms: 1) companies limited to shares: private if less than 50 shareholders and public if more than 50; 2) companies limited by guarantee:

mostly philanthropic organizations; and 3) unlimited public corporations: often private or statutory government-owned.

24 Davis, op.cit., pp.14—16.
25 Ibid., pp.14—16.
26 L.R. Pondy, 'Organizational conflict: concepts and models', *Administrative Science Quarterly*, vol.12, 1967, pp.47—60.
27 L. Coser, *The Functions of Social Conflict*, The Free Press, New York, 1956, pp.10—16.
28 Methods of conflict reduction.

1 Physical Separation:
   Adv: Can be done quickly.
   Disadv: Members of groups do not learn new behaviours or attitudes.
   Use: Where groups are not particularly interdependent *and* situation allows separation.

2 Limited Interaction:
   Adv: Same as above.
   Disadv: Same as above.
   Use: Where peacekeeping party has the power and situation allows, e.g. where situation is relatively stable and need for interaction focuses on subordinate goals or relatively stable routine issues.

3 Using Integrators:
   Adv: Can be used in conjunction with above, allows co-ordination to meet needs for interdependencies.
   Disadv: Requires individuals who are respected by both parties (the 'golden men' syndrome); does not encourage attitudinal change.

4 Negotiations Without Consultants:
   Adv: Groups must learn behaviours allowing interdependent activities.
   Disadv: Must be sufficient motivation to encourage parties to achieve cooperation.

5 Exchanging Members:
   Adv: Helps clear up important misconceptions, aids in learning of new behaviours and attitudes.
   Disadv: Takes time, exchanged members may not be acceptable to own group when returned.

6 Multilevel Interaction:
   Adv: Aids in development of changed attitudes and behaviour.
   Disadv: Must be sufficient motivation for members to work together even under conditions of conflict, high risk of hostility breaking out, takes time.

Appendix 2.A   A taxonomy of family life

Major characteristics of family stages

A number of authors (Glick, 1947 and 1955; Hall, 1975; Lopata, 1966) have identified the family stage phenomenon in the developed countries. Typically, families evolve through a series of stages in which there are different role demands on the husband and wife at each stage.

The Nigerian social system, which has mostly been dominated by the 'extended family system', is currently developing another form of family, influenced by education. This may be called the nuclear family. Unlike the stages identified in the industrialized nations, family stages are more complex, and may be identifiable as follows:

1   Newlywed couple: each assumes the role of a spouse and a parent to one or two younger relatives, with the man working in the farm or other retail trade, or government or private corporate office job;
2   Expansion: with the birth of their first child, which is usually expected nine months after marriage, roles as parents become more complex but mostly for the wife. It will not be unusual for this couple to settle down among parents and other kin;
3   Addition of more children: may not increase roles but increases role senders and demands. Increasing potential for inter-role conflict. Couples are expected by society to care for less fortunate relatives, parents and younger ones;
4   Maturing children: children grow, enter school, or join in farm work or learn some trade. Often the family grows bigger. Other less

fortunate relatives may find shelter in the family, helping out in the family business. The potential for the above happening depends on the wealth and income level of the family. The complexity of the demands are increased as the parental pair must deal not only with their own children, but with outside demands — school, neighbours, community development projects, clan activities, and others which require attention from the couple;

5 Role demands diminish as children and relations develop a trade, or find jobs, or get married. But often demands remain at the same level since the system is such that people usually live or build a home around the family when they get married.

Zukerman (1978) and others (Epstein, 1975; Okali, Gyekeye and Mabey, 1974; Harrison, 1965; Bassell and Roberts, 1963; and Akarele, 1978) found differences in the role demands of family at different stages of growth. It is not yet known how these Nigerian families cope with potential conflict. This problem and the relationship to the stages of development is one of the objectives of this study.

3 Macro-environments of Nigeria

Introduction

Environment is continually changing. However, an industrial business environment changes faster than the natural environment.[1] Many pivotal factors are responsible for these changes which influence industrial organizations, which in turn influence the quality of individual lives and the industrial society in general. But as evolutionary biologists suggest, organisms adapt to their changing environments, thus increasing their likelihood of survival. These influencing/initiating factors for business are both economical, political, and social in nature and are therefore unique to the cultures and stages of development of each nation.

There are noticeable differences in the levels of industrialization between developed countries, such as the USA, and developing countries, such as Nigeria.

From the above, it is therefore important to briefly describe here the general state of environment in Nigeria to enable readers to better understand the findings in this study. Furthermore, no economic or industrial development takes place in the absence of social change.[2] Social and economic changes are never mutually exclusive, and usually the former provide the milieu for the latter. This chapter therefore represents the profile of the Nigerian social and industrial environments.

The social environment

Nigeria's total area of 924,768 kilometres is inhabited by an estimated population of over 80 million people. Estimates of total population and of each of its major politico-administrative units (the ethnic groups) vary widely — a consequence of projections based on inadequate demographic data.[3] The last census, controversial and officially unacceptable, was conducted in 1973. Since 1973, population figures have been based on estimates of annual rates of growth, ranging from the United Nations' (UN's) 3.2 per cent to over 3.7 per cent. The inadequacy of the demographic data partly reflects the political and economic significance of the regional distribution of the country's population. Even more problematic than the estimates of total population is the breakdown of ethnic groups into the 19 states or into smaller entities. (See Table 3.1 for breakdown into states.)

These estimates of total population yield an average density of 85–100 persons per square kilometre in 1980. States (see Figure 3.1) were used as units for density measurement, and this application has masked the substantial internal variations in many of the groups.[4] Also, estimates of Nigeria's urban population and of trends in urbanization were subject not only to the demographic base, but also to ambiguities in definitions. The government considered settlements as urban population if they included 20,000 people or more, while other observers defined urbanization in such a way that not all the inhabitants of an urban area were considered.[5]

Long before the colonial era, some of the Nigerian regions and ethnic groups could be characterized by a large tribal settlement. However, extensive urbanization began after the Second World War and accelerated markedly in the 1960s and 1970s. This process reflected the beginning of the growth of the non-agricultural economy (and perhaps the neglect of the agricultural one) and the subdivision of three regions into twelve states after the Civil War and then to nineteen in the mid-1970s. The creation of the states increased urbanization as many rural towns were elevated to urban status.

Ethnicity and language, education and religion

Estimates of the number of ethnic groups and languages (often related but not necessarily coterminous) range from 250 to 500.[6] The determination of the number of ethnic groups has become more problematic because of the shifts in the defining characteristics. Categorization in the past had been more on a subjective, cultural basis (e.g. similar dialect), but with the Civil War and the creation of new states, this old framework has shifted with both history and situation.

74

Table 3.1 Censuses and estimates of the Nigerian population (in millions)

States	1952–53 Census		1963 Census		1978 Estimate[1,2]		Davidson Estimate 1979[2,3]	
	Numbers	%	Numbers	%	Numbers	%	Numbers	%
Ogun	–	–	1.6	2.9	2.2	2.8	3.4	
Ondo	–	–	2.7	4.9	3.8	4.8	5.1	
Oyo	–	–	5.2	9.4	7.3	9.3	9.5	
Lagos[4]	–	–	1.4	2.5	2.3	2.9	3.8	
Bendel	–	–	2.5	4.5	3.6	4.6	5.0	
Former Western Region Sub-total	6.4	20.3	13.4	24.1	19.2	24.4	26.8	
Anambra	–	–	3.1	5.6	4.4	5.6	5.5	
Imo	–	–	4.1	7.4	5.8	7.4	7.3	
Cross River	–	–	3.7	6.7	5.1	6.5	5.2	
Rivers	–	–	1.5	2.7	2.2	2.8	3.0	
Former Eastern Region Sub-total	8.3	26.3	12.4	22.3	17.5	22.3	21.0	
Kwara	–	–	1.7	3.1	2.4	3.1	2.3	
Benue	–	–	2.4	4.3	3.4	4.3	3.3	
Plateau	–	–	2.0	3.6	2.8	3.6	3.4	
Niger	–	–	1.2	2.2	1.7	2.2	2.2	
Sokoto	–	–	4.5	8.1	6.4	8.1	7.9	
Gongola	–	–	2.7	4.9	3.7	4.7	4.8	
Borno	–	–	3.0	5.4	4.2	5.3	5.8	
Kaduna	–	–	4.1	7.4	5.8	7.4	7.2	
Bauchi	–	–	2.4	4.3	3.4	4.3	4.4	
Kano	–	–	5.8	10.4	8.1	10.3	10.9	
Former Northern Region Sub-total	16.9	53.5	29.8	53.7	41.9	53.3	52.2	
Total	31.6	100.1	55.65	100.15	78.6	100.0	100.0	

Notes:

1 Deutsche Bank figures, presumably based on official Nigerian figures. Roughly 1.6 million greater than the United States Bureau of the Census and United Nations estimates for 1980.
2 Based on extrapolations to 1977 from 1963 census on a 1978 voter registration. Estimate for 1980 is 103.8 million.
3 In this column absolute numbers equal percentages.
4 An estimate made in 1972 put 80 per cent of the population of Lagos State in the metropolitan area (about seventy square kilometres).
5 Absolute and percentage sub-totals and totals are based on rounded figures.

Source: Nigeria: Study of a Country, Library of Congress, 1981.

Source: Federal Ministry of Information, Lagos, Nigeria.

Fig. 3.1   Federal Republic of Nigeria showing states

Despite the large number of ethnic groups, three groups — the Hausa, Yoruba and Ibo — comprised over 60 per cent of the Nigerian population in 1980. That proportion has probably not changed in the aggregate as of 1983. An additional 15 groups make up another 30 per cent (see Table 3.1). There were also 20 other groups, each of which consisted of 100,000 or more persons. However, when all these groups were included, the list of large and medium-sized groups in the country would total about 10 per cent of distinguishable ethnic entities.

The British colonial policy and practice of organizing the federal republic into three (later four) regions,[7] led to substantial regional rivalry. One probable consequence of this division was the Civil War of 1967–70. Each of the three regions was dominated by one of the largest ethnic groups — the North by the Hausa, the South-west by the Yoruba, and the South-east by the Ibo. Northerners were long regarded by Southerners — particularly the Ibos — as tradition-bound and ultra-conservative. This Northern behaviour contrasted with the traditional socio-political values of Southerners which proved more adaptable to the process of modernization initiated by the British.

The Ibo and other peoples of the South were personally competitive and their societies were free of rigid class structuring.[8] Placing great stress on individual achievement and initiative, they were willing to engage in any kind of work that offered a chance for personal advancement and a better way of life.[9] Among the Yoruba, also, there had been considerable room for personal advancement despite the presence of chieftainship recognition and some degree of stratification. That and the early impact of opportunities provided by the European presence[10] gave many Yoruba people a head-start in adaptation to Western-induced change.

In addition, the commoners and the traditional élite of the more slowly developing North regarded Southerners, especially the Ibos and other people associated with them,[11] as aggressive, heathen (non-Muslim), proud, disdainful of Northern customs and disrespectful of established authority. The Northern Muslims believed that Allah (God) created the wealthy and the commoners. The commoners should therefore serve and respect the rich while the rich had an obligation to provide for those commoners, especially, food. The commoners should not attempt to better themselves since this was not Allah's wish. In addition, Southerners aroused opposition among the Northern élites because, having taken advantage of formal educational opportunities, they were able to capture most of the available positions in government, private enterprise, and trade.

The cleavage between the Ibos and the Yorubas was accentuated by their competition for control of the machinery of economic development and modernization.[12] Thus, in this climate of ethnic and regional animosity, five coups d'état and a costly Civil War occurred in the decade between January 1966 and February 1976.[13] The formation of new states in 1970 created a different, additional framework for ethnic rivalry. In the ethnically mixed states, such as Anambra, tribes or groups that had been too small to be politically significant in the older, bigger regions or at national level began to have impact. Where the states were ethnically close to homogeneity, segments of the group, often defined by locality, became the competitive elements.[14]

Language diversity was another factor initiating rivalry. Of the four major language groups which were spoken in Africa, three were primarily spoken in Nigeria.[15] It is estimated that there were over 250 languages and over 1,200 dialects in the country, thus indicating that there were almost as many languages as there are ethnic groups. Table 3.2 presents some of the major languages which were related to the ethnic groups. Other minor languages spoken, by regions, include Zarma, Kambari, Kaje, Eggon, Angas, etc. in the North; Ekoi, Junkum, Chamba, Alago, etc. in the South-east; and Bini, Ijaw, Ischekiri, etc. in the South-west.

The language diversity as a national basis for ethnic grouping has substantially influenced the level of rivalries among the groups. Apart from the indigenous languages, two others, English (which is the official language) and 'Nigerian Pidgin'[16] (which is an adulteration of the English language), have played significant roles in the communication and interaction among various ethnic groups. English is used in all formal interaction — offices, industries, and schools. In education, it is introduced at primary school level and used exclusively in the secondary schools and universities. Unlike the English language, 'Pidgin' is mostly used in Southern ethnically mixed urban areas and among those with little or no formal education.

Even when they do not use English or 'Pidgin', many Nigerians have been forced by circumstances to become bilingual or multilingual. These circumstances were caused by trade activities across ethnic groups. Because of the large population of Hausa, their political dominance, and their conservatism and refusal to study English, their language became the usual second language among Southerners who had to live and trade in the North.

Over time, politicians, scholars and others have argued that Nigeria ought to have an African language as its official tongue — if not alone, at least in addition to English. It has also been suggested that such a language should serve as both symbol and as a means of national integration. Major political and ethnic conflicts over choice of the appropriate representative language have thwarted the adoption of a common language. It has been argued that selecting any of the ethnic languages would appear to be accepting that ethnic group as superior

Table 3.2 Major Nigerian ethnolinguistic categories (% total population)[1]

Ethnolinguistic Category[2]	%	Ethnolinguistic Category[2]	%
Hausa	21.0	Igala	1.0
Yoruba	20.4	Idoma	0.9
Ibo (Igbo)	16.6	Ebira (Egbirra)	0.8
Fulani (Fulbe)	8.6	Gwari	0.7
Kanuri	4.1	Ekoi (Ejagham)	0.6
Ibibio	3.6	Mumuye	0.5
Tiv	2.5	Alago	0.4
Ijaw (Ijo)	2.0	Ogoni (Kana)	0.4
Edo (Bini)	1.7	Isoko	0.3
Anaang	1.2	Sub-total	89.7
Nupe	1.2	Other[3]	10.3
Urhobo	1.2	TOTAL	100.0

Notes:
1 All categories listed comprised 200,000 persons or more in 1963.
2 Names in parentheses are commonly used alternatives.
3 An additional 15 ethnolinguistic categories, each comprising between 100,000 and 200,000 persons in 1963, constituted about 4 per cent of the population.

Source: Based on information from Nigeria, Federal Ministry of Information, *Nigeria: 1978–1979 Official Handbook*, Lagos, 1979, pp.273–4.

to others in the country, as well as possibly giving that ethnic group a head-start in any form of economic development.

English has not only been used as an official and formal language, but fluency in English has come to be regarded by many as a social 'class distinction'. People well-versed in English often tended to intersperse their conversation with single English words even when using an indigenous language.[17]

Formal education alone has not always been the only major criterion for social status; patronage within the community or tribe has also played as important part. However, in the South, class and social distinctions were mostly generated by 'Western education, modern methods of communication, urbanization and success in the growth of commerce',[18] while in the North (Hausa-Fulani and Kanuri areas) class formation occurred within the guidelines of a traditional order structured by the principles of aristocratic birth and socio-political rank.

Religion and educational levels were other distinguishing characteristics among the diverse groups of Nigeria. Two major religious groups
were distinguishable in Nigeria — the Muslims (Islam) in the North and
the Christians in the South. The 1973 census indicated that the Muslims
comprised over 47 per cent of the country's population while the
Christians comprised about 35 per cent, the remaining 18 per cent
being made up of small indigenous 'religions' such as the 'Aladura'
(prayer church), 'Qua Iboe' and other spirit-worship groups.

Neither Islam nor Christianity in Nigeria was characterized by a
unitary organization or by a single body of doctrine or practice. Among
Christians, there were the Protestants and the Catholics and, within the
Protestants, there were the Methodists (Yoruba and the Southern Ibo),
Presbyterian (Ibibio), Christian reformed, Salvation Army, Lutheran,
Sudan Interior Mission (SIM), and others. Most of the educated élite
in the South were professed Christians. Missionaries had come to the
West Coast of Africa in the company of the traders and colonial
government officials and in Nigeria, they were confined for some time
between the areas of Lagos and Ibadan. Catholic missionaries were
particularly active among the Ibos. Education generally became the
preserve of the missions and the missionaries played an important
part in the education of the Ibo people. Attempts to extend the
Christian mission to the North were discouraged by the Muslim leaders
and by colonial authorities who were careful to avoid offending the
sensitive Muslim leaders. Divisions also exist in Nigerian Islam which
consist mostly of the Sunnis,[19] Ahmadiyuo,[20] Bori,[21] Quadiriya and
Tijaniya.[22]

Generally, there has been major improvement in the educational
level of Nigeria, leading to a major improvement in the life and health
of Nigerian citizens. Many government policies[23] on education were
based on the

> nation's educational philosophy which was the moulding of the individual
> child into a sound and effective citizen and the provision of equal educational
> opportunities for all citizens of the country, at primary, secondary and
> tertiary levels, both inside and outside the formal school system.[24]

The universal primary education Act of 1976 increased primary school
enrolment from 5 million to 11.5 million and secondary enrolment
from 500,000 to 1.5 million between 1976 and 1983. Over the same
period, university enrolment has more than doubled from about 25,000
to 63,000. In 1983 there were also plans for an open university system
which would be available to adults over 25 years old. With the 'indigenization' programme[25] schools built and controlled by missionaries were
taken over by the government; however, some of these schools were

later handed back to the different missionary groups after several negotiations and agreements.[26]

Each of the three major ethnic groups has left its impact on the economic development of the country — the Northerners by virtue of their sheer numbers, democratic government policy, and military enrolment dominate the political seat; the Yorubas dominate Civil Service positions and professional service businesses; and the Ibos feature strongly in the development of private firms and businesses.

Economic/industrial environment

During the 1970s the revenues from oil were high, and the government took an active and significant role in attempting to encourage economic development. Although Nigeria's industrialization is yet to be fully realized, Nigeria, in comparison to its neighbours (Benin, Niger, Chad, Cameroon) and other African countries, has a fairly good supply of some minerals basic to industrialization. In addition to these natural resources, the 80 million-plus population offers a more than adequate supply of skilled and unskilled labour for the country's industries, as well as a good market for its products. Nevertheless, there has been inadequate exploration of the potential of these minerals. Most of all, the economic and political environment had not yet been stable long enough to encourage foreign and indigenous private investors.[27]

Complete industrial development requires mineral products in economic quantities as well as adequate infrastructural facilities. Table 3.3 presents the mineral deposits in Nigeria. (Those which are not in economic quantity or have not been identified as such in Nigeria, but may exist in smaller amounts are placed in brackets.) Figure 3.2 shows locations of the mineral deposits.

The above-mentioned table and map indicate that Nigeria has potential for industrialization. There are also high institutions of learning designed to develop and provide appropriately skilled man-power. The background description of the Nigerian industrial environment indicates that there are many factors influencing the status of the country's industrial development and the pattern of evolution of firms operating in the country.

Pre-independence — 1960

Attempts at industrialization and economic development in Nigeria date as far back as the mid-nineteenth century. During British colonization, trade and commerce with both the British government and other African colonies predominated. This period was characterized by exportation of raw materials and importation of manufactured goods.[28]

81

Table 3.3 Minerals and Mineral Products

Mineral Fuels	Coal; Oil; Gas
Iron and Ferro-Alloy Metals	Iron; (Manganese); (Nickel); (Chromium); (Molybdenum); Tungsten; (Vanadium); (Cobalt); Niobium
The Non-Ferrous Metals	Copper; Lead and Zinc; Tin; Aluminum
Minor Metals and Related Non-Metals	(Antimony); (Arsenic); Beryllium; (Bismuth); (Cadmium); (Magnesium); (Mercury); (Radium and Uranium); (Selenium and Tellurium); Tantalum; Titanium; Zirconium
Structural and Building	Lime and Cement; (Gypsum); (Magnesite); Bitumen; (Mineral Pigments)
Ceramic Materials	Salt; (Borax and Borates); (Potash); Soda; (Sulphur and Pyrite); (Nitrites); (Lithium)
Metallurgical and Refractory Materials	Flourspar; (Cryolite); Graphite; Limestone and Lime; Foundry Sands; Sillimanite
Industrial and Manufacturing Materials	Asbestos; Mica; Talc; (Barite); Glass Sands; Mineral Fillers; Mineral Filters; (Fullers Earth)
Fertilizer Minerals	(Potash); (Nitrates); Phosphates; Limestone and Lime; (Sulphur)
Abrasives	Diamond; (Conundum); Garnet; Diatomite

Note: Minerals and mineral products in brackets indicate those not in economic quantity or which may exist in small amounts.

Source: Dr C Raeburn, *Minerals and Industry in Nigeria*, Nigeria National Archives, MISF 110, Government Printer 3274/1148/500.

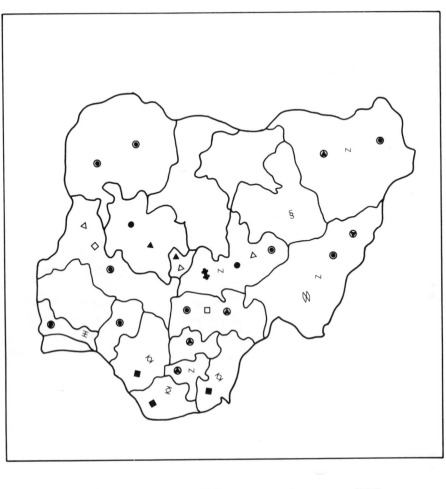

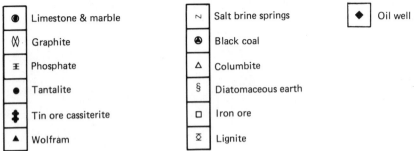

◉	Limestone & marble	∿	Salt brine springs	◆	Oil well
◊	Graphite	◓	Black coal		
⊞	Phosphate	△	Columbite		
●	Tantalite	§	Diatomaceous earth		
✽	Tin ore cassiterite	□	Iron ore		
▲	Wolfram	⦵	Lignite		

Fig. 3.2 Map of Federal Republic of Nigeria (mineral resources deposits)

The early twentieth century saw the development of such industries as timber (lumber) and later the formation of dealers' associations to develop and protect their interests in the industry.[29] In the 1940s, apart from the dominant retail and distribution industry, mining/extraction, and agricultural cash crop productions were starting up. Several 'ordinances' were established to develop and control these industries including the Mining Ordinance, 1912, reformed 1943; the Cooperative Societies Ordinance, 1948; and the Fish Farming Ordinance, 1951. The early 1940s also saw the establishment of such departments as the Commerce and Industries Department, which was responsible for the development and control of new and existing industries. The Federal Institute of Industrial Research was charged with conducting research on the feasibility of new industries using Nigerian raw materials, and also acting as a liaison and providing technical assistance on behalf of government corporations, private firms and international organizations. The search for petroleum in Nigeria, a major source of revenue by 1984, began as far back as 1908 when the Nigerian Bitumen Corporation drilled about 14 wells that were commercially unsuccessful. Oil prospecting licences were granted to parties such as Shell D'Arcy Exploration Co. in 1937 but this company was forced to suspend its activities in 1941 because of the Second World War. Between 1946—55 other prospectors (Shell BP; Mobil; AMOSEAS Texaco and Gulf Oil) drilled wells in several parts of the country without success.

Oil was first discovered in commercial quantities in 1956. Exportation of crude oil began in early 1958 along with many other findings of oil deposits. This discovery of oil in commercial quantities at this time in the history of Nigerian industrialization efforts was significant to the industrial environment of Nigeria after her independence from Great Britain in 1960.

As a result of the European traders' establishment of permanent posts along the Gulf of Guinea as early as the fifteenth century, cultural groups in the South became more acquainted with trade and modern education earlier than the Northerners.[30] Also, land availability and fertility had meant farmers were more concentrated in the North in contrast to the South (see Figure 3.3). In the South, however, hunting and gathering gradually gave way to some subsistence farming.

The Yoruba cities[31] functioned as political and religious centres and as emporia for some trade. The brass and bronze used by Yoruba artisans were in high demand by the Europeans.

Subsistence farming was practised in Ibo land which had always been over-populated in relation to its resources; however, the poor quality of the soil encouraged the Ibos to develop handicrafts and commercial skills more than any other group in the country. The Ibos relocated

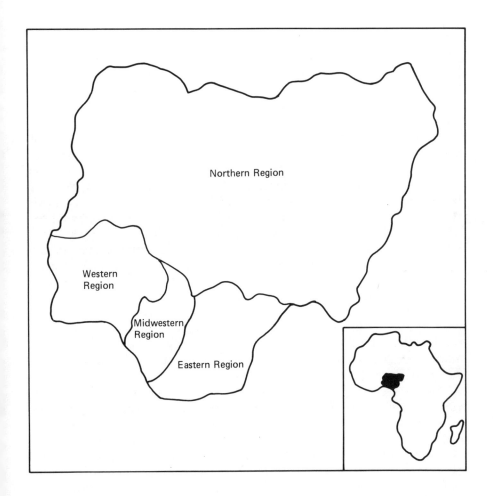

Source: Nigeria: Study of a Country, Library of Congress, 1981.

Fig. 3.3 Map of Federal Republic of Nigeria (regional areas, historical)

where any other trading activities would take them. Furthermore, in the North, tradition meant rulers benefited from trade but did not engage in it directly. Traders were Hausas,[32] not Fulanis,[33] whose trading instincts gave rise to a number of market centres on the caravan routes.

Between independence and the Civil War (1960–67)

Although the retail/distribution industry still dominated the nation's industrial environment, the effort at industrialization was increased by the Nigerian government after independence from Great Britain in 1960. In 1961, the government began discussion with the oil companies on the establishment of a refinery in Nigeria. Before the Civil War in 1967, oil production had increased from 6,000 barrels to 580,000 barrels per day according to a study by the Federal Ministry of Information in Lagos in 1979. Interest in the development of other industries was imminent, as indicated by the preliminary consideration for an iron and steel complex which dated as far back as 1958. However, definite steps were not taken until between 1961 and 1967 when a number of proposals were submitted to the federal government by various international companies. As was mentioned earlier in this section, steel is fundamental to the development of many other major industries, as well as the development of the infrastructures to support the growth of these industries. But despite the submission of proposals, high quality and commercial quantities of iron ore were not discovered until 1970. At that time a contract was signed with Techno-export of the USSR to develop and construct steel rolling mills and plants in the most desirable locations. The first iron and steel complex site was completed in 1975 at Ajakuta in Ibadan.

The six-year National Development Plan drawn up in 1962 for the 1962 to 1968 period emphasized industrialization, but was unevenly inclined toward the development of government corporations. Less emphasis and little or no incentives were established to encourage indigenous firms or private foreign investors, thus resulting in the existence of large numbers of public and government industries during this period. By 1966, for example, foreign ownership of private enterprises amounted to 92.9 per cent of all private enterprise, with British investment in fixed assets then constituting 52.3 per cent, US interests 17.3 per cent, and other foreign investment 30.4 per cent.

Also agricultural commodities accounted for over 80 percent of export values with major exports being Groundnuts [peanuts], Cocoa, Cotton, Palm Oil products, Beniseed and Soya. Major imports, on the other hand, included heavy and light industrial machinery, motor cars and parts, chemicals and drugs, industrial raw materials, electrical and electronic equipment.[34]

The three-year Civil War (1967—70) slowed down economic activities all across the country, but stopped activities completely only in the war-torn areas of the East. The areas most affected by the strife included the states of Anambra, Imo, and part of the Cross Rivers and Rivers States.[35]

Post-Civil War to 1983

In January 1970, the Nigerian Federal Military Government inherited the former civilian government's six-year National Development Plan established in 1962. This Plan anticipated Nigeria's transition from an essentially agricultural to a semi-industrialized economy based on the free market but including public participation to compensate for lack of locally generated private investment.[36] However, this military government was determined to create further situations that would not only meet the objectives of this second national plan, but also those of the third and fourth plans.[37]

With the above goals in mind (especially those concerning economic development), the federal government had designed and instituted various regulations and incentives aimed at increasing indigenous private enterprises. In 1970, when foreign ownership of enterprises in the country stood at 70 per cent, the federal government established the Enterprises Promotion Act 1972 (amended in 1977 and 1981), which was designed to put most Nigerians not only in the management positions but in control of many enterprises. (See Appendix 3.A.) The programme maintained three schedules of operations as follows: Schedule I must be fully owned by a Nigerian citizen; Schedule II must be jointly owned 40 per cent foreign to 60 per cent Nigerian, and Schedule III, 60 per cent foreign to 40 per cent Nigerian. In spite of considerable effort to avoid overlapping between the three schedules, difficulties have often been experienced in sorting out under which schedule an enterprise actually falls. Other major regulations on businesses included approved status, immigration laws, technology transfer, loan capital application, royalty and earnings transfer, and an economic stabilization programme (see Appendix 3.B), established to control imports of certain goods into the country.

However, various incentives were established to encourage both indigenous Nigerians and foreign investors to do business in Nigeria. These incentives included the establishment of the National Industrial Development Bank (NIDB) to provide loans to qualifying indigenes, tax breaks in forms of accelerated depreciation of capital investments, drawback regulations, excise tax reduction, extra concession for integrated agro-based industrial concerns, quasi-loans approved user scheme, pioneer industry status, and others (see Appendix 3.C).

Major financial contributions to the implementation of the government plans came from oil revenues, which by the year 1973 had become almost the only source of major revenue to the government in the country.[38] Although most of the oil revenue was earmarked for investment in economic development and diversification, poor management and resulting high inflation brought about increased unemployment in the urban cities as large numbers of farmworkers surged into the cities in search of higher-wage employment. Appendix 3.D presents the Gross Domestic Product contribution at 1973 cost and demonstrates the decrease or slow growth in agriculture compared to petroleum and wholesale (import) trade. However, Appendix 3.E, which presents the classification and frequency table of a sample of almost 1,000 firms, shows that service and trade industries dominated the economy at the end of 1983.

However, attempts by many private firms to benefit from the various incentives available in the country have resulted in a pattern of extensive diversification into related and unrelated industries. Also, in many cases, backward integration and joint action by competent relatives were the outcome of the government-initiated development plans.

Predictions and directions for Nigerian business and industry

Analysis indicated that firm-type economic development flourished in the 1970s. The industries making the most profit were the construction, and automobile and vehicle retail dealership industries. Construction was a relatively easy industry to enter, but was relatively difficult to exist in. This industry had the greatest number of new entrants as the result of reconstruction activities created by the Civil War. The automobile and vehicle dealership also flourished as most citizens who made 'quick money' during and after the Civil War needed and wanted to own a car so badly that they were willing to pay high prices for vehicles. The ownership of a vehicle and the type of vehicle owned became a basis of class distinction among civil servants, professionals, small and medium businessmen, and entrepreneurs with larger firms. Popular automobiles were Volkswagon, Peugeot and Mercedes Benz and, as a result of the growing market, the makers of these automobiles established assembly plants in various parts of the country.

Breweries and the soft drink bottling industry, like the above two, also became an attraction for many of the established organizations. Apart from the low capital involved in starting up a brewery, the market for its products remained almost perpetually growing as a result of the tropical weather which exists around the year in the country. The number of breweries grew from one plant in 1947 to 33 in 1984, with over 25 of these plants established between the 1970s and 1980s. Analysts with the Nigerian *Financial Punch* and the London *Financial Times* predict that the brewery industry will continue to top Nigeria's industrial 'profit league' in the latter half of the 1980s despite the general economic depression. Evidence indicates that while construction, merchandising, automobile and other industries are slowing down their operations as a result of the depression, breweries and soft drinks are making a 'killing' selling stocked inventories. The only problem affecting these industries are the middlemen who are taking advantage of the 'price control' policies and increasing their profit through hoarding practices.

Nigerian businessmen are rather inclined to take advantage of any industry that shows signs of increasing profit and thus will readily enter that promising market with a new business. In addition, government incentives have been extended to many manufacturing enterprises. Manufacturing operations with relatively simple technologies are usually owned and operated by Nigerian businessmen. Most manufacturing requiring more complex technologies is usually initiated through joint ventures with foreign partners with technical expertise or experience.

Summary and conclusions

Cultural and religious differences among the ethnic groups have created rivalry and problems which delayed various attempts at unified economic efforts. An example was the Civil War,[39] which interrupted the second National Economic Development Plan (1962–68). Unlike the Northern, Western and Midwestern states, where class distinction was an ingrained characteristic of the social order, most of the Eastern states rejected class distinctions and emphasized individual achievement. This emphasis on individual achievement gave impetus to the early development of trade organizations[40] before the arrival of the British traders from the West. Although firm-type economic development started in the early 1920s, enterprise activities were mostly in the hands of British expatriates. By the early 1950s few firms were owned and established by Nigerian indigenes. However, the 1972 Enterprises Promotions Act and its amendments (1977 and 1982) changed the situation by making it possible for more Nigerians to own and operate these businesses. But the timing of the programme created an uneven distribution of ownership opportunities since most of the people from the East were not in the position to buy most of the firms.[41] Most of the expatriates were willing to sell to, or go into joint ownership with, indigenes who were already running their own businesses and had potential for management. The situation resulted in the involvement of indigenous business Nigerians in various industrial enterprises. Furthermore, the owners of these firms took advantage of government incentives to develop other businesses and thus diversified their business interests. Many got into agriculture-based businesses or pioneer industries (see Appendices 3.B and 3.C), in order to benefit from the associated tax breaks and other benefits offered by the government. The government incentives, together with the rebuilding efforts following the war destruction, greatly encouraged such industrial sectors as building and construction, consulting and service, the wholesaling/retail trade, small-scale food processing, and manufacturing firms. The situation also affected the pattern of development of organizations. For example, all of the eight participating firms in this study operate in the construction and merchandising industries, four out of the eight are in integrated farming, and all are in at least one type of pioneer-classified industry. Interestingly enough, these businesses were all in the favoured industries for incentives and were established.

By mid-1983, however, the fast-growing Nigerian industrial economy appeared to be crumbling under the falling price of oil, high inflation, and corrupt practices. The military council headed by General Buhari, which took over the government in December 1983, inherited an empty federal treasury with a billion naira in foreign and internal government debts.[42] Traditional traders were badly hit by the debt situation as foreign trade partners became hesitant about forwarding more goods. Peugeot and Volkswagen Nigeria Limited made arrangements to finance their own loans from their home office, thereby leaving most indigenous trading companies and the government export credit agencies to battle with the exchange problem.

During an interview after the takeover of government, General Buhari[43] vowed that he and the Supreme Military Council would work to renew the country's industrial base, fight corruption, and pay Nigerian foreign debts. Fourteen months after the military takeover (February 1985), the same agency reported 'that the government has achieved much, although some demanding times lie ahead before the economic corner can be turned'.[44] In the economic and industrial sectors, analysts indicated that austerity measures still existed nationwide and specific positions (autumn 1985) in various sectors stood as follows:

— *Economy*: 'Failure of the IMF's loan arrangements promised a continued period of austerity and slower but continued economic growth.'

90

- *Capital markets*: 'Expected to see some industrial and banking parastatus, owned by the state governments (breweries, soap manufacturers, etc.) being sold in the securities markets.'
- *External debts*: 'The seemingly endless permutation of servicing the country's debts are compounded by the question over oil earnings in 1985, which itself is dependent on world conditions.'
- *Industry*: 'This sector forsees another tough year ahead. Many factories such as breweries and pharmaceuticals, who have shut down factories because of shortage of raw materials or machinery spare parts, were making profit selling stock.' But the question is how long will the stock last? Import restrictions are forcing manufacturers to reorganize as they struggle to find alternatives to imported raw materials.
- *Construction sector*: 'Bulldozers, scrappers and other construction equipment were gathering dust following federal and state cutback on project spending.' Companies were devising new strategies to survive, while over 220,000 workers (two-thirds of the sector's work force) had been laid off. Uncertainty still prevails as the government investigates past contract awards.
- *Trade sector*: 'As Nigeria continued to reduce its import levels, traditional suppliers [Britain, France, etc.] face new competitors [e.g. a big trade deal $1 billion with Brazil], and counter trade seems likely to increase. Improved import licence distribution gives hope to traders.'
- *Oil sector*: Leaves little room for manoeuvre. The country's oil industry is once more on edge with an urgent need to produce oil for sale constrained by price conditions in the world market. The natural gas industry, this nation's richest resource, is yet to be tapped.
- *Service sector*: 'Communication, electricity and other utilities have improved with the year. Nonetheless, there is still much room for improvement.'
- *Agricultural sector*: 'Although the military government claims that the success of its agricultural policy [government incentives – Appendix 3] is already apparent. Critics say this boost [increased poultry and fertilizer markets] was due more to the fortuitous arrival of good rain and the protection from imports.'[45]

All the firms participating in this study operate in most of the industrial sectors briefly analyzed above. Each company, by autumn 1984, was involved in retrenching of employees, as well as temporarily closing facilities in the absence of raw materials. Many had received new import licence quotas allowing importation of scarce materials and papers and were making plans to resume operations.

The political instability in Nigeria, resulting from coups and counter-coups, brought in another military president in autumn 1985. During his broadcast on 28 June 1986, President Ibrahim Babangida, reflecting the adverse economic development, introduced some radical measures and changes in the national budgets. These measures amount to major changes in the way Nigerians see the nation's budgets as well as the way that business has previously been done in Nigeria.

Despite the depressed economy, there was a 2.4 per cent growth in the 1985 GDP in contrast to the decline of 55 per cent in 1984. The government's effort to reschedule its foreign debts has been frustrated by its creditors' insistence that Nigeria accept an IMF-sponsored programme, while a national debate rejects the idea. President Babangida announced a budget which was built on policies rather than projects.

The broad policy objectives were to restructure and diversify the productive base of the economy and reduce dependence on oil and imports. These include proposing programmes that will stimulate agricultural production.

In an effort to raise the capacity utilization of Nigeria's import-dependent industries, a decision to set up a Second-tier Foreign Exchange Market (SFEM) was announced by the president. It is hoped that by trading the naira freely in this market, its value will massively decrease, thus removing the last obstacle for getting approval from the IMF. This approval will allow Nigeria's debt to be rescheduled.

Furthermore, the SFEM, which became operative in October 1986, appears certain to revolutionize the business environment in Nigeria since most exchange control regulations (an important feature of the economy) have been relaxed. Import licensing has also been phased out, and the 30 per cent import surcharge dropped, with the revenue from it expected to be more than covered by government profits from selling foreign exchange to the SFEM.

The SFEM is not expected to be risk-free. The over-regulated economy is not used to the level of freedom which may come from the second-tier market and there is bound to be confusion as businesses decide how to pay for and price their goods. The guidelines, processes and impact of the SFEM on the business community will be discussed in detail in Chapter 6.

Notes

1   Lawrence, P.R. and Dyer, D., *Renewing American Industry*, The Free Press, New York, 1983. The USA maintained that American industries were failing because they were not changing with environment.

2   Everett E. Hagen, *On the Theory of Social Change*, A Study from the Center for International Studies, Massachusetts Institute of Technology, Dorsey Press, Homewood IL., 1962.

3   The last completed and yet controversial census was in 1973. However, since then, the United States Bureau of the Census, on the basis of one projection, estimated the 1979 population at 74.6 million, an estimate close to the UN's estimate of 76 million. The Population Reference Bureau, basing its estimates on figures used by Nigerian Federal Government, estimated the 1980 population at 85.6 million. The highest estimate recorded was that given by economist R.A. Davison of the University of Calabar. Basing his estimate on the 1963 census, the latest officially accepted, and some assumptions, he came up with a population of 100 million for 1979 and 107 million for 1981.

4   Density ranges from fewer than 25 in Niger state to 600 per square kilometre in Lagos state.

5   In some cities with over 100,000 people, farmers whose farmlands lay at the outskirts of the city were excluded. *Nigeria − A Country Study*, Area Handbook Series, 4th edn, 1982.

6   Nigerian Federal Ministry of Information, *Nigeria: 1980−81*, Official Handbook, Lagos, 1982.

7   Initially they were the Northern, Western and Eastern regions but by early 1963, the Midwestern region was carved out between West and East to create four regions. This action was probably a result of the influence of a prominent politician from that area.

8   It was believed that the Ibo had no natural rulers. They were mostly small groups of individuals who believed that hard work could put one in any class one wished to belong to.

9   Again, because of the scarcity of fertile land in the area occupied by the Ibos, they were mostly traders and craftsmen and would move to other parts of the country to take any advantage it might offer.

10   The European traders as well as the missionaries with their education landed first in the Western part of Nigeria because of its proximity to the coast. The Yoruba tribes occupied the Western part of the country.

11   The other groups associated with the Ibos were the Ibibios and the Ikwerre peoples of the Cross Rivers and Rivers states. Sometimes part of the Midwestern was also associated with the Ibos, primarily because of some cultural similarities.

12   With the Yoruba's early opportunity at education and the Ibo's undaunted spirit to compete, the two groups formed two of the few eligible groups for modern government and commercial positions. With many qualified applicants and few positions great

resentment was generated by favouritism shown by authorities to members of their own ethnic groups.

13   The four recorded coups d'état were:
     January 1966 — bloody, many were killed.
     July 1967 — outbreak of the Civil War.
     June 1975 — bloodless takeover.
     February 1976 — bloody, assassination of the military leader.
     31 December 1983 — army takeover from civilians, bloodless.

14   In Anambra state, for example, the group from the North were accusing the Southern members of dominating the government offices, as well as controlling the industrial establishments of the states. This attitude has created an animosity that initiates non-cooperation in both political and social situations.

15   Of the four — Indo-European, Afro-Asiatic, Niger-Kordofanian and Nilo-Saharan — only Indo-European was not identifiable in Nigeria. *Nigeria — A Country Study*, Area Handbook Series, 1982.

16   'Pidgin' language is characterized by a structure related to the Nigerian languages, mostly those of the South, and by a lexicon that borrowed much from the English. This language is common among Southerners and people from diverse ethnic groups who use it in lieu of English when they are among non-Nigerians, even the highly educated indigenes.

17   Common among the formally educated élite was the practice of interspersing some English words, such as 'please', 'sorry', etc. when indigenous languages were being used. These practices sometimes occurred unconsciously or where certain English terms had no equivalent in the indigenous language.

18   *Nigeria — A Country Study,* Area Handbook Series, 4th edn, 1982, p.20. Indigenes who were highly formally educated or had acquired some substantial wealth through commerce were accorded reasonable class distinctions on that basis and not as a birth right which was common in the North.

19   The larger of the two greater divisions in Islam (the other is Shia), Sunnis, believe they are the true followers of the Sunna, the guide to behaviour composed of the Koran and the Hadith (the established traditions of Mohammed's deeds and words).

     Sunnis Islam requires of the faithful five fundamental duties (the pillars of faith): (1) profession of the faith — no god but God, with Mohammed as his only prophet; (2) prayer at five specified times of the day; (3) alms-giving to the poor by the wealthy; (4) fasting in the month of Ramadan; and (5) pilgrimage to Mecca.

20   Almadiya — a movement originating in India and considered deviant, if not heretical, by Sunnis. Popular among South-western Nigerians.

21 Bori (Spirit) Cult — popular among women, butchers, hunters, blacksmiths, and others of a socially subordinate status.

22 Qadiriya and Tijaniya — brotherhoods popular among the Hausa, Fulani and Yorubas, emphasize the principle of regimen of prayer and other activities conducive to mystical experience of God.

23 Some education policies included the system of primary, secondary, technical adult and university, as well as non-formal, special and teacher education. The above was designed to increase the literacy level of Nigerian citizens.

24 Education: The 4th National Development Plan, 1980—85, Federal Government Printers, Lagos, Nigeria, pp.13—14. See also note 23.

25 'Indigenization' — a programme designed by the Nigerian Federal Government to place, upon implementation, majority business ownership in the hands of Nigerians.

26 The missionary schools were taken over by the federal government as a sort of punishment to the missions for their charitable activities (air-lifting of food) in 'Biafra' during the Civil War. As the wounds of the war began to heal and the loss of the education provided by these missionaries was felt, Christian parents began to put pressure on the government to return schools to missionaries as a means of restoring discipline.

27 See note 13 for the series of coups d'état experienced in less than two decades.

28 Ordinance for Management and Regulation of Customs and Trade, 1907.

29 African and Eastern Trade Corporation Limited Timber Licence, 1929; African Timber Association, 1928; Co-operative Timber Products Societies, 1941.

30 The first British colony in Nigeria was established in Lagos in 1861.

31 While the Yorubas were governed by chiefs or Obas appointed by a King, the Benin in the Midwest were governed by members of a royal family who assigned land and territories. Also, while the Northerners were ruled by traditional leaders, the Ibos had been the only stateless society.

32 Hausas (translation: kings, leaders) were descendants of Chadic-speaking migrants from Sudan. Land occupied extended across Niger-Volta basins (in Nigeria — Kano, Zavia and Sokoto are traditionally Hausa lands).

33 The Fulanis were pastoral people forced south from the Sahara. They peacefully entered Hausaland in the early thirteenth century and consisted of a fiercely religious, educated élite who made themselves indispensable to the Hausa kings as government

officials, Islamic judges, teachers, or sometimes remained pastoral or cattle herders outside the cities.

34 ICON, *Nigerian Company Handbook*, 1983 edn, Jikonzult Management Services Ltd., Lagos, 1983.

35 This situation existed because the war was fought in the East as the battleground.

36 *Nigeria's Economic Development and Income Distribution*, Government White Paper, Lagos, 1984.

37 Objectives of the Fourth National Plan (1981–85) (which was similar to the previous ones) included among others:
   - Increased participation of citizens in the ownership and management of productive enterprises;
   - Reduction of the dependence of the economy on a narrow range of activities, and
   - Balanced development, that is the achievement of better balance in the development of the different sectors of the economy and the various geographical areas of the country.

38 Crude oil production (thousands of barrels) rose from 580,000 in 1966 to 750,675,000 in 1973 and continued to rise until 1975. Oil export ranged from $6,033 million in 1978 to $11,935 million in 1981. *Petroleum Economist*, October 1982.

39 The Civil War was the consequence of ethnic group rivalry which was escalated by the killing and massacre of Ibos living in the North by the Northerners.

40 History shows that the British traders travelled down to Onitsha and its environs in the eastern state of Anambra to buy produce, but soon established a buying depot in the early fifteenth century. By 1984 Onitsha hosted the largest commercial market in West Africa.

41 Easterners were still trying to recover from the effects of war and had insufficient funds to buy businesses. Northerners and Westerners who had continued business operations during the war period bought substantial numbers of firms, often resulting in their involvement in many diversified and sometimes unrelated industries.

42 Although the country's basic statistics at this time showed a per capita income of N527 (1 naira = $1.328, 1982), debts were estimated at 4 billion to 5 billion naira.

43 Interviewed by London *Financial Times* newspaper, January 1984.

44 Ibid., February 1985.

45 Ibid., Autumn 1985.

Appendix 3.A Nigerian Enterprises Promotion Amendment Act 1982

The Act classifies business into Schedules I, II, and III. Enterprises under Schedule I are those reserved exclusively for indigenous exploitation. Schedule II allows a maximum foreign participation of 40 per cent and a minimum Nigerian participation of 60 per cent, while Schedule III allows a maximum foreign participation of 60 per cent and a minimum indigenous participation of 40 per cent. The principal body charged with the responsibility of implementing the Act is the Nigerian Enterprises Promotion Board.

The Nigerian Enterprises Promotion Act 1977

SCHEDULE I

1. Advertising and public relations business.
2. All aspects of pool betting business and lotteries.
3. Assembly of radios, radiograms, record changers, television sets, tape recorders and other electric domestic applicances not combined with manufacture of components.
4. Blending and bottling of alcoholic drinks.
5. Blocks and ordinary tile manufacture for building and construction works.
6. Bread and cake making.
7. Candle manufacture.
8. Casinos and gaming centres.

9. Cinemas and other places of entertainment.
10. Commercial transportation (wet and dry cargo and fuel).
11. Commission agents.
12. Departmental stores and supermarkets having an annual turnover of less than N10,000,000.
13. Distribution agencies excluding motor vehicles, machinery and equipment and spare parts.
14. Electrical repair shops other than repair shops associated with distribution of electrical goods.
15. Estate agency.
16. Film distribution (including cinema films).
17. Hairdressing.
18. Ice-cream making when not associated with the manufacture of other dairy products.
19. Indenting and confirming.
20. Laundry and dry-cleaning.
21. Manufacturers' representatives.
21A. Industrial cleaning.
22. Manufacture of suitcases, brief cases, handbags, purses, wallets, portfolios and shopping bags.
23. Municipal bus services and taxis.
24. Newspaper publishing and printing.
25. Office cleaning.
26. Passenger bus services of any kind.
27. Poultry farming.
28. Printing of stationery (when not associated with printing of books).
28A. Paper conversion.
29. Protective agencies.
30. Radio and television broadcasting.
31. Retail trade (except by or within departmental stores and super-markets).
32. Singlet manufacture.
33. Stevedoring and shorehandling.
34. Tyre retreading.
35. Travel agencies.
36. Wholesale distribution of local manufactures and other locally produced goods.
36A. Storage and warehousing — the operation of storage facilities and warehouse for hire to the general public.

SCHEDULE II

1. Banking — commercial, merchant and development banking.

2. Basic iron and steel manufacture.
3. Beer brewing.
4. Boat building.
5. Bottling of soft drinks.
6. Business services (other machinery and equipment rental and leasing) such as business management and consulting.
7. Canning and preserving of fruits and vegetables.
8. Coastal and inland waterways shipping.
9. Construction industry.
10. Departmental stores and supermarkets having annual turnover of not less than N10,000,000.
11. Distribution agencies for machines and technical equipment.
12. Distribution and servicing of motor vehicles, tractors and spare parts thereof or similar objects.
13. Fish and shrimp trawling and processing.
14. Grain mill products except rice milling.
15. Industrial cleaning.
16. Internal air transport (scheduled and charter services).
17. Insurance — all classes.
18. Lighterage.
19. Manufacture of bicycles.
20. Manufacture of biscuits and similar dry bakery products.
21. Manufacture of cosmetics and perfumery.
22. Manufacture of cocoa, chocolate and sugar confectionery.
23. Manufacture of dairy products, butter, cheese, milk and other milk products.
24. Manufacture of food products like yeast, starch, baking powder, coffee roasting; processing of tea leaves into black tea.
25. Manufacture of furniture and interior decoration. Manufacture of metal fixtures for household, office and public building.
26. Manufacture of leather footwear.
27. Manufacture of matches.
28. Manufacture of paints, varnishes or other similar articles.
29. Manufacture of plastic products such as plastic dinnerware, tableware, kitchenware, plastic mats, plastic machinery parts, bottles, tubes and cabinets.
30. Manufacture of rubber products, rubber footwear, industrial and mechnical rubber specialities such as gloves, mats, sponges and foam.
31. Manufacture of tyres and tubes for bicycles and motorcycles; of tyres and tubes for motor vehicles.
32. Manufacture of soap and detergents.
33. Manufacture of wire, nails, washers, bolts, nuts, rivets and other similar articles.

34. Other manufacturing industries such as non-rubber and non-plastic toys, pens, pencils, umbrellas, canes, buttons, brooms and brushes, lampshades, tobacco pipes and cigarette holders.
35. Mining and quarrying.
36. Oil milling, cotton ginning and crushing industries.
37. Paper conversion industries.
38. Printing of books.
39. Production of sawn timber, plywood, veneers and other wood conversion industries.
40. Publishing of books, periodicals and the like.
41. Pulp and paper mills.
42. Restaurants, cafes and other eating and drinking places.
43. Salt refinery and packaging.
44. Screen printing on cloth, dyeing.
45. Inland and coastal shipping.
46. Slaughtering, storage associated with industrial processing and distribution of meat.
47. Tanneries and leather finishing.
48. Wholesale distribution of imported goods.
49. Photographic studios, including commercial and aerial photography.
50. Tin smelting and processing.
51. Establishments specializing in the repair of watches, clocks and jewellery, including imitation jewellery for the general public.
52. Garment manufacture.
53. Manufacture of jewellery and related articles including imitation jewellery.
54. Rice milling.

Note: No.50 above was moved from Schedule III to II while 51—54 were moved from Schedule I to II.

SCHEDULE III

1. Distilling, rectifying and blending of spirits such as ethyl alcohol, whisky, brandy, gin and the like.
2. Tobacco manufacture.
3. Manufacture of basic industrial chemicals (organic and inorganic) except fertilizers.
4. Manufacture of synthetic resins, plastic materials and man-made fibres except glass.
5. Manufacture of drugs and medicines.
6. Manufacture of pottery, china and earthenware.
7. Manufacture of glass and glass products.

8. Manufacture of burnt bricks and structural clay products.
9. Manufacture of miscellaneous non-mineral products such as concrete, gypsum and plastering products, including ready-mixed concrete; mineral wool, abrasive; asbestos products; graphite products.
10. Manufacture of primary non-ferrous metal products such as ingots, bars and billets; sheets; strips, circles, sections rods, tubes, pipes and wire rods; casting and extrusions.
11. Manufacture of (fabricated metal) cutlery, hand tool and general hardware.
12. Manufacture of structural metal products — components of bridges, tanks, metal doors and screens, window frames.
13. Manufacture of miscellaneous fabricated metal products except machinery and equipment, such as safes and vaults; steel springs, furnaces; stoves, and the like.
14. Manufacture of engines and turbines.
15. Manufacture of agricultural machinery and equipment.
16. Manufacture of metal and wood working machinery.
17. Manufacture of special industrial machinery and equipment, such as textile and food machinery, paper industry machinery, oil refining machinery and equipment, and the like.
18. Manufacture of office, computing and accounting machinery.
19. Manufacture of other machinery and equipment except electrical equipment, pumps, air and gas compressors; blowers, air-conditioning and ventilating machinery; refrigerators, and the like.
20. Manufacture of electrical industrial machinery and apparatus.
21. Manufacture of radio, television and communication equipment and apparatus.
22. Manufacture of electrical applicances and houseware.
23. Manufacture of electrical apparatus and supplies not elsewhere classified, such as insulated wires and cables, batteries, electric lamps and tubes, fixtures and lamp switches, sockets, switches, insulators and the like.
24. Ship building and repairing (excluding boat building).
25. Manufacture of railway equipment.
26. Manufacture of motor vehicles and motorcycles.
27. Manufacture of aircraft.
28. Manufacture of professional and scientific and measuring and controlling equipment, such as laboratory and scientific instruments, surgical, medical and dental equipment, instruments and supplies and orthopaedic and prosthetic applicances.
29. Manufacture of photogaphic and optical goods.
30. Manufacture of watches and clocks.
31. Ocean transport/shipping.

32. Oil servicing companies.
33. Textile manufacturing industries.
34. Hotels, rooming houses, camps and lodging places.
35. Data processing and tabulating services (on a fee or contract basis).
36. Production of cinema and television films (or motion picture production).
37. Machinery and equipment rental and leasing.
38. Fertilizer production.
39. Manufacture of cement.
40. Manufacture of metal containers.
41. Plantation agriculture for tree crops, grains, and other cash crops.
42. Plantation sugar processing.
43. All other enterprises not included in Schedule I or II not being public sector enterprises.

Note: Nos.38—42 of Schedule III were moved from Schedule II to III by recent legislation to encourage greater foreign participation in these industries.

Investors seeking to comply with the provisions of the Nigerian Enterprises Promotion Act 1977 are advised to contact the offices of the Nigerian Enterprises Promotion Board, 72 Campbell Street, PMB 12253, Lagos, Nigeria. Financial institutions performing Issuing House functions are also willing to offer useful advice and assistance to prospective investors wishing to comply with the provisions of the Act.

Note: The Authorities have reviewed the Act with a view to stimulating new and increased foreign investments.

Appendix 3.B   Economic Stabilization (Temporary Provisions) Import and Export Prohibition Order 1983

The Order provides, among others, for the prohibition of export and import of certain goods while placing others under licence.

SCHEDULE I

GOODS THE IMPORTATION OF WHICH IS
ABSOLUTELY PROHIBITED

PART I

ABSOLUTE PROHIBITION
(OTHER THAN TRADE)

1.   Air pistols.
2.   Airmail photographic printing paper.
3.   Base or counterfeit coins of any country.
4.   Beads composed of inflammable celluloid or other similar substances.
5.   Blank invoices.
6.   Coupons for foreign football pools or other betting arrangements.
7.   Cowries.
8.   Exhausted tea or tea mixed with other substances. For the purposes of this item, 'exhausted' tea means any tea which has been deprived of its proper quality, strength or virtue by steeping, infusion, decoction or other means.

9. Implements appertaining to the reloading of cartridges.
10. Indecent or obscene prints, paintings, books, cards, engravings or any indecent or obscene articles.
11. Manillas.
12. Matches made with white phosphorous.
13. Materials of any description with a design which, considering the purpose for which any such material is intended to be used, is likely in the opinion of the President to create a breach of the peace or to offend the religious views of any class of persons in Nigeria.
14. Meat, vegetables or other provisions declared by a health officer to be unfit for human consumption.
15. Piece goods and all other textiles including wearing apparel, hardware of all kinds, crockery and china, or earthenware goods bearing inscriptions (whether in Roman or Arabic characters) from the Koran or from the traditional commentaries on the Koran.
16. Pistols disguised in any form.
17. Second-hand clothing.
18. Silver or metal alloy coins not being legal tender in Nigeria.
19. Spirits —
(1) other than —
    (a) alcoholic bitters, liqueurs, cordials and mixtures admitted as such in his absolute discretion by the Director and which are not deemed to be injurious spirits within the meaning of any enactment or law relating to liquor or liquor licensing;
    (b) brandy, i.e. a spirit —
        (i) distilled in grape-growing countries from fermented grape juice and from no other materials; and
        (ii) stored in wood for a period of three years;
    (c) drugs and medical spirits admitted as such in his absolute discretion by the Director;
    (d) gin, i.e. a spirit —
        (i) produced by distillation from a mixed mash of cereal grains only saccharified by the diastase of malt and then flavoured by a re-distillation with juniper berries and other vegetable ingredients and of a brand which has been notified as an approved brand by notice in the Gazette and in containers labelled with the name and address of the owner of the brand; or
        (ii) produced by distillation at least three times in a pot-still from a mixed mash of barley, rye and maize saccharified by the diastase of malt and then rectified by re-distillation in a pot-still after the addition of juniper berries and other vegetable materials;

(e) methylated or denatured spirits, i.e. —
   (i) mineralised methylated spirit mixed as follows: to every ninety parts by volume of spirits nine and one-half parts of volume of wood naphtha and one-half of one part of volume of crude pyridine and to every 455 litres of the mixture 1.7 litres of mineral naphtha or petroleum oil and no less than 0.7 grammes by weight of powdered aniline dye (methylviolet) and so in proportion for any quantity less than 455 litres; and
   (ii) industrial methylated spirits imported under licence from the Director and mixed as follows: to every ninety-five parts by volume of spirits five parts by volume of wood naphtha and also one-half of one part of volume of the mixture; and
   (iii) spirits denatured for a particular purpose in such manner as the Director in any special circumstance may permit;
(f) perfumed spirits;
(g) rum, i.e. a spirit —
   (i) distilled direct from sugar-cane products in sugar-cane growing countries; and
   (ii) stored in wood for a period of three years;
(h) spirits imported for medical or scientific purposes, subject to such conditions as the Director may prescribe;
(i) spirits totally unfit for use as potable spirits admitted to entry as such in his absolute discretion by the Director; and
(j) whisky, i.e. a spirit —
   (i) obtained by distillation from a mash of cereal grains saccharified by the diastase of malt; and
   (ii) stored in wood for a period of three years.
(2) Containing more than forty-eight and one-half percentum of pure alcohol by volume except denatured, medicated and perfumed spirits, and such other spirits which the Director, in his discretion, may allow to be imported subject to such conditions as he may see fit to impose.
20. Weapons of any description which in the opinion of the Director are designed for the discharge of any noxious liquid, gas or other similar substance, and any ammunition containing or in the opinion of the director designed or adapted to contain any noxious liquid, gas or other similar substance.
21. All passenger cars whose value (C and F) exceed N15,000.

PART II

ABSOLUTE PROHIBITION (TRADE)

1. Basketwork, wickerwork and other articles of plaiting material, made directly to shape include coir door mats, articles made up from goods falling within Heading Nos.46.01 or 46.02 in the Customs Tariff.
2. Floor mops.
3. Bread, chips, biscuit and other ordinary bakers' wares not containing sugar, honey, eggs, fats, cheese or fruits.
4. Box files, letter trays, storage boxes and similar articles, of paper or paperboard, of a kind commonly used in offices, shops and the like.
5. Cigarettes.
6. Fur clothing, that is furskins, raw, tanned or dressed (including pieces or cuttings of tanned or dressed furskin, heads, paws, tails and the like) and articles of furskins.
7. Live poultry, that is fowls, ducks, geese, turkeys and guinea fowls (excluding day-old chicks).
8. Stone, sand, gravels, excluding refractory bricks and industrial grinding stone.
9. Household utensils of wood excluding ice cream and confectionery sticks.
10. Vegetable, roots and tubers, fresh or dried, whole or sliced, cut or powdered and sago pitch.
11. Wood in the rough, roughly-squared or half squared, but not further manufactured.
12. Worked monumental or building stone (including road and paving sets, curbs and flagstones) and articles thereof (including articles of agglomerated slate and mosaic cubes), other than goods falling within Chapter 69 of the Customs Tariff.
13. Eggs in the shell, including those for hatching but excluding those imported by recognized hatcheries approved in that behalf by the Minister.
14. Vegetables, fresh or chilled.
15. Pastry, biscuits and cakes (Tariff No.19.08).
16. Fresh or dried edible nuts, including coconuts, other than koala-nuts and nuts for extracting oil.
17. Fresh fruits.
18. Fruits, temporarily preserved.
19. Fruits, preserved, and fruit preparations and fruit juices excluding concentrated fruit comminutes and fruit juices unfermented and not containing alcohol imported by the manufacturer approved in

that behalf by the Minister (Tariff Nos.20.01, 20.03, 20.04, 20.06 and 20.07).

20. Potatoes, fresh or chilled.
21. Potatoes other than fresh or chilled.
22. Tomatoes, fresh or chilled.
23. Vegetables other than fresh or chilled.
24. Vegetable products, fresh or chilled.
25. Vegetables, roots and tubers preserved or prepared, excluding tomato puree and paste.
26. Sugar confectionery and other sugar preparations including flavoured or coloured syrups and molasses (Tariff Nos.17.04 and 17.05).
27. Textile fabrics of all types, including woven, knitted pile, coated, narrow, embroidery, imitation leather with textile backing, elastic or rubberised, excluding —
    (a) trimmings and linings;
    (b) importation excluding jute fabrics for local manufacture of goods by a manufacturer approved in that behalf by the Minister (chapters 50—60 and headings 43.c4 and 70.20);
    (c) tracing cloth.
28. Woven labels and badges excluding badges used by approved international organisations.
29. Towels (Tariff Nos.59.03A and 62.02A).
30. Other made-up articles of textile (Tariff Nos.62.03 and 62.05).
31. Travel goods of all kinds including shopping bags, handbags, brief-cases and wallets but excluding spectacle cases (Tariff No.42.02).
32. Stoppers and closures of common glass (Tariff No.70.10).
33. Ornaments and other fancy glassware of a kind used for domestic purposes (Tariff Nos.70.19D and 70.21).
34. Other articles of glass (Tariff No.70.21).
35. Domestic articles and wares made of plastic materials excluding babies' feeding bottles (Tariff No.39.07G).
36. Enamelware and galvanised buckets (Tariff No.73.38A).
37. Bottled beer (Tariff No.22.03).
38. Bottled stout (Tariff No.22.03).
39. Furniture made of stone or of plaster or of asbestos cement (Tariff Nos.68.11 and 68.12).
40. Evian and similar waters (Tariff No.22.01).
41. Carbon papers.
42. Lace, tulle (excluding tulle grass) and net fabrics (Tariff Nos.58.08 and 58.09).
43. Fresh milk (Tariff No.40.01).
44. Flavoured or coloured beet sugar (Tariff No.17.02).

45. Macaroni and spaghetti (Tariff Nos.19.03 and 21.07D).
46. Beer and stout (Tariff No.22.03).
47. Vitaminised malt extract drinks (Tariff No.22.02B).
48. Footwear, uppers, soles and heels, excluding soles, heels, industrial footwear, gloves, boots and apparel for all disciplined forces imported by manufacturers and users approved in that behalf by the Minister.
49. Carpets, carpeting and rugs (Tariff Nos.58.01 and 58.02).
50. Furniture, excluding medical, dental, surgical or veterinary furniture (Tariff Nos.94.01 and 94.03).
51. Matches (Tariff No.36.06).
52. Jewellery and imitation jewellery (Chapter 71).
53. Men's and boys' outer and under garments of all kinds, women's, girls' and infants' outer and under garments of all kinds including headties but excluding sport jerseys, track suits, industrial protective gloves, apparels imported by approved users and professional robes accepted as such by the board (Tariff Nos.39.07B, 40.03A, 43.04A, 60.05, 60.06B (2) 60.01–60.06 and 70.20A).
54. Household candles (Tariff No.34.06).
55. Pearls, precious stones and semi-precious stones.
56. Christmas cards and other greeting cards.
57. Calendars, almanacs and diaries.
58. Tooth-picks.
59. Rice in packets or in containers of less than 50 kilogrammes.
60. Artificial flowers or fruits or parts thereof (Tariff No.67.02).
61. Fireworks (Tariff No.36.05).
62. Toothpaste (Tariff No.33.06B).
63. Bicycle tyres and tubes sizes 28x10, 26x1–3/8 and 26x1–5/8.
64. Gaming machines (Tariff No.97.04A).
65. Chilled or frozen poultry of all kinds including chicken, duck, goose, turkey and guinea fowls and any part of such poultry (Tariff No.0.2.03).
66. Primary cells and batteries (1.5 volts) of size "D", "UMI", "R20" and other batteries of a size similar to those aforesaid as specified in Tariff No.83.03c.
67. Components of all the above goods imported unassembled or disassembled.

SCHEDULE II

GOODS CONDITIONALLY PROHIBITED

PART I

GOODS PROHIBITED FROM BEING IMPORTED EXCEPT AS PROVIDED HEREIN

Column I — Articles

Column II — Exceptions

1. (a) Advertisements or notices as such or contained in periodicals or books or as labels on packets, bottles, boxes or other enclosures, relating to the treatment of any venereal disease or any disease or condition in respect of which section 56(1) of the Poisons and Pharmacy Act prohibits advertisements or relating to aphrodisiacs.

   (b) Any packet, box, bottle or other enclosure containing any drug or preparation with which there is any advertisement or notice or on which there is any label, which advertisement, label or notice is prohibited under paragraph (a) above.

Except advertisements in publications of a technical character for circulation amongst —
(a) Registered medical or veterinary practitioners;

(b) selling dispeners or chemists and druggists;
(c) the governing body or managers of hospitals, nursing homes or mental hospitals.

2. All goods which bear a design or imitation of any currency or banknote or coin in current use in Nigeria or elsewhere.

Except books for use in schools.

3. Ammonium nitrate, pure

Except under licence from the Director of Food and Drugs Administration, Federal Ministry of Health or Minister of Mines and Power.

4. Apparatus which in the opinion of the Director is suitable for the distillation of alcohol or the rectification or redistillation of spirits.

Except such as may be licenced under any enactment or law relating to liquor or liquor licensing.

5.	Calcium carbide	Except when enclosed in substantially closed metal vessels with screw press on or lever opening themselves clearly marked in conspicuous characters with the words "Calcium Carbide — Dangerous if not kept dry".
6.	Cyanide of potassium and all poisonous cyanides and their preparations.	Except under license from the Chief Inspector of Mines or the Inspector-General of Police, and subject to such conditions as they may see fit to impose.
7.	Gold coin	Except under licence from the Minister.
8.	Raw or rolled precious metals	Except by a manufacturer of jewelry approved in that behalf by the Minister and approved to be imported by the Minister charged with responsibility for mines and minerals.
9.	Motor Vehicles fitted or adapted for solid tyres and parts thereof including solid tyres.	Except under licence from the Minister charged with responsibility for Federal highways.
10.	Naval, Military, Air Force or civil accoutrements or uniforms or any dress having the appearance of or bearing any resemblance of such uniform, or which may in the opinion of the proper officer be used to convey the impression that a person wearing the dress holds any office or authority under the Government of the Federation or of a State therein.	Except such as are imported by serving members of Nigerian Armed Forces or with the authority of the Commander-in-Chief of the Armed Forces.
11.	Firearms of all descriptions and ammunitions.	Except for the Nigerian Armed Forces or those imported with the approval of the Minister charged with responsibility for police affairs.
12.	Nets, gins, traps, snares, spring guns, missiles containing explosives, apparatus for setting guns and all similar or other mechanical engines or appliances including any parts thereof or accessories thereto designed, calculated or	Except such articles as may be imported with the approval of the Director on specific occasions if required for scientific purposes on condition that they are either destroyed or exported from Nigeria after they have been used for the scientific purposes aforesaid.

intended to be used to capture, injure or destroy any animal: Provided that no gin or trap or similar article shall be deemed hereby to be prohibited from being imported solely or by reason of the fact that it has jaws, if the jaws are not capable of being opened to a greater width than 10 cm. measured at the widest part: Provide further that the decision of the Board shall be conclusive in any dispute which may arise as to what is to be considered a prohibited import within the meaning of this item.

13.	Percussion caps.	Except those adapted for use with cap guns.
14.	Reel-fed rotary ticket printing presses.	Except under licence from the Minister.
15.	Spirits —	
	(a) of all descriptions	(a) Except in a ship of more than 100 tonnes registered or in an aircraft.
	(b) in casks or drums	(b) Except under license granted by the Director and subject to the payment of 5k per liquid litre for every one per cent of pure alcohol in excess of 43 per cent or such other fees as the Minister shall from time to time determine.
	(c) Denatured, other than methylated spirits as defined in Schedule I, totally unfit for use as potable spirits.	(c) Except under licence from the Director.
	(d) Methylated, industrial as defined in subparagraph (ii) of paragraph (e) of item 19 of Schedule I.	(d) Except under licence from the Director.
	(e) Spirits other than potable spirits mentioned in paragraph 19(1) of Part I of Schedule I to this Order imported for medical or scientific purposes.	(e) Except under licence from the Director.
16.	Tear gas.	Except under licence from the Minister.

17.	Terne-plate and all goods made from terneplate.	Except under licence from the Import Licensing Authority.
18.	Machines for duplicating keys	Except under licence from the Inspector-General of Police and subject to such conditions as he may see fit to impose.
19.	Salk anti-poliomyelitis vaccine	Except under licence from the Director of Medical Services to the Government of the Federation.
20.	Petroleum products including:— (i) gas or diesel oils; (ii) illuminating oils including kerosine and others; (iii) lubricating oils; (iv) motor spirits, benzine, bensoline, naphtha, gasoline, petrol and petroleum shale and coal tar spirits.	Except under licence from Minister for Petroleum Resources.
21.	Armoured Vehicles	Except under licence from the Minister for Defence.
22.	Eaves-dropping equipment, probe microphones, mini-size dynamic microphones, contact microphones, pocket-size tape recorders, lie detectors, door-step microphones, pocket wireless transmitting and receiving sets, pocket electronic stethoscope, wireless telephone and space monitoring sets, micro-cameras and all forms of mini-transmitters.	Except under licence from the Minister.
23.	Photocopying machines capable of reproducing in colour.	Except under licence from the Minister.

PART II

PROHIBITION – (TRADE)

GOODS PROHIBITED FROM BEING IMPORTED EXCEPT UNDER IMPORT LICENCE

Articles

1. Unmanufactured tobacco, tobacco refuse (Tariff No.24.01).
2. Other manufactured tobacco (Tariff No.24.02).
3. Packaging containers excluding those made of glass.
4. Manufactured articles of wood of all types whether or not for domestic or decorative use including flush doors (Tariff Nos.44.19 to 44.28).
5. Stout imported in tanks for blending by a manufacturer approved in that behalf by the Minister (Tariff No.22.03).
6. Duplicating paper (Tariff No.48.01).
7. Pre-printed papers and forms with or without carbon papers inserted.
8. Kraft paper (glazed or unglazed) excluding kraft paper imported by a manufacturer approved in that behalf by the Minister (Tariff No.48.01).
9. Paper board, including liner and corrugated board excluding paper board imported by a manufacturer approved in that behalf by the Minister (Tariff Nos.48.01–48.07).
10. Bed linen, table linen, toilet linen, kitchen linen, curtains, pillow cases, and other furnishing articles but excluding mosquito nets (Tariff Nos.62.02 and 94.04).
11. Typewriter ribbons (Tariff No.98.08) excluding computer ribbons.
12. All non-alcoholic beverages including all soft drinks and waters (Tariff Nos.20.07, 21.07B, 22.01 and 22.02).
13. Cornflakes, rice crispies and similar cereals (Tariff No.19.05).
14. Structural scaffolding pipes.
15. Radio receiving sets, record players, tape recorders, video cassette recorders, tape decks and stereo sets (Tariff Nos.85.15A and 92.11A).
16. Television sets (Tariff No.85.15).
17. Air-conditioners (Tariff No.84.12) and domestic refrigerators (Tariff No.84.15).
18. Paints (Tariff Nos.32.09 and 32.10).
19. Cigars and Cheroots (Tariff No.24.02).
20. Copper or aluminum electric wire, uninsulated, other than those imported by a manufacturer approved in that behalf by the Minister (Tariff Nos.74.03 and 76.02E).

21. Motorcycles (Tariff No.87.09).
22. Lorries, trucks, including tankers, tippers, pick-ups and four-wheel drive vehicles (Tariff Nos.87.02D and 87.02F).
23. Chilled or frozen meat of all kinds but excluding importations from neighbouring countries (Tariff Nos.02.01 to 02.04 and 02.06, 05.04 and 16.01).
24. Frozen beef.
25. Computer and similar data processing machines.
26. All passenger cars.
27. Jams and marmalades.
28. Tomato puree and tomato paste.
29. Tapestries and all floor coverings excluding linoleum of all types in rolls.
30. Mats and mattings.
31. Mattresses, mattress supports and cushions.
32. Gramophone records (complete).
33. Record tapes.
34. Toys.
35. Sporting goods.
36. Salted or dried meat.
37. Salted, dried or smoked fish.
38. Tarpaulins.
39. Loudspeakers, amplifiers and microphones.
40. Soups of all descriptions.
41. Spices.
42. Cameras, projectors, photographic and all cinematographic goods, excluding unexposed films and chemicals for developing and printing films.
43. Ceramic products other than industrial ceramic products accepted as such by the Board including ceramic sinks, water basins, bidets, water closets, pans, urinals, baths, wall tiles and the like sanitary fixtures.
44. Musical instruments and parts and accessories of musical instruments.
45. Clocks and watches.
46. Brandy, bitters, gin, liqueurs, rum, schnapps, spirits and whiskey in bottles or cans.
47. Wines of all kinds including cider and perry in bottles or cans.
48. Binoculars and sunglasses and the like other than medical.
49. Socks and stockings.
50. Ties, bow ties and cravats.
51. Primary cells and batteries (1.5 volts), size "D", "UMI", "R20" and all batteries of physical size similar to "U2 Size D" (Tariff No.85.03C).

52. Polythylene and regenerated cellulose film (Chapter 39).
53. Blankets (Tariff No.62.01).
54. Corrugated asbestos roofing sheets (Tariff No.68.12B).
55. Tubes and pipes of cast iron or steel (not excluding 8 cm in diameter) (Tariff Nos.73.17C and 73.18C).
56. Corrugated galvanized or coated roofing sheets (Tariff No.73.13A).
57. Paper napkins, paper serviettes and similar tissue paper (Tariff No.48.21).
58. Cosmetics and perfumery (Tariff No.33.06).
59. Sewing thread of all kinds.
60. Trailers (Tariff No.87.14B).
61. Sewing machines (Tariff No.84.41).
62. Jute fibre and similar vegetable fibre (Tariff Nos.57.03 and 57.04).
63. Wheat and meslin (mixed wheat and rye) (Tariff No.10.01).
64. Rye (Tariff No.10.02).
65. Barley (Tariff No.10.03).
66. Oats (Tariff No.10.04).
67. Rice in containers of 50kgs and above (Tariff No.10.06) provided that Import Licences on Rice shall be awarded only to Federal, State and Local Government Agencies.
68. Buckwheat, millet, canary seed, grain sorghum and other cereals (Tariff No.10.07).
69. Butter (Tariff No.04.03).
70. Cheese (Tariff No.04.04).
71. Radio broadcasting and television transmission and reception apparatus and television cameras (Tariff No.85.15).
72. Electric filament lamps (domestic type bulbs) (Tariff No.85.20).
73. Galvanised or coated flat sheets.
74. Asbestos flat sheets.
75. Structures and parts of structures (Tariff No.76.08).
76. Starch.
77. Empty beer bottles.
78. Umbrella handles.
79. Plastic pipes (Tariff Nos.39.02(D) and 39.07).
80. Concentrated malt extracts.
81. Auto-cycles.
82. Yarn of man-made fibre, continuous and discontinuous.
83. Motor tyres for cars and similar sizes of sectional width exceeding 102mm to 304mm.
84. Cotton yarn of all types.
85. Cereal flour (Tariff No.11.01).
86. Nails.
87. Bolts and nuts (including bolt ends and screw studs).
88. Processed barite and bentonite.

89. Assembled road and agricultural tractors (Tariff No.87.01).
90. Vegetable oil.
91. Real Madras (Tariff No.55.09D).
92. Cement (Tariff No.25.23).
93. Tea (Tariff No.09.02).
94. Stockfish (including fish dried, salted or in brine; smoked fish, whether or not cooked before or during the smoking process) (Tariff No.03.02).
95. Fishing nets (Tariff No.59.05).
96. Furniture fabrics.
97. Jute and other vegetable fibres (Tariff Nos.57.03, 57.04).
98. Asbestos cement pipes.
99. Sugar (Tariff Nos.17.01, 17.02).
100. Delivery and panel vans.
101. Louvre window frames (Tariff No.73.21B).
102. Insulated electric wire and cables (Tariff No.85.23).
103. Printing ink (Tariff No.32.13).
104. Paper labels (Tariff No.48.19).
105. Ladies sanitary pads and children's disposable nappies made of tissue paper (Tariff No.48.31C).
106. Spades and shovels (Tariff No.82.01C).
107. Wheel barrows (Tariff No.87.14B).
108. Soap and detergents (Tariff No.34.01).
109. Automotive lead/acid batteries or electric accumulators (Tariff No.85.04).
110. Finished alkyd resins (Tariff No.39.01).
111. Saw mill equipment (Tariff No.82.02).
112. Arc-welding electrodes (Tariff No.85.240).
113. Sticks imported for use in the confectionery industry (Tariff No.44.28C).
114. Prefabricated buildings of wood (including flush doors and sashes).
115. Fabricated building materials other than glass.
116. All building bricks, other than glass bricks.
117. Roofing tiles (Tariff Nos.44.19 to 44.28).
118. Baby food.
119. Frozen fish.
120. Maggi cubes.
121. Maize.
122. Tinned fish.
123. Glassware.
124. Insecticides.
125. Kerosine stoves.
126. Lamps and lantern.

127. Mosquito coils.
128. Paper.
129. Petroleum products.
130. Plastic goods.
131. Sporting goods.
132. Stationery (No licence required by FEDECO).
133. Calculators.
134. Baby goods.
135. Magazine (49.02 Magazine only).
136. Combs.
137. Crash helmets.
138. Electrical accessories.
139. Fans and parts (85.06A only).
140. Flash light.
141. Kitchen ware.
142. Mosquito nets.
143. Shoe parts.
144. Special types of dentrifices.
145. Hats and caps.
146. Locksets.
147. Plates and plate circles.
148. Polish.
149. Ropes and twine.
150. Water filter.
151. Zippers.
152. Lampholders.
153. Bags.
154. Beads.
155. Belts.
156. Brushes.
157. Buckets.
158. Buttons.
159. Cartridges.
160. Cookers.
161. Cutlery.
162. Disinfectant.
163. Enamelware.
164. Flasks.
165. Aircraft and parts.
166. Engines and parts.
167. Industrial machinery.
168. Laboratory equipment.
169. Matchet.
170. Catering equipment.

171. Compressors and parts.
172. Concrete mixers.
173. Construction equipment.
174. Kitchen equipment.
175. Meters.
176. Moulding machines.
177. Photocopying equipment.
178. Photocopying machines.
179. Printing equipment.
180. Storage equipment.
181. Textile machinery.
182. Typewriters.
183. Diesel engine and parts.
184. Sewage plants and parts.
185. Dye stuff.
186. Enamel frits.
187. Electric fittings.
188. Glass sheets.
189. Tin plate.
190. Wire.
191. Rubber soles.
192. Shoe soles.
193. Acid.
194. Aluminum foil.
195. Brass fittings.
196. Cable.
197. Copper.
198. Carbon.
199. Caustic soda.
200. Cotton wool.
201. Electrodes.
202. Iron angles.
203. Light fittings.
204. Louvre glass.
205. Lime.
206. Lubricating oil.
207. Leather.
208. Metal fittings.
209. Sockets and plugs.
210. White tallow.
211. Printing materials.
212. Petroleum derivatives.
213. PVC compounds.
214. Plastic sheets.

215. Reinforcing bars.
216. Steel angles.
217. Day-old chicks.
218. Safety glass consisting of toughened or laminated glass shaped or not (Tariff No.70.08).
219. Caustic soda, solid or liquid (Tariff No.28.17).
220. Industrial salt (Tariff No.25.01B).
221. Crown corks (Tariff No.83.13A).
222. Margarines (Tariff No.15.13).
223. Buses (Tariff No.87.02(E)).
224. Electrical motors of less than 500 watts (Tariff No.85.01(B2)).
225. Knives with cutting blades serrated or not (including pruning knives falling within heading No.82.06 and blades thereof) (Tariff No.82.09).
226. Essential oils (Tariff No.33.01A).
227. Groundnut oil (Tariff No.15.07B).
228. Lanolin BP (wood grade and fatty substances derived therefrom including lanolin) (Tariff No.15.05).
229. White petroleum jelly (Tariff No.27.12).
230. Other articles of plastic nature (Tariff No.39.07(M)).
231. Milk powder (Tariff No.04.02).
232. Waxes (Tariff No.27.13).
233. Comminuted juices (natural yeast and other food preparations) (Tariff Nos.21.06 and 21.07(D)).
234. Zinc dust (other articles of zinc) (Tariff No.79.06).
235. Ball, roller or needle roller bearings (Tariff No.84.62).
236. Springs of iron or steel (Tariff No.73.35(B)).
237. Malleable iron chain belling (Tariff No.73.29(B)).
238. Electric industrial heating apparatus (Tariff No.85.12).
239. Oscillator (other electrical line telephonic and telegraphic apparatus) (Tariff No.85.13(B2)).
240. Bailing wire/cable (other standard wire and cable of iron and steel (Tariff No.73.25(B)).
241. Other copper wire and cables (Tariff No.74.10B).
242. Other stranded aluminum wire and cables (Tariff No.76.12(B)).
243. Other insulated electric wire and cables (Tariff No.85.23B).
244. Coils — (other electrical starting and ignition equipment for internal combustion engines).
245. Metal lining (other gauze cloth, grill, netting, fencing, reinforcement and similar materials of iron or steel wire, expanded metal of iron or steel (Tariff No.73.27(C)).
246. Tooth brushes.
247. Nail files (Tariff No.82.13).
248. Bearings and bushings (other machinery parts not electrical) (Tariff No.84.65B).

249. Leather (Tariff No.41.02).
250. Articles of iron or steel (Chapter 73).
251. Components of the above goods imported unassembled or disassembled excluding those components imported under Approved User Licence.

SCHEDULE III

PART A

GOODS THE EXPORTATION OF WHICH IS ABSOLUTELY PROHIBITED

ABSOLUTE PROHIBITION (TRADE)

1. Beans.
2. Cassava-tuber.
3. Groundnut oil.
4. Maize.
5. Palm oil.
6. Rice.
7. Timber, excluding Blad Wood, Ebony — sawn or unsawn in logs, in the rough, roughly-squared or sawn into any shape.
8. Milk.
9. Sugar.
10. Flour.
11. All imported food items.

PART B

COUNTRIES TO WHICH EXPORTATION OF GOODS IS ABSOLUTELY PROHIBITED

1. South Africa.
2. Namibia (South-West Africa).

PART C

GOODS PROHIBITED FROM BEING EXPORTED EXCEPT UNDER LICENCE

1. Cigarettes
2. Columbite

3. Gold, raw as defined in the Goldsmith's Act 1948 (No. 81 of 1948).
4. Goods manufactured outside Nigeria
5. Goods made wholly or partly of imported components (excluding imported containers or containers manufactured wholly or partly of imported materials used for purpose of conveying goods made in Nigeria).
6. Petroleum products
7. Tantalite
8. Tobacco
9. Beniseed
10. Raw cocoa beans
11. Raw cotton
12. Cotton seed
13. Groundnuts
14. Palm kernels
15. Soya beans
16. Copra
17. Grape-fruit
18. Lemons
19. Cotton linters
20. Cotton seed cake
21. Cotton seed oil
22. Cotton seed meal
23. Groundnut cake
24. Groundnut meal
25. Palm kernel cake
26. Palm kernel meal
27. Palm kernel oil
28. Zirconium
29. Slag resulting from the processing of tin
30. Raw coffee
31. Cassava flour
32. Gari
33. Yam-tuber and flour (elubo)
34. Hides and skins undressed

These provisions may be subject to changes. Exporters and importers are advised to ensure that they are up to date with possible amendments to the above schedules. To facilitate prompt payment, importers and exporters are advised to give full descriptions of merchandise.

Appendix 3.C Incentives to invest in Nigeria

Industrial Incentives

The Nigerian Federal Government, which has exclusive powers in the fields of company taxation and tariff policy, offers special incentives to industrial enterprises where such incentives are considered necessary in the overall economic interest of Nigeria. These incentives are embodied in four Acts — the Industrial Development (Income Tax Relief) Act, 1958 as amended by Decree No. 22 of 1971; the Customs Duties (Approved User Scheme); the Customs Duties (Dumped and Subsidized Goods) Act, 1958; the Customs (Drawback) Regulations, 1959 and the Income Tax (Amendment Act 1959).

Industrial Development (Income Tax Relief) Act 1958
— as amended by Decree No. 22 of 1971:

The object of the Act is to encourage the establishment and development of such industries as the government may consider to be beneficial to Nigeria and assistance to which would be in the public interest. By making relief from income tax possible during the early years of public companies engaged in pioneer industries, this Act is designed to attract capital to Nigeria in the development of her natural resources and the expansion of her industrial capacity.

Before benefits provided by the Act can be obtained, it is necessary that the industry or the products which it is proposed to establish, develop or produce should be declared a pioneer industry or pioneer products. Application for the pioneer status can be made to the Federal Ministry of the Industries on Form AP/2 by a public company incorporated in Nigeria. A successful applicant will be issued with a pioneer certificate. A company which desires to engage in an industry or products which have not been designated 'pioneer' may submit a representation for its industry or products to be granted 'pioneer status' on Form AP/1. Only a public limited liability company registered in Nigeria is eligible for a pioneer certificate, or where it is not feasible for a company to go public at start-up, there must be an undertaking to do so within the shortest possible time. A period of four months is given, if necessary, for the registration of the company after the award of a certificate has been approved. The grant of a pioneer certificate entitles the company to enjoy relief from income tax, subject to the observance of the conditions stipulated in the certificate. The most important of these conditions are that:

(i)   The company shall not engage, during the tax relief period, in any enterprise except the pioneer industry in respect of which the pioneer certificate is granted, and

(ii) The company shall start to operate the factor, or where a mining company is concerned, begin operations — within one year of the date estimated by the company in its application.

Every application for an industry to be included in the list of pioneer industries or pioneer products shall be addressed to the Permanent Secretary, Federal Ministry of Industries, Lagos, and shall be in such form as he may from time to time specify.

The application shall be accompanied by a fee of N100, which sum shall not be refundable to the applicant, whether or not the application is approved.

No application for the issue of a pioneer certificate to any company shall be made unless the estimated cost and qualifying capital expected to be incurred by the company on or before production day (if the application is approved) is an amount which:

(a)   in the case of an indigenous-controlled company, is not less than N25,000 or

(b)   in the case of any other company, is not less than N150,000.

The tax relief period of a pioneer company shall not exceed three years in the first instance. At the end of the three years the tax relief period may be extended:

(a)   for a period of one year and thereafter for another period of one year, or

(b)   for one period of two years.

In granting extension of tax relief period some of the points considered are as follows:

(a) The rate of expansion, standard of efficiency and the level of development of the company;

(b) The implementation of any scheme —
    (i) for the utilization of local raw material in the processes of the company; and
    (ii) for the training and development of Nigerian personnel in the relevant industry;

(c) The relative importance of the industry in the economy of the country;

(d) The need for the expansion, having regard to the location of the industry; and

(e) Such other relevant matters as may be required.

If losses are incurred during the tax holiday, a further extension may be given. For such accounting period within the tax holiday in which a loss is incurred, the tax relief period is extended by the same period.

There is also provision for capital expenditure, and the type which normally attracts relief from income tax and which is incurred in a tax relief period, to be written off wholly from the taxable profit arising after the period.

As a corollary to the exemption from tax on profit earned by the company in its tax relief period, shareholders can be exempted from tax on dividend up to the amount of such profit.

For the time being, we have listed below the schedule of pioneer industries and main pioneer products as announced by the Federal Ministry of Industries:

SCHEDULE OF:

Pioneer Industries	Main Pioneer Products
1. Cultivation and processing of foodcrops, vegetables and fruits	Preserved/canned foodstuffs and fruit, tea, coffee, refined sugar, tomato puree/ juice, etc.
2. Manufacture of cocoa products	Cocoa powder, cocoa butter, cocoa cake, chocolates, cocoa wine.
3. The processing of oilseeds	Coconut oil, meal, cake; shell and shell flour, cotton-seed oil, meal, cake; flour and linters; lecethin; benniseed oil, meal and cake; soya oil, meal, cake and

flour; sheanut oil, meal and cake; essential oil, meal and cake; castor-seed oil, meal and cake; cashew-nut oil, meal and cake; sun-flower-seed oil, meal and cake; kernel cake.

4. Integrated Dairy Production

Butter, cheese; fluid milk, milk powder; ice-cream. (By products:– Livestock, minor edible dairy products.)

5. Cattle and other Livestock Ranching

Livestock.

6. Bone Crushing

Glue, gelatine, bone meal, bone flour, crushed bone, oil grease and tallow.

7. (a) Deepsea trawling and processing)
   (b) Coastal fishing and shrimping)
   (c) Inland lake fishing and processing)

Preserved sea foods, fish and shrimps, fishmeal.

8. Manufacture of salt

Refined edible salt (sodium chloride); crude salt.

9. Mining of lead/zinc ores by underground mining methods

Lead-zinc ores.

10. The manufacture of iron and steel from iron ore

Iron and steel products.

11. The smelting and refining of non-ferrous base metals and the manufacture of their alloys

Refined non-ferrous base metals and their alloys.

12. Mining and processing of barytes and associated minerals.

Barytes and associated minerals.

13. Manufacture of oil well drilling materials containing a predominant proportion of Nigerian raw materials

Oil well drilling materials containing a predominant proportion of Nigerian raw materials.

14. The manufacture of cement

Cement; clinker.

15. Manufacture of glass and glassware

Sheet glass; Pharmaceutical and Laboratory glassware; Household glassware (excepting lamp fittings); Glass envelopes for electric lamps and electronic valves.

16.	Manufacture of lime from local limestone	Lime.
17.	Quarrying and processing of of marbles	Marble and processed marbles.
18.	Manufacture of ceramic products	Refractory and heat-insulating constructional products; Tableware; Sanitaryware; Laboratoryware.
19.	Manufacture of basic and intermediate industrial chemicals from predominantly Nigerian raw materials	(i) Basic and intermediate organic chemicals; (ii) Basic and intermediate inorganic chemicals; (iii) Fertilizers; (iv) Petrochemicals; (v) Synthetic textile fibres; (vi) Caustic soda and chlorine.
20.	Manufacture of pharmaceuticals	Pharmaceuticals.
21.	Manufacture of surgical dressings	Cotton wadding, dressings, bandages, sanitary protection.
22.	Manufacture of starch from plantation crop	Starch.
23.	Manufacture of yeast, alcohol and related products	Yeast, alcohol and related products.
24.	The manufacture of animal feedstuff	Animal feedstuff.
25.	Manufacture of paper-pulp, paper and paperboard	Paper-pulp, paper, paperboard.
26.	Manufacture of articles of paper-pulp, paper and paperboard	Paper-pulp, paper, paperboard.
27.	Manufacture of leather	Sole leather, upper leather and leather products.
28.	Manufacture of textile fabrics and man-made fibres	Yarn, thread, twine, cardage; bags, sacks; water-proof canvas; textile piece goods.
29.	Manufacture of products made wholly or mainly of metal	Pipes and tubes, Nuts, Bolts, Rivets, Washers, Screws, Nails, Wire, Extruded metal sections.

30.	Manufacture of machinery involving the local manufacture of a substantial proportion of components thereof	Office and industrial machinery equipment and apparatus (whether or not electrical).
31.	Manufacture of goods made wholly or partly of rubber.	Tyres, tubes, compounded rubber sheeting, camelback; rubber solution, rubber flooring compound, rubber flooring.
32.	Manufacture of nets from local raw materials	Fishing nets, mosquito nets and related products.
33.	The processing of local wheat-flour milling	Flour and offal.
34.	Oil palm plantation and processing	Palm oil, palm kernel, offals.
35.	Rubber plantation and processing	Rubber.
36.	Gum Arabic plantation and processing	Gum Arabic.
37.	Integrated wood projects	Furniture, decorative veneer, blackboard, particle board, sawn-timber, plywood.
38.	Manufacture of fertilizers	Superphosphate and nitrogenous fertilizers.
39.	Commercial vehicles manufacture	Commercial vehicles.

Approved User Scheme

The Scheme was based on the recommendation of a committee set up to advise on the stimulation of Nigerian industry by giving it relief from import duty and tariff protection.

The Scheme allows for either exemption from import duty or grants a concessionary low rate of import duty on materials brought into Nigeria for use in the manufacture or processing of goods or in the provision of services, provided that certain conditions are fulfilled.

To qualify for relief under the Approved User Scheme an applicant must satisfy the Federal Government that it is impossible to provide the goods or services in question at prices low enough to compete with the imported equivalent; or that the imported finished article bears a lower proportion of import duty than the materials imported to manufacture the same article in Nigeria.

The Federal Government must also be satisfied that any relief to be made is to the overall economic advantage of Nigeria having regard to certain criteria.

As with income tax relief, import duties relief is intended as a measure of temporary assistance in order to enable a new industry to become established in Nigeria, or for an already established industry to be developed on a scale suitable to the country's overall economic requirements.

Under the Approved User Scheme, manufacturers, approved in that behalf by the government may be permitted to import either duty-free or at a concessionary rate of duty, certain materials specified in the Customs Tariff, for a period not exceeding three years. Applications under this Scheme should be made to the Federal Ministry of Industries on Form Sale 65 — accompanied with the following documents:

1   a copy of the Certificate of Incorporation,
2   a copy of the Tax Clearance Certificate,
3   a copy of the feasibility study or IPQ Form,
4   a copy of the Business Permit if foreign partner is involved,
5   a copy of the Technical Service Agreement,
6   evidence of excise duty paid, if the company had enjoyed AUS before.

Importation of any goods under the Approved User Scheme is subject to the provisions of Section 41 of the Customs and Excise Management Act No. 55 of 1958 which stipulates that the goods must not be used, other than for the approved purpose of the item of the tariff except with prior permission of the Board of Customs and Excise and only after payment of the full duty of such proportion thereof as the Board may direct.

The exemption from import duty or a granting of a concessionary lower rate of import duty may not apply to any articles which are manufactured locally and which an approved manufacturer can purchase from this source but which he chooses to import. Benefits under the Approved User Scheme can be varied by budgetary announcement and embodied in tariff amendments. Further enquiries in respect of the Approved User Scheme should be addressed to the Permanent Secretary, Federal Ministry of Industries, Lagos.

The Customs Duties (Dumped and Subsidized Goods) Act 1958

This Act permits, when necessary, the imposition of a special duty on any goods which are being dumped in Nigeria or are subsidized by any government or authority outside Nigeria. The right to exercise this power is vested in the Federal Government which must be satisfied that material injury will be threatened or caused by the entry of such goods to a potential or established industry in Nigeria and that the imposition of a special duty will not conflict Nigeria's obligations under the General Agreement on Trade and Tariffs.

The Customs (Drawback) Regulations 1959

Under these regulations importers may, in certain circumstances, claim repayment of import duty. Repayment will be made in full:

(a) if goods are exported in the same state as that in which they were imported;

(b) if materials are imported for use in the manufacture of goods which are exported.

In the case of certain composite goods which contain wholly or partly duty-paid ingredients and are manufactured in Nigeria according to standard formulas, the Board of Customs and Excise may grant to bona fide applicants a 'fixed rate' drawback on proof of exportation of such goods or their disposal in an approved manner.

Companies Income Tax Act (Accelerated Depreciation)

This Act grants to companies a much quicker write-down of their capital assets in the early years of production so as to enable them to amortize their capital assets during their formative years, and so build up liquid reserves at an early date. The capital allowances involved are as follows:

Qualifying Expenditure	Initial Allowance	Annual Allowance
1 Plant and machinery including furniture, fittings, motor vehicles	20%	12.5%
2 Building		
(a) Industrial	20%	12.5%
(b) Non-industrial; residential	5%	10.0%
3 Plantation	25%	15.0%
4 Mining	20%	12.5%

Approved Status

Foreign investors in the Nigerian economy are required to obtain approved status for their original investment in order to ensure future unimpeded repatriation of their capital, dividends, etc. Approved status is a recognition that the original investment comes into the country from abroad in the form of equity either by way of cash and/or parts, equipment and machinery. Approved status can be granted in principle or as final.

Approved status in principle

Applications for the grant of approved status in principle, to enable non-residents to bring capital into the country, should be made to the Permanent Secretary, Federal Ministry of Finance, Exchange Control Department, New Secretariat, Lagos, supported with the following documents:

(a)   a photostat copy of certificate of registration of Company;
(b)   copy of Memorandum and Articles of Associations;
(c)   photostat copy of business permit;
(d)   two copies of answers to Federal Ministry of Finance standard questionnaire;
(e)   evidence of compliance with section of Nigerian Enterprises Promotions Decree (foreign participation in Schedules II and III is 40 per cent and 60 per cent respectively).

Note: Approval in principle has a life span of 12 months within which the foreign equity must have been brought into Nigeria. It may be extended.

Final approved status

Application for final approved status must be accompanied by the following:

(a)   Central Bank Certificate of Capital Importation in the case of subscription by cash;
(b)   original Customs Bill of Entry for machinery/equipment;
(c)   certificate of value by the Inspectorate Division of the Federal Ministry of Industries in the case of machinery/equipment.

Financing of projects with external loans

External loans for financing of projects can be undertaken only with the approval of the Federal Ministry of Finance.

Application for approval of an external loan agreement must be supported with the following documents:

(a) a copy of the loan agreement;
(b) a copy of offer of loan from the lender;
(c) terms of conditions of the loan showing maturity, interest rate, schedule of repayment, principal and interest and moratorium, etc.;
(d) two copies of feasibility studies and cash flow projections which will show profitability as a result of the loan and ability to repay;
(e) most current audited account.

Repayment of external loan

Applications in Form 'A' should be supported with evidence that:

(a) the loan has been imported into the country — Central Bank Certificate of Capital Importation showing the importation of the loan must be produced;
(b) evidence to show that the loan was approved by the Ministry;
(c) the necessary demand notice showing the principal and the interest due for payment;
(d) evidence of tax payment on the interest where appropriate.

Local borrowing

Any company with substantial foreign equity participation (i.e. in Schedule III) that intends to avail itself of local credit facilities must seek and obtain the approval of the Federal Ministry of Finance before enjoying such facilities, for example, overdrafts, medium- and long-term loans.

In making applications for permission to obtain local loans the following information should be supplied:

(a) Letter of Intent from the local bank;
(b) duration;
(c) purpose of loan;
(d) the amount;
(e) scope of the company's/firm's business activities;
(f) latest audited account.

Capitalization of retained profits

Applications for approval to capitalize retained earnings should be made to the Federal Ministry of Finance, accompanied by the following:

(a) Board Resolution authorizing such capitalization;
(b) latest audited account of the company;
(c) receipt for the payment of stamp duty in case of increase in capital;
(d) letters of consent from Central Bank of Nigeria in the case of commercial and merchant banks;
(e) evidence of compliance with NEPB 1977.

Payment for technology transfer

It is recognized that the owner of technology must have acquired it at a cost and should therefore be compensated. However, Technical/Management Service Agreement must be cleared with Federal Ministries of Finance and Science and Technology. The requirements are:

(a) the agreement should clearly show the services to be carried out by the foreign technical partners;
(b) the agreement should also spell out the arrangement, through training and on-the-job learning processes, the effective and orderly transfer of the technology to Nigerian personnel, during the period of the agreement.

Applications for remittance of Technical/Management Service Fees must be supported with the following documents:

(a) a copy of the audited account for the relevant period;
(b) Tax Clearance Certificate issued by the Federal Inland Revenue Department referring specifically to the technical service fees;
(c) evidence of approval of the Technical Service Agreement by the Federal Ministry of Science and Technology.

The approved fee for Technical Service Agreement in the 1980 fiscal year was 2 per cent net profit before tax.

Consultancy fees

It is recognized that certain specialized jobs can only be performed by foreign consultants because of the basic lack of indigenous expertise in these areas. As a result these foreign consultants are retained by

132

business for specific assignments of fixed duration and for which these consultants expect to be financially compensated.

Application for the remittance of such fees must be accompanied by:

(a) evidence of prior approval of the consultancy agreement by the Federal Ministry of Finance;
(b) copy of consultancy agreement;
(c) evidence of local payment;
(d) Tax Clearance Certificate referring specifically to the fees. In fiscal year 1980, a maximum of 30 per cent of the Consultancy Fees was allowed as offshore.

Remittance of proceeds from disposal of assets other than securities

Applications under this category must be accompanied by the following documents:

(a) copy of the sale agreement;
(b) payment receipt of capital gains tax, if any;
(c) evidence that the original investment was imported into Nigeria;
(d) evidence to show that the beneficiary is leaving or has left the country finally;
(e) evidence of valuation by an independent third party.

Royalties

A maximum fee of 1 per cent of sales value is allowed as royalties.

Home remittance

Home remittance allowance for both male and female expatriates who have not obtained Nigerian citizenship is 50 per cent of net salary.

Transfer of payments of dividend to non-resident shareholders

For fiscal year 1980, government allowed a distribution of dividends to non-resident shareholders of either a maximum of 60 per cent of profits after tax or 25 per cent of paid-up capital, whichever is higher, provided such distributions were made out of current year profits.

Applications for remittance of dividends of non-resident shareholder must be accompanied by the following:

(a) evidence of approved status on non-resident capital investment or evidence of previous approval to remit dividend;
(b) Tax Clearance Certificate issued by the Federal Department of Inland Revenue on the amount to be remitted;
(c) audited accounts for the year dividends were declared and two preceding years;
(d) Board of Directors' resolution;
(e) declaration that the dividend declared has not exceeded the maximum allowed by the current policy.

Other fiscal measures which are meant to preserve foreign exchange as well as protect local industries include:

(i) imposition of high customs tariffs on imported goods
(ii) import restrictions
(iii) prohibition of importation of certain goods
(iv) full repatriation of dividends or capital provided the industry already has an approved status.

Compiled by:
Nigerian Investment Information and Promotion Centre
Federal Ministry of Industries
Lagos.
Phone: 680794

Appendix 3.D   Contributions of industries to Nigeria's gross domestic product

Table 3.D.1   **Gross Domestic Product at 1973—74 factor cost (N million)**

Activity Sector	1973—74	1974—75	1975—76	1976—77	1977—78	1978—79	1979—80
1. Agriculture	2,183.3	2,203.8	2,143.1	2,251.9	2,336.6	2,406.7	2,486.6
2. Livestock	488.8	491.2	393.9	399.6	408.9	422.2	440.6
3. Forestry	215.0	302.7	328.8	355.1	383.5	412.2	443.2
4. Fishing	465.0	567.6	573.8	607.1	658.7	698.2	743.6
5. Crude Petroleum	2,771.6	2,797.6	2,345.3	2,676.8	2,715.7	2,480.6	2,866.5
6. Other Mining and Quarrying	198.8	247.8	310.5	372.6	436.0	492.7	544.4
7. Manufacturing	611.0	601.4	729.7	854.4	943.0	1,040.6	1,151.0
8. Utilities	45.2	51.8	59.7	74.4	95.2	117.3	136.6
9. Construction	884.1	1,108.4	1,411.4	1,693.6	1,981.8	2,239.7	2,474.7
10. Transport	429.6	403.1	468.2	636.8	764.1	878.7	966.9
11. Communication	33.2	38.9	47.7	54.9	60.3	65.2	71.7
12. Wholesale and Retail Trade	2,268.1	2,295.1	2,491.5	2,788.5	3,043.9	3,245.2	3,492.2
13. Hotels and Restaurants	32.4	35.6	39.1	43.0	47.5	52.0	57.2
14. Finance and Insurance	140.5	155.0	170.4	187.6	206.4	226.7	249.4
15. Real Estate and Business Services	61.1	67.3	74.0	81.4	89.5	98.5	108.3
16. Housing	625.9	688.2	756.6	832.4	915.6	1,006.4	1,107.7
17. Producer of Government Services	664.4	743.4	1,049.1	1,082.4	1,208.5	1,299.3	1,399.8
Total	12,118.0	12,798.9	13,392.8	14,992.5	16,285.2	17,182.2	18,740.4

Table 3.D.2 Gross Domestic Product at 1973—74 factor cost (N million)

	Activity Sector	1980	1981	1982	1983	1984	1985
1.	Agriculture	2,583.9	2,687.3	2,821.7	2,976.9	3,140.5	3,290.8
2.	Livestock	463.5	488.2	521.8	558.8	603.3	642.5
3.	Forestry	496.4	521.2	550.5	591.9	636.6	684.6
4.	Fishing	791.9	847.3	910.8	983.7	1,062.1	1,143.1
5.	Crude Petroleum	2,988.6	3,222.5	3,183.5	3,114.1	3,079.6	3,105.2
6.	Other Mining and Quarrying	588.9	637.4	698.5	770.7	862.0	948.2
7.	Manufacturing	1,315.1	1,504.9	1,763.4	2,090.6	2,540.3	2,995.5
8.	Utilities	175.7	220.9	272.9	299.0	329.2	385.9
9.	Construction	2,676.7	2,897.2	3,174.8	3,503.2	3,981.1	4,310.0
10.	Transportation	1,063.2	1,169.5	1,286.5	1,415.1	1,556.7	1,712.4
11.	Communication	78.9	86.7	95.4	104.4	115.4	126.9
12.	Wholesale and Retail Trade	3,807.1	4,170.3	4,466.9	4,857.9	5,331.0	5,799.4
13.	Hotels and Restaurants	64.1	71.8	80.8	90.8	102.3	114.8
14.	Finance and Insurance	279.4	312.9	352.0	396.0	445.5	500.6
15.	Real Estate and Business Services	121.3	135.9	132.9	171.9	193.5	217.5
16.	Housing	1,240.9	1,389.6	1,563.3	1,758.3	1,978.4	2,223.1
17.	Producer of Government Services	1,509.7	1,628.0	1,756.3	1,895.5	2,046.5	2,208.2
	Total	20,245.3	21,982.6	23,652.0	25,578.8	27,941.1	30,408.7

Source: Fourth National Development Plan, Federal Ministry of Planning, Lagos, Nigeria.

Appendix 3.E Industrial classification of major companies in Nigeria

	Frequency of companies	%
General services (insurance, banking, printing, transportation)	290	30.34
Manufacturing	105	10.98
Agriculture: farm, food processing	69	7.21
Wholesale and retail trade	230	24.06
Construction and engineering services	262	27.41
	956	100.00

Source: INCH Classification, 1983.

4 The evolution pattern of Nigerian enterprises

Introduction

The cases in the study present the clinical data needed to respond to the specific questions covering the theme of this book. These questions are:

1. How do firms evolve in the developing nation, Nigeria? (Are patterns of evolution in a developing country similar to or different from those found in a developed country such as the USA?)
2. How does family structure influence the firms' pattern of evolution?
3. How do conflict resolution mechanisms influence a firm's ability to move from one stage to another?

This chapter describes the evolution of strategy and structure in Nigeria. Although Chapter 3 described the industrial environment of Nigeria, some of these data may be repeated for emphasis. Models described in this chapter include:

(a) Stages in pre-enterprise development:
   - Cash crop production
   - Retail activities
   - Enterprise
(b) Stages in the evolution of enterprise:
   - Formation/Registration
   - Early expansion
   - Economic growth
   - Major/induced diversification
   - Reorganization/consolidation

138

(c) Characteristics of the stages: these characteristics are described under the following headings:
  — Product line
  — Distribution
  — Organizational structure
  — Research and development
  — Performance appraisal
  — Rewards/motivation
  — Control systems
  — Strategic choices

Stages in pre-enterprise development

Examination of the country's historical setting shows that there are two major stages to the development of Nigerian business organizations. Figure 4.1 presents these stages, which include the pre-colonial stage (I) and the early colonial stage (II).

Data show that, although agricultural activities were dominant in the life of the people of Nigeria, there was no organized system for this activity.[1] However, the different groups in Nigeria often needed commodities which could not be produced by some particular group. For example, climate in Nigeria was such that the northern savannah area produced grains, cottons, and groundnuts (peanuts), while the southern areas, with abundant rainfall, cultivated oil palm, cocoa, yams, cocoyams, etc. Until the late sixteenth century when these became major export crops, Nigerian citizens met to exchange crops by barter. Trade by barter is the first step towards the development of organized enterprises.

The second stage of mixed exchange and retail trade was initiated by the colonial slave traders. With the abolition of slave trade, legitimate trade in commodities attracted a number of British merchants to the River Niger regions. In addition, some formerly engaged in the slave trade changed their line of wares. The large trader[2] subsequently opened depots in several delta cities (e.g. Onitsha, Calabar, Lagos) for their trade transactions. These companies (e.g. United African Company (UAC), Royal Niger Company) were often ruthlessly competitive and frequently used force to compel potential suppliers to agree to contracts and to meet their demands. Year by year the UAC extended its direct jurisdiction to territory it had acquired by treaty and which was policed by a British-led native 'constabulary' that also protected trade. Treaties were entered into with the Sokoto, Kano, Boru and Nupe tribes (all in the Northern states of the country) guaranteeing the company exclusive access to trade in those areas in return

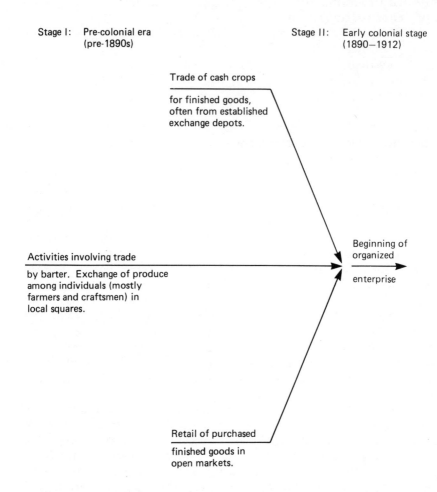

Stage I: Pre-colonial era
(pre-1890s)

Stage II: Early colonial stage
(1890—1912)

Trade of cash crops

for finished goods,
often from established
exchange depots.

Activities involving trade

by barter. Exchange of produce
among individuals (mostly
farmers and craftsmen) in
local squares.

Beginning of
organized

enterprise

Retail of purchased

finished goods in
open markets.

Fig. 4.1 Stages in the development of organized enterprise

for the payment of an annual tribute which often comprised arms and ammunition. The same type of treaty was entered into with tribes in other parts of the country.

Trade activities at this stage involved the exchange, at the established depots, of raw materials and finished goods between the individuals (mostly farmers and craftsmen) and the European traders. After this initial exchange, retail of the goods obtained from the European traders was undertaken at central markets and small bazaars. Daily market centres were established in the cities while weekly market meetings were organized in the rural areas.

Although the indigenes exchanged goods and engaged in retail activities, organized retail business never materialized until after the First World War, when the Ibos (partly because of the poor quality of their wool) began to engage more aggressively in trade and craft activities as a full-time occupation. This small retail occupation was often seen as a prelude or step towards organized enterprise. In this study, as presented in Table 4.1, 50 per cent of the companies studied had a historical background of retail activities involving farm cash crops while the other 50 per cent (Francis, Onyeukwu, Amadi, Nwoke) started out as retailers of manufactured goods. In addition, one should note that the founders of all the four firms which started out as retailers of goods were from the Eastern, Ibo-dominated, regions. Of the others, Ntiki originated from the Cross River oil palm basin, and the Oko and Ginano from the Midwestern and Northern agricultural areas, respectively. Standards, whose founder also came from the Eastern region, practised 'medicine' and sold herbs.

The above period often served to provide capital (fund) development, as well as a learning (trade apprenticeship) stage for the founder of the firm. For example, in the Ntiki group of companies, the father of the founder who provided the initial fund for the Palm Produce Marketing Company (the first company in the group) was a palm produce farmer who sold his produce to the South-eastern government. In the early 1920s Chief Ntiki, the founder of Palm Marketing Company, had no centralized place of business, but sold whatever he produced to the government depot. It was not until after Chief Ntiki's death that his successor, the eldest son, took over the farms and gradually organized a palm produce marketing company to buy from rural subsistence farmers and to sell to the government or large foreign companies for export.

The firms that subsequently emerge usually develop an emotional attachment to these basic business activities and retain them in the diversified organization even when they have become economically non-viable.[3]

Table 4.1 Pre-organized enterprise activities

Companies:	Ntiki Group of Cos.	Nwoke & Sons Ltd.	Francis Group of Cos.	Oko Holdings Limited	Onyeukwu & Sons Limited	Amadi & Sons Limited	Ginano Holdings Limited	Standard Entprs. Limited
Background Activity:								
1. Supply/ sales of crops	X (palm produce)	–	–	X (rubber)	–	–	X (groundnuts, grains)	X (herbs)
2. Retail of finished goods	–	X	X	–	X	X	–	–
3. Retail of goods and crops (comb.)	–	–	–	X	–	X	X	X

Key: – not applicable
X pre-organized enterprise activities

Stages in the evolution of enterprises

Based on data collected primarily from interviews of owners and managers of companies and from review of company records, five phases of evolution were identified. These include:

- *Stage I:*   Formation/registration — this stage is described as a small-scale, one-man operation (usually retail activities), with less than N1,000 in capital. It carries multiple product lines distributed through one outlet.

  Vertical and horizontal
integration of products

- *Stage II:*   Early growth — described as volume and facility expansion, with one or two employees and the founder as overall controller. Expansion into wholesale, importation of diverse goods, more defined outlets (dealership). Maintains over N5,000 in capital.

  Horizontal diversification

- *Stage III:*   Economic growth — operating in more than one industry. Managerial activities — functional/holding structure. Professional employees, with increased non-integrated channels of distribution. Capital is over N1-million.

  Major diversification

- *Stage IV:*   'Accelerated' growth — into major manufacturing operations, induced by government incentives. Both forward and backward integration. Increased diversification into several industries. Beginning of systematic planning. Holding company.

  Reorganization

- *Stage V:*   Reorganization — consolidation of business units, major restructuring through holding/functional. Holding/divisional.

Table 4.2 presents the above five stages and the level of each company's involvement at each stage. Appendix 4.A and 4.B, respectively, define both the degrees or levels of diversification and structures as identified in these cases.

Stage I: formation/registration

This stage describes the period of formal establishment of an organized enterprise. It involves the registration of the company name according to the Nigerian Companies Act 1958 and its amendments.[4] This stage directly follows the period of unorganized, informal business activities

Table 4.2 Stages in evolution

Companies / Stages:	Ntiki Grp of Cos.	Nwoke & Sons Ltd.	Francis Grp of Cos.	Oko Holdings Limited	Onyeukwu & Sons Limited	Amadi & Sons Limited	Ginano Holdings Limited	Standard Entprs. Limited	Fidesco
1. Formation/registration	+	+	+	+	+	+	+	+	
2. Early growth	+	+	+	+	+	+	+	+	
3. Economic growth	+	+	+	+	+	+	−	+	
4. Accelerated growth	++	++	++	++	++	?	++	+	+
5. Re-organization	+	+	+	+	+	−	+	+	

Key: + stage identified in the firm's evolution
++ diversified into more than 6 industries
− not applicable
? no information on company's status

144

when the founder was invariably testing his or her skill in business and most of all trying to build up some capital. All the eight cases in this study went through this registration stage, but changed the initial company name to reflect the increased breadth of their activities. Only Amadi and Sons Limited has retained its original company name and has continued to carry on other business operations under this name. The other seven companies, although known by the end of 1983 under a new name, continued to retain their original names and original companies as subsidiaries. Examples include Oko and Okome Fisheries, and Francis Group of Companies with Francis Enterprises Limited.

Registration as a sole proprietorship under the Business Names Act 1961 was still common by the end of 1983. Most small-scale businessmen, craftsmen/artisans and petty traders find this legal vehicle very convenient. Thus, this type of organization prevails in the first stage of evolution. It is also important to note that individuals and professionals (engineers, doctors, lawyers, surveyors) may carry on business in their real names without registering under the Business Names Act.[5] Amadi and Sons Limited, for example, started trade activities in the late 1920s but registered the business in 1948. Also Francis Enterprises started business in 1961 but was registered in 1970. These business activities or concerns prior to registration are what this study has grouped as pre-organized enterprise activities.

Stage II: early growth

Stage II, 'early growth', is described as a period of expansion in volume and facility. Expansion was usually brought about by efforts to extend the market and thereby increase sales. It also depicts the stage at which the companies have performed satisfactorily and thereby have accumulated funds for possible economic growth. Among the cases in this study, Oko Holdings, Nwoke and Sons, Francis Group of Companies, and Ntiki Group of Companies have depicted this stage very clearly. A brief description of each of these companies at this stage is in order.

Oko Holdings Limited: With the establishment of Okome Sea Food in 1957, the company spent the subsequent year of operation creating frozen fish distribution centres all over the country. Within two years of entering the frozen fish business, 'the name Okome became almost synonymous with frozen fish', explained Mr Obi, one of the company's directors. Mr Obi also maintained 'that the fish business had been responsible for the development of the greater business operation. The fish business was basic to the building of the necessary funds and collateral required for obtaining loans from banks as well as attracting foreign investors for joint ventures.' Okome Sea Foods, as of the end of 1983, distributed fish from more than 70 centres in Nigeria and, according to Mr Obi, 75 per cent of these distribution centres were created within the first two years of operations.

Nwoke Group of Companies: The founder, Sir Nwoke reported,

> . . . after the Civil War in 1970, our former customers of pre-war days came back to us as a result of our high quality and timely construction jobs . . . . We had more jobs than we needed, but were able to complete all of them on a timely basis . . . . We were carrying on construction work in all parts of the country for the federal and state governments as well as individuals and companies.

Explaining further, he continued,

> the company expanded its operations on the supply of building materials; however, we generated so much funds in less than five years that we started looking for other areas to invest our profit.

Ntiki Group of Companies: The head of the firm, Prince Ntiki, described his expansion activities thus: 'My brother and myself built our capital or fund for establishment of the construction business through expansion of our commodity sales, volume and facility.' Explaining, the prince described how he acted as the purchasing officer, 'travelling all over the country in pursuit of any product in demand' while his brother became the sales person 'creating new distribution centres and discovering new lines of product to be added'. In conclusion, the prince added that the family was encouraged to enter the construction business as a result of the funds generated through expansion of the marketing company.

Francis Group of Companies: Mr Nwoji,[6] the foreign trades manager, in response to the question 'How and why do you decide to enter or invest in a new business?' stated, 'Basically we have continued to behave just like we did in our first major investment move. This move was triggered by the availability of funds which were accumulated through expansion of operations between 1972 and 1975.' Mr Nwoji then explained further:

> After the company was registered in 1971, the founder continued to expand through addition of other product lines — tyres, tubes, and then motorcycles, spare motor parts, etc. Soon we had to move to a new and larger facility, followed by introduction of electronic equipment and parts and so on . . . . Business was good and the company made profits . . . . By 1974, we had

started thinking of investment into other viable industries which finally became a reality in 1978 with the establishment of Auto filters and Utensil Manufacturing industry.

Stage III: economic growth

The third stage of development, termed 'economic growth', described a period in the history of the companies' evolution when attempts were made to diversify into new markets or industries. This stage depicts the founders' efforts to be more formalized and economically create a viable, financially strong and lasting operation. Upon accumulating a substantial sum of liquid assets through expansion of volume and facility, these companies then set out to establish more capital-intensive operations, such as the manufacturing operation. The only exception was the Amadi and Sons Limited, a medium-sized company with a 71-year-old head who was interested in moving back to his home town.

In the cases studied in this project, the initial step into economic growth seemed to be in the construction industry for the Ntiki and Ginano Groups in the early 1970s. Nwoke and Amadi, who entered the construction industry in the 1950s, also increased their construction industry activities in this decade. This tendency to enter the industry or increase these activities may be explained by the fact that the Civil War, which ended in January 1970, created a lot of reconstruction jobs. In addition, there were a number of jobs created by the government to fulfil the objectives of developing appropriate infrastructural facilities to aid economic growth.[7] Also, further examination of the cases shows that, in addition to the companies mentioned above, Onyeukwu, Oko and Fidesco of Standard Enterprises were also operating in the construction industry. Francis Group, which started its economic growth through the establishment of the filter and utensil manufacturing company, had plans to enter the construction industry sometime in the mid-1980s.[8]

Diversification in this growth stage appeared to be into both related (Francis Group, Onyeukwu), and unrelated (Ntiki Group, Ginano, Oko, Amadi, etc.) markets or industries. Again, in over 60 per cent of cases (Francis Group, Oko, Amadi, Ginano, Nwoke), the strategy was that of backward integration as opposed to forward integration. For example, Francis Enterprises marketed motor spare parts for several years before entry into motorfilter manufacturing. Oko Holdings, under the name Okome Sea Foods (1963), made profits by selling imported frozen fish for several years before establishing Osajeve Fishing Company Limited (1971) to catch, process, and distribute fish, as well as prawns and shrimps, to supplement the imported frozen fish.

Organizations were more formalized at this third stage as their owners attempted to be effective and at the same time maintain control. A popular structure among the firms studied was a blend of functional and holding company structures. With each organization operating in two or three different industries or markets, the holding company structure, or what was described as Group of Companies included positions designated as 'group general manager', 'group accountant', 'group secretary' or 'group engineer'. These titles applied to individuals who held these positions in the holding company. These group officers had limited autonomy, if any, and reported to the founder or his successor. The limited autonomy which did exist often related to the freedom to market the products in the most profitable manner. Thus, profitability became a measure of success. In the Oko Holdings, Ntiki Group, and Ginano where this type of success criterion was explicit, individual companies in the group often competed against each other (especially in Oko) for resources, even though they belong in different industries.[9] In this third stage of development it was common to see organizations operating in at least two or more industries or markets. The above situation has therefore made it difficult to draw a clear line on where Stage III ended and Stage IV began.

Stage IV: major diversification

Stage IV was marked by horizontal diversification into more than five unrelated businesses. From the cases in this study this 'accelerated'[10] diversification became popular in the 1970s. The Oko Holdings Limited and Ginano Group of Companies represent good examples of companies involved in this major diversification stage.

Oko Holdings Limited: This organization made its mark in the Nigerian business sector through distribution of frozen fish and other imported goods. In 1968 Oko also entered the automobile distribution business. However, major diversification took place in the early 1970s and, by the end of 1984, resulted in the addition of more than 40 companies in the 'Okome Organization'. By 1984 Okome was operating in such industries as the food manufacturing and processing industry, construction, merchandise/service, brewery and soft drink manufacturing, oil and timber milling, marine services, and transportation industries. There were more than six individual companies under each of the above industry groupings.

It is important at this point to indicate that Oko Holdings and Ginano Groups were among those companies who had and took the opportunity offered by the Federal Government through the

Enterprises Promotion Act and used the tax and other incentives to diversify into various business concerns. Such companies as the Rutham Limited, F. Steinar and Company, Lilleshal Nigeria Limited and W.F. Clark Nigeria Limited (which at the end of 1984 belonged to 'Okome Organizations') represent examples of companies which foreign investors were forced to sell to Nigerian indigenes, to operate with indigenes on an established percentage basis (see Appendix 3.A), or to liquidate operations.

Ginano Group: This company also went into joint ventures in the early 1970s in such operations as the Sugar Manufacturing Company, Nigerian Wire Production Company and the Gino Marine Company. By the end of 1984, there were about 13 individual business operations in the Ginano Organization.

Unlike Oko and Ginano Organizations which have partially diversified through acquisition, all the other cases (which operate an average of seven businesses) had diversified through establishment of a new business in the new industry or market. Most diversification into integrated agriculture was induced by both the government incentives and the growing demand. Four of the eight companies studied operated integrated agricultural and food processing businesses.

Structure at this Stage IV level still remained a blend of a holding company and a functional position, or holding/central structure. However, the companies in 'Okome' or Oko Organization were organized under nine different holding companies. The groups, according to Group General Manager, Dr Onori, were classified according to the company's function, location and administration. Dr Onori also described the groups' structural set-up thus: 'Our management set-up is very complex with nine holding companies and a central control at the top. It is more of a matrix structure than anything else.'[11]

Stage V: reorganization

Stage V depicts a period of planned reorganization in the organizations. This period included mostly managerial and structural reorganization rather than growth strategies. In response to the question, 'Are you or rather has your organization developed as far as it can go or as far as you desire? Please explain what the organization's plans are at the moment and for the future', the following represent some of the responses from managers and/or owners of the organizations.

Ntiki Group of Companies: According to Justin Ntiki, second son of the co-founder and a director of all the companies in the group, 'No, we are not fully diversified. My parents have plans for the further growth of this organization. For an example, my father just came back yesterday from Lagos after registering a new company designed to deal with shipping operations.'[12] Continuing, Mr Ntiki maintained that the Group's major concern in 1984 had been primarily that of re-organization. 'My father and uncle, in cooperation with the other officers of the organization, have been working on a reorganization programme which will somehow consolidate related operations and possibly relocate the main facilities of some,' added Justin. For explanation Justin produced the draft copy of the new organizational chart. He pointed out that there were plans to grant full autonomy to the insurance company as well as increase its lines of services.[13] Also, the Century Transportation office was being relocated to Calabar and was to be integrated with the new shipping concern. Both businesses would be carried on under the name of Century Transportation, with the distinctions as Shipping and Bus Service divisions. This relocation of Century operating headquarters from Uyo to Calabar was a strategic move to have offices closer to the third largest sea port in the country.

Adding to Justin's statements, the senior group general manager, Mr Etinem, said, 'You see, we expect the shipping line to grow faster than the bus services, which had already begun to decline.' Then, in response to the question of whether the company planned to liquidate the bus services, Mr Etinem emphatically replied, 'Oh no! The bus service is primarily our way of serving and helping the community. You know how difficult it is to travel from one place to another in Nigeria? Our bus services will continue to alleviate this problem for this community.' Other major reorganization activities planned by the group include plans to establish a separate business unit to carry on the operations of Mercedes Benz vehicles and spare parts when Century moves to Calabar.

Company characteristics

Table 4.3 presents the characteristics examined and identified at each of the development stages. The following paragraphs describe the findings.

Product line

All the large companies reviewed and studied started out as retail trading organizations. This situation was probably the consequence of the trade-oriented economic development of the country. That is, the country was initially agriculturally based, with trade beginning with

Table 4.3 Company characteristics at stages of development

Stages: Company characteristics:	Formalization	Early Expansion	Economic Growth	Major Diversification	Reorganization/Consolidation
1. Product Line	Diversified/Multiple product line	More diversified	Multiple	Multiple	Diverse but more focused
2. Distribution	One channel	More than one channel (branches)	Sets/Multiple channels	Unintegrated sets of channels	Diverse channel
3. Organizational Structure	One-man or two-man operation	More formalized with few employees	Functional structure mostly for professional activities	Holding/Central structure with SBUs	Holding/Division structure/SBU
4. Research & Development	N/A	N/A	Feasibility Study by Prof. Consultant	Professional Consultation	Quality Control Group
5. Performance Appraisal	Subjective	Subjective	Objective	Standardized Criteria	Standardized Criteria
6. Rewards/Motivation	Unsystematic	Unsystematic	More Formalized	Systematic	Systematic
7. Control System	Owner control of strategic and operational decisions	Owner control of strategic and operational decisions	Professional involvement, limited delegation	Planned but mixed with owner's final decision	Planned but mixed with owner's veto power
8. Strategic Choices	Depends on owner's goals and objectives	Depends on owner's goals and objectives	Owner/Plus consultants analysis, entry into industry	Rate of growth entry and exit into industries investment	Integration of SBUs, structural choices, consolidation

Source: Format and Company Characteristics from B.R. Scott, *Stages of Corporate Development*, 1971.

colonization. Unlike the single product or single line identified by Scott and his associates in Stage I, Nigerian firms carried multiple product lines which were continuously added to with any indication of demand. The Ntiki Group and Nwoke Group of Companies in describing this early stage maintained that the strategy 'was to stock anything that was demanded by more than five to ten customers'. 'There were never any plans for specialization as far as product line was concerned,' stated Prince Utuk of the Utuks Group of Companies. This multiple product line usually continued into the later stages with a more defined product line associated with the business that then formed the organization.

Distribution strategies

Distribution strategies ranged from one channel at the early stages to several integrated channels in the later stages. However, organizational structures were identified as informal/unstructured in Stage I, a little formalization in Stage II, a form of functional structure in Stage III, a holding/centralized/divisional structure in Stage V (see Appendix 4.B for definitions).

Research and development

Research and development (R&D), systematic performance appraisal and reward/activation issues were never a major concern for these organizations until about Stage IV. Even then, with the degree of diversification and size of the organizations, R&D was often left with outside marketing or industrial analysts.

Control strategies

The control strategies, especially with the large family organizations, ranged from owner/founder controlled to limited involvement of professionals on an advisory basis. Structures were usually selected so that the founder and/or the members of the family could retain control. In the early stages, strategic choices were based on balancing family and company needs to the third stage, where the need for economic growth forced companies to compromise some of the family objectives and beliefs. The Ginano Group presents a good description of the case where a company compromised belief by shifting responsibility to professionals. Ginano was the only case in this study with a Muslim family as owner. According to the Muslim religion, rigorous or intensive pursuit of economic wealth is against the commandments.[14] But after several years of declining business after the initial expansion, the family elected to retain strategic control and give management to professionals outside its religion. By 1984, most of the Ginano Group's individual businesses were managed by indigenous and expatriate professionals.

Summary and conclusions

Data show that an enterprise in Nigeria developed either through horizontal or vertical expansion of product lines, or through expansion or discovery of new market, or from diversification into other industries. Five stages of development were identified with all firms starting off in a retail trade organization, but developing into large organizations mostly through diversification strategies.

All companies studied were horizontally diversified into some related, but mostly unrelated, businesses. When companies initiated related activities, the major approach was more of backward integration, with distribution and sales of purchased products preceding diversification into manufacturing of products. The Ntiki Group, for example, entered into the manufacture of asphalt and graphite seven years after establishing a road and sewage construction business; Oko started a fishing business after marketing imported frozen fish for several years; and Ginano established the Anadriya farm after several years of operating a food processing company.

Only two of the eight firms studied use a holding/functional structure with another variation — holding/divisionalization — developing into the reorganization stage. The other six appeared to retain a functional/centralized structure from the third stage of formalized structure into the fifth stage. Broadly stated, Nigerian companies had become more diversified than the American companies studied by Chandler (1962), Wrigley (1970) and Rumelt (1974). These Nigerian firms tended to coordinate and control their diverse operations through the creating of a holding company with the founder and members of the family dominating the board. This central head office was often designated or registered as '. . . Group of Companies' as exemplified by Ntiki Group, Ginano Group and Francis Group. Six out of the eight cases controlled 5—45 subsidiaries under one or more holding companies.

Unlike the holding company defined by Rumelt and Pavan, in which there is a parent company with financial control of a number of largely autonomous subsidiaries, the subsidiaries under the Nigerian holding company had little or no autonomy. Autonomy, when granted, was usually granted for the marketing of products. With the later stages of development, data indicated trends towards the introduction of a divisional structure combined with the holding structure developed in the middle of evolution stages. This reluctance to decentralize but to retain a controlling holding company seemed to be an effort by the founder and the family to retain structural as well as financial control of their organizations.

Further, there was a prevalence of diversification through establishment of a new business rather than through acquisition of an on-going business. Only two of the eight companies studied had partially diversified through acquisition of on-going firms (Ginano, Oko). However, this strategy of diversification might be due to the fact that there were no maturing businesses to purchase nor enough large businesses initiating some divestments. It should also be emphasized that the companies acquired by Ginano and Oko were available as a consequence of the Federal Government action designed to reduce the number of private enterprises held by foreign investors (see Enterprises Promotion Act, Appendix 3.A).

Table 4.4 presents the classification of strategy and structure of the enterprises. However, evidence exists to show that the prevailing strategies and structures among enterprises in Nigeria were strongly influenced by not only the natural ecology but also by several government planned actions,[15] designed to effect national economic development. These strategies and structures could be expected to change as the country achieved further economic and industrial development and the government relaxed some of the current regulations. The market continued to expand in the country and most firms were still diversifying into new markets with new business in order to benefit from the growing market and the incentives. But attempts to maintain better control had some firms (such as Oko) thinking in terms of integration of related firms and possible divestment of the 'question marks' and the unrelated. Also as more individuals or families go into organized business activities, competition in many industries, which was almost negligible in 1983, was bound to increase and thereby force the exit of some incompetent businesses through liquidation or divestment.

In conclusion, there were similarities as well as differences in the pattern of evolution of firms in the USA, Western European countries, Japan and in Nigeria. Similarities are common in the framework of development stages, while differences occurred in the internal as well as external characteristics of the enterprises.

Table 4.4 Classification by strategy* and structure** of enterprises studied (1983)

Classification by strategy:	No. of companies	%
No diversification*	—	
Moderate diversification (related businesses)	2	25
High diversification (unrelated)	6	75
Diversification by acquisition	2	22
Diversification through establishment of new business	7	78
Classification by structure:		
Functional and holding/functional	6	75
Holding/divisional (holding/centralized)	2	25
Reorganizing (holding/decentralizing)	3	37.5

* See Appendix 4.A for description.
** See Appendix 4.B for description.

Note: One company can appear in multiple classifications.

Notes

1   *Nigeria — A Country Study*, Library of Congress, Cataloging of Public Data, 1982, Chapter 1, 'Historical setting'; *History of economic activities in Nigeria, 1982*, National Archives of Nigeria, EP #4423, Lagos, Nigeria.
2   The most important of these firms, United African Company (UAC), was founded in 1871 by George Goldie. In 1886 this company was granted broad concessionary powers in 'all the territory of the Niger Basin'. The terms of the charter specified the maintenance of free trade in the Eastern region, a principle that was systematically violated as the company strengthened its monopoly to forestall French and German trade expansion.

3   Five examples will illustrate: The Ntiki Group still maintains one facility of the old palm produce marketing which has not done any business since 1979–83. Oko still maintains a rubber farm, Standard sells herbs, Nwoke continues retailing miscellaneous merchandise, and the Francis Group continues retailing motor-parts and motorbikes.

4   According to the Companies Act 1958, 'indigenes and foreigners alike may engage in private enterprise in Nigeria through any or all of the following mediums', (a) sole proprietorship, (b) partnership, and (c) company with or without limited liability. Appendix 5.C presents the characteristics of these mediums.

5   This probably explains why most of the companies of the study were able to carry on business activities for years prior to the formal registration.

6   Mr Nwoji was the first employee the company hired when it started business in 1970. Thus, apart from the founder, Chief Abana, he is the oldest member of the organization. Mr Nwoji was responsible for the description of the company's history in this research.

7   One of the objectives of the Second National Development Plan (1962–68) was to develop the necessary infrastructure facilities to aid economic growth. Even prior to the start of the Civil War the construction industry had become an attractice venture for many businesses because of existing jobs.

8   Mr Nwoji, during an interview session, explained that the company had a blueprint of plans for further diversification and that this diversification 'may include entry into a specialized area of the construction industry'. He would not explain what he meant by 'specialized area' in the construction industry.

9   Dr Onori, the Group General Manager, maintained that individual businesses were encouraged to expand their market and sales either through introduction of a new product line or entry into a new market. 'Where potentials for improvement were indicated, this company may be allocated additional funds to develop this potential,' he reiterated.

10   The term 'accelerated' was used here to describe the degree of diversification (see also Appendix 4.A) because of the intro-duction of the Enterprises Promotion Act 1972 which not only forced foreign investors to transfer some categories of business to Nigerian citizens, but also provided funds through the Industrial Development Bank for them to develop private businesses.

11   By 1972, two years after the Civil War, the war-devastated and depressed citizens of the Eastern regions were still very sceptical of venturing outside their states of origin and so did not get into

the business action in Lagos until the mid-1970s (see dates of new business establishments in Kwoke's Group, Francis, Standard and Onyeuku in the cases).

But Ginano, originating from the Northern state, had the opportunity, as did Okome from the Midwest and Ntiki from the Cross Rivers. Although Cross Rivers belonged in the East, it was liberated early in the war and so the people were able to communicate with Lagos.

12 This interview took place on 19 September 1984.

13 Destiny Insurance was established in response to the increasing number of auto insurance referrals being made by Utuks Motors to other insurance companies. Concluding that the market looked promising, the company went into the business just for all types of auto insurance. In this expansion programme, plans were to introduce all other types of insurance except life.

14 'Ethnic Groups and Religions: The Hausa Group', *Nigeria — A Country Study*, op. cit.

15 Examples of government actions designed to influence economic and industrial development in Nigeria include:
 — Enterprises Promotion Act 1972, 1977 and 1981
 — Economic Stabilization Orders 1983
 — Tax Incentives 1974
 — Industrial Development Acts 1958, 1962.

Appendix 4.A Degrees of diversification

Low diversification: *

Horizontal expansion of product line: Firms which continued to grow by marketing of finished goods. These firms expanded the product line both horizontally and vertically, often growing from retail activities to wholesale.

Moderate diversification** (related business):

Firms which grow from expansion by means of entry into related markets or businesses. By getting involved in a manufacturing enterprise but related activities. May be forward or backward integration.

High diversification*** (unrelated business):

Firms which grow horizontally into new markets and new industries mostly unrelated to the original business. Often operates in more than five different industries.

Examples: *   Amadi and Sons Limited
       **   Standard Enterprises Limited
      ***   Oko Holdings Limited

Appendix 4.B   Organizational structure

Functional company:

Specialized functional position (usually accounting, personnel/administration), who report hierarchically to the chairman and founder of the organization (e.g. Amadi and Sons Limited).

Holding/Functional:

A parent company with overall control of all subsidiaries who are largely non-autonomous. Functional positions are titled group function, whereby the individual, for example the group personnel officer, was responsible for hiring and firing of all positions in the subsidiaries. Also regarded as functional/centralized structure (e.g. Ntiki Group of Companies).

Holding/divisionalization:

Where further autonomy had been granted to the subsidiaries and there has been some integration of firms (either related by location or market). Here the parent company maintains mostly financial control and overall policy-making, while the manager of the subgroup or the strategic business units receive reports from the divisional manager and then report to the chairman or founder through the group general manager (e.g. Ginano Group of Companies and Oko Holdings).

This structure is also known as the 'Holding/decentralization'.

Appendix 4.C   Legal forms of companies in Nigeria

Sole proprietorship:

Most common among small scale businessmen, artisans and petty traders. Requires the registration of company name under the Business Names Act 1961, as a sole proprietor. However, professionals carrying on business in their real name need not register under this Act. They are not, however, allowed to operate as limited liability companies.

Partnership:

Essentially the same as sole proprietor except that there is more than one party involved. Partnership must also be registered under the Business Names Act 1961.

Limited liability companies:

A limited liability company is regarded in law as a legal entity or 'person', separate or distinct from its members and with a perpetual existence until dissolved. Third parties (especially creditors) feel reassured dealing with this abstract and artificial body. This is becoming the most favoured vehicle for entrepreneurs wishing to invest sizeable amounts in the Nigerian economy. Investors also feel comfortable investing in a joint stock enterprise, knowing that their liability is limited (in case of liquidation) to the extent of the unpaid share capital, if any. Such companies have less than 50 investors.

Unlimited companies:

The law often requires professional persons like insurance brokers to carry on business by incorporating a company with unlimited liability. This requirement is to protect the interest of creditors, since the creditors have recourse to the individual members of the firm in the event of liquidation.

5 Remote and internal environmental factors in strategy and structure development

Introduction

In Chapter 4 it was observed that enterprises in Nigeria evolved through five stages. In the firms studied, a strategy of diversification was very prominent in this growth effort while three major management structures were also identified. These structures include functional, holding/functional (or holding/centralization), and holding/divisionaliz-ation (or holding/decentralization).

In this chapter, several factors which may have influence on these evolution patterns,[1] especially family 'constellation'[2] are described. The influence of family constellation was observed at two major levels, (a) strategic and (b) structural. At both levels the natural/ecological factors, which included family constellations or forms, and the government actions were identified. The ecological and governmental factors include:

1 Ecological factors:
   (a) social milieu
   (b) family constellations or forms
   (c) economic milieu

2 Governmental factors:
   (a) national development plans
   (b) Enterprises Promotion Programme
   (c) Economic Stabilization Orders
   (d) Pioneer Industries Programme

Table 5.1 summarizes the profile of the families studied while Tables 5.2 and 5.3 summarize the levels of influence of the above factors on the evolution patterns.

Family 'constellation'

For the purposes of this study, families were classified into 'nuclear' (or small) and 'extended kinship' (or large).[3] These two forms were defined as:

1 *Nuclear (small)*: Refers to family forms where responsibilities or obligations were confined to the immediate small family (i.e. father and mother, sons and daughters, sometimes grandchildren). Usually these groupings were six or fewer members.
2 *Extended kinship (large)*: Refers to family forms where obligations or responsibilities went across and beyond the boundaries of immediate family. Obligations included relationships based on a complex set of norms and on culture.

Six of the eight companies studied were 'extended kinship' families with high family involvement in the running of the business (see Table 5.1). These companies (Ntiki, Oko, Amadi, Standard, Onyeukwu and Francis) were founded by Christian[4] families with ethnic origins in the old Eastern region.[5] The other 25 per cent of the companies in the study consisted of one Moslem[6] family organization, founded by a Northern Hausa ethnic origin with low family involvement, and Nwoke Group, a medium-sized organization with high family involvement.

The Ntiki family, for example, consisted of three brothers working together to maintain the family. The oldest brother (Chief Ntiki) married four wives and had over 27 children. The next brother (Prince Ntiki) had a wife and four children, while the youngest, Mr Ntiki, had nine children (four from his deceased wife and five from the next). Responsibilities, as well as authority for actions, rested more with the oldest brother, who was the father figure to the others and their families. Culture and norms, which gave authority to and demanded respect and obedience for the elders, constituted the basis for the family relationships and thus its structure. The Ntikis formed one large family unit until 1968 when disagreement over the management and control of the business organization brought about a break-up of the private family business. However, members of the family have continued to look out for each other on a non-business basis. For example, with the death of Chief Ntiki in 1973, the Prince and his younger brother continued to sponsor the education as well as career development of their nephews, nieces, etc.

Table 5.1 Profile of families studied

Company	Family 'Constellation' or Form	Religious Background	Ethnic Origin	Founder's Children Male	Founder's Children Female
1. Ntiki Group of Companies	Large(++)	Christianity (Catholic)	Ibibio (Cross River State)	3	1
2. Nwoke Group of Companies	Medium/Small(++)	Christianity (Catholic)	Ibo (Anambra State)	7	2
3. Francis Group of Companies	Large(++)	Christianity(?)	Ibo (Imo State)	2	5
4. Oko Holdings Limited*	Large(++)	Christianity(?)	Urobo (Bendel State)	4	4
5. Amadi and Sons Limited	Large(++)	Christianity(?)	Ibo (Anambra State)	6	10
6. Onyeukwu and Sons Limited*	Large(++)	Christianity(?)	Ibo (Anambra State)	8	11
7. Ginano Group Limited	Large(+)	Moslem	Hausa (Kano State)	?	?
8. Standard Enterprises Limited	Large(++)	Christianity(?)	Ibo (Anambra State)	2	1

Notes:

*   Headquarters located in Lagos, Capital of Nigeria.
?   Not specific as to whether Anglican, Methodist, Baptist, etc.
+   Low family involvement in business.
++   High family involvement in business.

164

The Amadi's family structure was similar to the Ntiki's. The older brother, Noah, took care of not only his immediate family but his brothers' as well. This complex relationship created a web of conflicting ties among brothers, half-brothers, nephews, nieces, and cousins. Major characteristics of this structure (which were common among the six firms) were the unclear and undefined responsibilities among the family members; only the set of responsibilities of the oldest brother or 'patriarch' of the family was clearly understood.

In all the firms, involvement of family members in the organization appeared to be a 'given'. Except for Ntiki's and Amadi's, where some members of the next generation were observed to have taken initial employment outside the family business, the other firms immediately absorbed members of the family soon after completion of or quitting school.

Nwoke's family has remained between nuclear and extended kinship in its relationships or interaction with members outside the immediate family. Although family involvement in the organization remained high, the extension of responsibility towards others outside the immediate family is very limited. Also the family appeared to be more actively involved in the practice of their religion than the other Christian families in the study. The Ginano family, on the other hand, appeared to have maintained low involvement in the family business because of their religious beliefs.[7]

In all the families studied, the educational levels of the females appeared to have improved with the second generation. This observation appears to be the consequence of such factors as 1) the social time period in Nigeria, 2) increasing affluence of the family, 3) the needs of the business, and 4) religious beliefs. All the founders, with the exception of the Okos, had either not finished primary school, or had primary or high school diplomas. The Oko founder, Dr Chief Moses Okome, was awarded an honorary doctorate degree by a Nigerian university in his home state because of his contribution to the community and the university in particular. Among the generations following the founders, family members were college degree holders with over 50 per cent of the degrees earned at universities outside Nigeria (usually in the USA or UK).

In summary, wherever the 'extended kinship' family constellation existed, the business became a source of provision for the needs of the kinship. These needs included food, shelter, education, employment and old age support. Sometimes certain needs (general assistance and community improvement projects) were expected from the family by its immediate community.

Factors and levels of influence

Ecological factors

Apart from family constellation, two other factors (social and economic milieu) have been listed under the ecological factors. These two factors were closely related to the forms of families, especially the social milieu, whose culture, norms and religious beliefs have basically influenced the family units. All the families studied were located in the major cities[8] of the country. In these urban locations the traditional norms and culture were influenced by Western civilization. A typical example of the characteristic difference was well put in a remark by Prince Ntiki, during one of the interview sessions in which his nephew Justin was present. Justin was the general manager of the insurance company, a subsidiary in the group. The Prince explained the reasons for the relationship he maintained with his older brother's children. 'As much as I feel obligated to watch over them and give as much assistance as I can, I do not need to hire them into this organization, knowing what happened with their father's section of the business and assets.' At this point Justin intervened with a remark that the Prince had not responded to his question. After dismissing Justin, the Prince remarked, 'That is what I call Western influence, even in the villages today, younger people do not speak to their elders until they are spoken to. But as my sons indicate, it is the "order of the day" and personally I love it,' concluded the Prince with his tongue in his cheek. What the above incidents indicate was that Western influence in the cities has changed some cultural norms guiding relationships among members of families. Children raised in the cities are more outspoken, alert, individualistic and often very achievement-oriented. The last characteristic is more true about Southern Nigerian families than the Northerners.

Demographic factors, especially population, have implications for the family forms and strategic patterns of evolution. The Ibos had a considerable population and occupied a small section of the country (see Imo and Anambra States in Figure 3.1, page 76) with very poor soil. Unable to pursue agricultural activities with much success, almost 75 per cent of this ethnic group has become business owners or civil servants. Furthermore, Nigeria's early economic development history shows that trade played an important part in the lives of the indigenes who exchanged their crops for finished goods.

As indicated in Table 5.2, ecological factors such as social and economic status had implications more for the strategic patterns of evolution, while family constellation (partially influenced by the social milieu) had implications for the structural patterns of evolution.

Table 5.2 Ecological factors: levels of influence

Companies:	Ntiki Group of Cos.	Nwoke & Sons Ltd.	Francis Group of Cos.	Oko Holdings Limited	Onyeukwu & Sons Limited	Amadi & Sons Limited	Ginano Holdings Limited	Standard Enterprises Limited
Factors:								
Social milieu	+	+	+	+	+	+	?	+
Economic milieu	+	+	+	+	+	+	+	+
Family 'Constellation'	/+	X	/+	/	/	/+	+	/+

Legend:
+   Has reasonable influence on strategic patterns
−   Least influence on strategic patterns
/   Has influence on structural patterns
X   Least influence on structural patterns
?   Unknown or influence not observed

167

(See Appendix 5.C for the industries and organizational structures of the companies.) In the Ntiki Group of Companies, for example, both strategic and structural patterns were observed as being strongly influenced by the family constellation. The senior group manager, Mr Etinem, was asked to respond to the question, 'How do you see relationships among members of the Ntiki family and how do they fit into the organization?' His remarks included the following:

> Of course they own the company, and we expect them to come in as directors and high officers of the organization. But for one thing, they are qualified to hold their respective positions. Take Justin, for example, he returned from the United States of America, three weeks ago with a diploma in Insurance Marketing. Just a day after he got back, he resumed work at the Destiny Insurance, sharing an office with the acting General Manager, a position we all expect him to assume soon. Not only that, the Insurance Company is undergoing a major reorganization in both management and product line and all these are geared toward adaptation to Justin's new skill and family satisfaction . . . . As a matter of fact, this was not unusual . . . . A general reorganization was made in the entire organization when Uwa, the older son obtained his MBA, and Retail Motor Co. also with Vincent's degree in Mechanical Engineering . . . . Don't get me wrong, this is one happy family determined to operate a profitable organization and believe me, they are doing it. In this family, both parents and children work hard for the good of the family as well as the business — why else would Justin be spending one year with another insurance company prior to assuming full responsibility in the family subsidiary.

Also, Justin explained that the position of Chairman and Managing Director, which his uncle held, did not indicate that the Prince owns more shares than his father, but is a result of cultural respect to the older brother.[9] He reiterated that both 'brothers share business responsibilities and decision-making equally' (see Appendix 5.A for excerpts of the interview with Mr Etinem and Justin).

The Francis Group represents another example of the effects of family constellation on the evolution of structural patterns. Although the founder and the middle brother later broke up, the initial strategies were to develop a business where they could all work together for the benefit of the family. Early structures included the positions of manager and assistant manager for the two brothers. Also later, upon the younger brother's return after graduation from college, a position of assistant managing director was created for him, and an almost identical facility as the headquarters was constructed at Iba in Imo State. This facility controlled almost all the industrial subsidiaries located in Imo State. This reorganization was planned to maintain family relationships and form.

In the same company, in less than five years, another major re-organization took place as a result of the arrival of the third and youngest brother of the family. Damian, the youngest brother, graduated with a doctoral degree in finance. He joined the organization as the financial controller, a new position in the organization. The family proceeded to reorganize the accounting system, as well as other systems in the organization, and positioned relatives and clansmen in more strategic spots like accounting and inventory control. The founder maintained that, apart from the existence of appropriate facilities in his home town, he was motivated to locate the Integrated Farm Project there in order to provide a means of livelihood to his relatives (uncles, aunts and others) who were less fortunate and, therefore, had relied on him for some support. With the creation of the Project, these people became gainfully employed and thus lessened his responsibility. 'Culture demands that I take care of these relatives', he added, 'and I am happy that the project is providing the means.' In addition, this farm project will be the main source of supply for the food processing unit which is being planned by the company (forward integration).

Another example of family form implications for evolution pattern is the Amadi and Sons. In this company, the founder entered into the transportation service industry to provide a job/career for his younger brother who graduated from vehicle driving school. Furthermore, this non-profitable venture was continuously supported in order to maintain cordial family relationships. The timber business provided a haven for the school drop-outs in the family, while the highly educated abstained from joining the organization. These informal relationships among members of the family have strongly contributed to the informal structure and uneconomical strategies observed in the company, even 50 years after it started.

In Oko Holdings, where subsidiaries were grouped under several sub-holding companies (forward diversification to give control to members of the family), and others like Nwoke and Standard Enterprises, where positions were created to accommodate family members (related diversifications initiated because of family skills), the structural patterns appeared to be much more influenced by family forms than by planned strategies for the organization.

Governmental factors

Just as social and economic factors had greater influence on the formation/initiation of strategic patterns, most of the government actions were observed to have more influence on diversification or growth strategies (see Table 5.3). In summary, the 1981–85 National Development Plan is the fourth of its kind by the Federal Government

Table 5.3 Government actions: levels of influence

Companies: Factors:	Ntiki Group of Cos.	Nwoke & Sons Ltd.	Francis Group of Cos.	Oko Holdings Limited	Onyeukwu & Sons Limited	Amadi & Sons Limited	Ginano Holdings Limited	Standard Enterprises Limited
National Development Plans (1972–1985)	+	+	+	+	+	–	+	+
Enterprises Promotion Programme (1972, 1977, 1982)	+X	+X	/+	+	/+	–	+	–
Economic Stabilization Programme (1983)	X	X+	X	X+	X	?	?	+
Pioneer Industries Programme (1971)	+	+	/+	+	+	?	+	–

Legend:
+ Has reasonable influence on strategic patterns
– Least influence on strategic patterns
/ Has reasonable influence on structural patterns
X Least influence on structural patterns
? Unknown or level of influence not observed

since the country attained political independence in 1960. The Fourth National Development Plan, like its predecessors,[10] was a deliberate instrument for harnessing the country's natural resources for the benefit of her people. To this end, the plan re-emphasized these specific objectives:

1 Greater evenness of income distribution among individuals and socio-economic groups;
2 Reduction of the dependence of the economy on a narrow range of activities;
3 Balanced development — that is, the achievement of better balance in the development of the different sectors of the economy and the various geographical areas of the country;
4 Increased participation by citizens in the ownership and management of productive enterprises; and
5 Greater self-reliance — that is, increased dependence on Nigerian resources in seeking to achieve the various objectives of society. This also implies increased efforts to achieve optimum utilization of Nigerian human and natural as well as other forms of resources.[11]

The above objectives laid the foundation and framework for the development of the specific programmes and/or Acts which actually influenced evolution patterns of Nigerian enterprises. Outstanding among these programmes was the Enterprises Promotion or 'indigenization' Programme which actually made it possible for many private citizens to own and control firms. This Programme actually inspired the development of many family firms started around the early 1970s. Many brothers, fathers and sons in civil service organizations or corporations resigned their jobs and pooled their savings to go into their own businesses. The Economic Stabilization and the Pioneer Industries Programmes, respectively, inspired and encouraged development of alternative sources of raw materials and establishment of basic industries such as farming and processing operations.[12]

In this study, Oko Holdings and Ginano Group of Companies demonstrate the influence of the government indigenization efforts on major diversification strategies. Oko, at the end of 1983, was operating with over 45 individual companies involved in over five unrelated industries, ranging from retail distribution of commodities to the manufacturing of agricultural and industrial chemicals. Ginano Group was operating in over 14 companies, ranging from distribution of apparel to the processing and packaging of food items.

The Economic Stabilization Order (1983) and the Pioneer Industries Programme influenced the strategic decisions in J. Nwoke Group of Companies. Both the brewery and the soft drink bottling companies were located in a rural part of the country, to enable the company to comply with the Federal Government's plea to locate industries in rural areas in order to decrease the influx of labour into the cities and to hasten the development of the rural sections of the country. Companies complying benefited from the corporate tax reduction (10 per cent) incentive programme. Also, the Nwoke Group of Companies was lured initially by the Pioneer Industries Programme to enter the package manufacturing industry in a joint venture agreement in which the Japanese firm provided mainly the technical expertise. However, with the establishment of the Economic Stabilization Order which restricted importation, including raw materials, the company, in 1984, renegotiated its joint venture agreement. This time the foreign partners agreed to provide for the major part of raw materials. Under this agreement the company did not have to worry too much about the foreign exchange restriction since payment for purchase, shipment and handling was the foreign partner's responsibility.

In the Francis Group, Oko Holdings, Onyeukwu and Sons and Ginano Group, the establishment of integrated farm projects was also initiated in response to the institution of the Pioneer Industries Programme. The locations for these farms and processing factories were also in rural areas. As a result of the prohibition of the import of some of the commodities in their product line, the Oko Holdings strategy called for forward integration. Plans were underway in 1984 to set up a processing plant to produce the canned fruits and juices which were a major line of products distributed by T.B. Clarke (Nig) Limited, a subsidiary of Oko. Ginano Group, on the other hand, integrated backward with its farm business, Main Foods Company Limited, a wholly owned subsidiary of the Group. Other businesses such as the steel and wire industry of Ginano, the chemical company of Onyeukwu, and ceramic and marble business of Standard qualified as pioneer industries. Establishing these activities provided some tax benefits to the companies. Data also show that most of the above companies were established after the initiation of the government incentive programmes. Even Ginano Steel, which was established before 1971, was refiled under the Pioneer Industries Programme.

Summary

This section summarizes the findings on how family constellation influences the pattern of evolution. Data indicated that the 'extended kinship' family form was more prevalent in the Nigerian society than the nuclear form. Evidence exists that the more gifted members of the family often went beyond the call of duty to support and also take responsibility for the care of the younger and less fortunate relatives outside their immediate families. Society and culture demands this behaviour and the family members in this study have responded. These extended relationships, coupled with responsibility for the welfare of others, are sometimes referred to by many who had been exposed to Western culture (especially the USA) as the 'social security system' for the developing country.

Although the original research question was 'How does family constellation influence a firm's evolution pattern?', it was impossible to separate the influence of ecological and governmental factors. This decision relates to the fact that both the social, economic, and governmental factors operate simultaneously with family constellation relationships in one of several ways. The traditional social milieu was responsible for the pattern of interaction which required respect for the unquestioned leadership and wisdom of the elders. The society was also responsible for the predominant family form of extended kinship. The economic status of the country initially influenced the type of business established by each family, as well as the level and type of career developed among members of the family. During the time period covered in this study, the actions, programmes and activities instituted by the government (educational, health and industrial economic programmes) improved the standard of living of the people and thus changed the socialization and interaction patterns among family members. For example, the influence and acceptance of Western culture by members of the younger generation has slowly increased the number of families classified as nuclear in the society. Thus, the number of children per couple has decreased; however, interaction still remained that of the extended kinship type as defined in this study.

Thus, although the study was designed to explore the influence of family constellation on evolution patterns of enterprise, it seemed appropriate to examine other factors which have indirectly influenced family forms and the patterns of family firms.

Two major levels of evolution pattern were determined — strategies and structures. Strategies refer to the pattern of decision choices, distribution methods, manufacture versus purchase, control systems and the like. Structure refers to the relationship and interaction/communication set-up. Broadly, data show that half of the firms studied indicated that family forms had influence on the structural patterns of evolution, but little influence on strategic patterns. However, both the socio-economic status and government actions show strong influence on the strategic patterns adopted by the enterprises.

The structural influences were displayed in the process of the family's attempt to create appropriate employment for family members and especially in the attempt to accommodate them in the management positions of the organizations. The structures of holding/functional and holding/decentralization were dominant among companies where family constellation influenced the patterns that evolved (Ntiki, Oko and Amadi in Appendix 5.C). It is apparent that these companies maintain the above structures under the following conditions:

1 Holding/functional when the younger members of the family were still in school and the founder and patriarch would use professionals at the functional positions while he maintained control through the holding structure;
2 Holding/decentralization gradually evolved as the children or relatives graduated from colleges and were able to take over some responsible, professional position which the founder was at that point willing to accommodate through relinquishment of some autonomy.

However, founders often tried to maintain control and coordination through, once again, the holding structure. The only company (Ginano) in the study in which family involvement was very low was a consequence of the family's religious beliefs which discouraged intensive pursuit of wealth especially by women. In this company, both strategies and structures for the operations of the business were based mostly on the economic development of the firm and these decisions were usually made by professionals consisting mostly of Ibo and Yoruba ethnic groups.

The socio-economic influence on the strategies is also evident. The dominance of trading activities at the formation stage was a consequence of the interaction between the European traders and the colonial government. Major diversification, which was largely influenced by government-planned action, was predominant among the companies studied. How are these family/private firms able to sponsor and maintain so many diversified companies in a growing country? Government actions not only created incentives for indigenes to go into business and be involved in industrial development, they also provided several funding programmes (see Appendix 5.B) for the benefit of its citizens. Nigerian Industrial Development Banks (NIDBs), special arrangements of term loans and overdrafts through commercial banks, and 'private placements', are a few of the programmes designed to provide funding for enterprise development.

Another widely used financing method was equipment leases or 'quasi-loans'. 'Quasi-loans' were a new phenomenon, designed to help investors facing the problem of financing large and expensive, but essential, machinery and equipment. This funding technically provided a means of 'leasing' the equipment from a financial institution and thus indirectly obtaining what is in actual fact a loan or quasi-loan. This arrangement is an attempt by the financial institution, in collaboration with the government, to ensure the importation and maintenance of appropriate technology or high quality equipment for use by the firms. This method is increasingly being adopted by many private firms in the country. It has the advantages of simple budgeting, improving liquidity, freeing working capital, and leaving the credit lines unimpaired.[13] Most of the companies (Ntiki, Oko, Ginano, Onyeukwu and Nwoke) have applied this source of funding to capital-intensive projects.

Notes

1   Evolution patterns under strategies include types of product and diversity/concentration of product lines; purchasing vs. manufacturing of products; distribution methods; motivation, appraisal, control methods, etc. Structural patterns include functional and all variations of holding structure.
2   Constellation includes patterns of family dynamics, relationships, emergent structures, and often also includes birth order.
3   For other forms of families and definitions examined, see Chapter 2.
4   In general, most adherents to the Christian faith in Nigeria, especially Catholics and the Anglicans, practised monogamy. Whenever a Catholic married more than one wife (which continued to happen often) the major punishment was to deny him and the second wife communion and other sacraments in the Church.
5   The old Eastern region comprised Anambra, Cross River, Imo, Bendel and Rivers states. Ethnic groups in these states include Ibos, Ibibios and Ijaws.
6   The Muslim faith allows for four to eight wives according to the status of the individual. The tenets of this religion discouraged the intensive pursuit of wealth.
7   See note 6 above.
8

	Families	Cities
(i)	Ntiki	Uyo (second largest city in Cross River State)
(ii)	Nwoke	Onitsha (largest commercial city in country)
(iii)	Francis	Enugu (capital of Anambra State)
(iv)	Oko	Benin (capital of Bendel State)
(v)	Amadi	Enugu (capital of Anambra State)
(vi)	Onyeukwu	Onitsha (largest commercial city)
(vii)	Ginano	Kano (capital of Kano State)
(viii)	Standard	Enugu (capital of Anambra State)

9   Justin's father, D. Ntiki, was the assistant chairman/managing director of the group.

10 Other National Development Plans include the following periods:

1st	1962—68
2nd	1970—74
3rd	1975—80

11 Source: Fourth National Development Plan 1981—1985. Nigerian Federal Ministry of Planning, Lagos, Nigeria, 1982.

12 See Appendix 3.C for the provisions of the programme.

13 For more details on the quasi-loan, see Appendix 5.B.

Appendix 5.A   Tracing the influence of family on evolution patterns of the Ntiki Group of Companies

The following text shows excerpts of a conversation between Mr Etinem, senior group manager, and Justin Ntiki, director of all the companies in the group, during the discussion of how the family has affected, or fits into, the organization's growth.

Researcher: Mr Etinem, if you are free to discuss further on the family members and their relationships with the company, could you please trace the history back from where the firm started to the involvement of the third generation?

Mr Etinem: As I mentioned earlier, there is no doubt in the community and among us employees that this company belongs to the Ntiki family. They all join the company at the management level and as members of board of directors. This is expected and we all accept it. Besides they have all been very good workers/managers.

Researcher: Thank you, could you trace the entry points of each of the family members currently working in the organization? Also where possible, would you include the changes made (if any) in the organizational policies and set-up as a result of this entry?

Mr Etinem: I joined the organization after the break-up between the brothers in 1968, but as a native of the town and member of the community, I can recall some of the characteristics of the earlier organizational set-up. When the three brothers — Chief Ntiki, the Prince and the youngest, D. Ntiki — took over the management of the palm produce marketing company (I can't think of the exact year now), the Chief was in control of everything, while the younger brothers worked in the afternoon and went to school in the mornings.

However, soon after graduation, both younger brothers joined the company on a full-time basis. The Prince was made the purchasing manager while Damian [the youngest] became the assistant purchasing officer. These positions which were created basically to accommodate the brothers were filled by age and not skill.

Then after the Prince and Damian branched out, they started out working together, performing any task that needed to be done. As business improved, clerks were hired to perform some regular functions. These functions included bookkeeping, secretarial duties and others.

Researcher: Would you describe the above as a formal organization?

Mr Etinem: In a way, yes, since every employee was assigned some form of specific duty, but actual formalization of the company came with the establishment of the construction in 1971. With the hiring of engineers and construction workers, the Prince formally assumed the position of the chairman while the co-founder (as a result of birth) became the vice chairman. So things moved pretty well with this form of structure.

Personally, I think we have witnessed one major reorganization following the entry of Vincent, the chairman's oldest son, into the company. Vincent joined the company in 1976 as the Administrative Director of the group. This position made him the third highest manager in the organization, after his father and the co-founder.

Two years later, he [Vincent] supervised the development of the organizational chart that is about to be reorganized with the entry of Justin into the organization.

But the current organizational chart has three members of the family at some expected position [see the Ntiki Group's organizational chart, Appendix 5.C].

I believe that the only changes that may be reflected in the planned reorganization will be the extension of more autonomy to the companies and the decentralization of administrative activities, which are being controlled by members of the family.

It was time for Mr Etinem's next meeting, and he referred me to Justin Ntiki (who was about to take over the management of the Insurance Company).

Justin confirmed the planned reorganization explaining that, apart from family involvement, efficiency was also one of the reasons for moving from a holding/centralized structure to one of holding/decentralized. However he confirmed Mr Etinem's theory that the parents now have more confidence in their generation and 'were willing to release some reasonable lengths of the rope', concluded Justin.

Appendix 5.B Project finance and the Nigerian capital market

Source: Abdulai, Iaiwo and Co., *Establishing A Business in Nigeria*, 2nd edn, Academy Press Ltd, Nigeria, 1983.

I. THE ISSUES

The author, in her experience, has observed that most Nigerian and foreign would-be entrepreneurs are often vague and imprecise about the possible sources of finance for projects being contemplated. While these entrepreneurs are aware of Government's positive attitude towards private initiative, they are generally unaware of potential sources of project finance.

The discussion that follows in this Chapter VI, therefore, focuses attention *inter alia*, on the following: (a) Equity contribution by shareholders and proprietors as a source of project finance, (b) Term loans and overdrafts, (c) Raising of project finance from the public by the issue of shares and debenture stock, (d) Equipment Leases — a new phenomenon with great potential etc.

Whereas most of what is examined in this Appendix would broadly speaking be familiar to businessmen from Commonwealth countries, it is, however, necessary to emphasize the fact that the information is presented against the background of the Nigerian Companies Act 1968; the Nigerian Enterprises Promotion Act 1977; the Nigerian Securities and Exchange Commission Act 1979; the Listing Requirements of the Nigerian Stock Exchange; and the general monetary and financial policies operative in the country for the time being.

II. FINANCING PRIVATE LIMITED LIABILITY COMPANIES

A. Equity Contribution by Shareholders or Proprietors

Like most other countries, private limited liability companies in Nigeria, to a very large extent, rely on the resources or finances of their proprietors or shareholders. Where the contributions of members are insufficient, such companies may apply to commercial or merchant banks, insurance companies, etc. for additional funds. While this state of affairs is in no way unique or unexpected, it must be explained that the policy of banks in Nigeria towards a particular company is usually influenced by its categorization under the provisions of the Nigerian Enterprises Promotion Act 1977. For example, while companies in Schedules I and II (Nigerian majority interests with NEPB Compliance Certificates) may easily raise additional project finance (i.e. term loans backed by adequate collateral) and overdrafts from local banks, Schedule III companies may only enjoy these financing arrangements with the approval of the Federal Ministry of Finance. The rationale here is to oblige Schedule III companies (which have majority foreign interests) to bring sufficient capital into Nigeria for their projects rather than rely on the local capital market.

In the light of the above, the question to which the foreign investor must address his mind is this: Is it always prudent to insist on a Schedule III classification rather than a Schedule II where there is an option? This is obviously a subject to which considerable thought has to be given by the foreign investor in view of the restrictions imposed on Schedule III companies as regards local borrowings; and considering that a majority shareholding is usually not necessary in Nigeria in order to have a secure and permanent position in a company.

B. Term Loans and Overdrafts

The expansion of the banking industry in the last decade has been matched by a corresponding reliance on the services of the institutions. This observation is particularly true with the introduction of development and wholesale or merchant banking in Nigeria. Through the expertise of the corporate finance departments of these banks, it is now possible for projects requiring funds to be objectively appraised and for funds to be provided to augment the contributions of project sponsors.

C. Private Placements

An alternative to the above methods of financing private limited liability companies is the concept of 'private placement' which is now quite common in Nigeria. With this method of financing, the company arranges for an Issuing House to purchase its securities and 'place' them with its own clients, or, alternatively, to 'place' them without itself first purchasing these securities. The first instance is, in effect, similar to an offer for sale, the only difference being that the placement is private and not made to the public generally. The second instance is more or less a private prospectus issue where the Issuing House acts as the agent of the company in the disposal of its shares.

A private placement which is, of course, very much cheaper than an offer for sale or subscriptions to the public by the issue of prospectuses, is only advised if the issue can be taken up by a few selected well-known institutions or individuals. While privately placed shares are not quoted on the Stock Exchange, there is every effort to ensure that the NEPB Act is complied with and that the shareholding is as widespread as practical.

In the last few years private placements in the Nigerian capital market have been much more numerous than either offers for sale or subscriptions through prospectuses. Generally, therefore, private placement as a means of financing private companies would continue to be significant.

III. PUBLIC COMPANIES AND THEIR FINANCES

Until 1970, public companies (i.e. companies with more than fifty shareholders) were very few in Nigeria. Most successful industrial and commercial enterprises were in the hands of private alien individuals or tightly controlled companies with majority foreign interests. With the 'indigenization' in 1972 and 1977—78, the whole scene has now changed. As part of its efforts to achieve economic independence, enterprises controlled by aliens were asked to 'go public', that is, to 'admit' Nigerians. This was to be accomplished either by an 'Offer for Sale' of a part of their shareholding or an 'Offer for Subscription' for new shares in the company. In either situation, the objective was the same — that is, the admission of Nigerians into the company on a non-preferential or discriminatory basis — in compliance with the provisions of the Nigerian Enterprises Promotion Act, 1977.

From the practical point of view the indigenization exercise was a temporary measure. What Nigeria should, therefore, be more concerned about is the question of project finance for a public company on a continuing basis.

182

A. Unlisted or Unquoted Public Company

One of the advantages of incorporating a 'public company' is that it affords the promoters of such an entity the opportunity to collect funds from an unlimited number of persons. Or, looked at differently, a public company enables the investing public to share in the profit of an enterprise without taking any part in its management. In this type of company, which is economically (but not numerically) by far the most important, the company may be viewed simply as a device analogous to a 'trust', which is specifically designed to facilitate the raising and putting to use of capital by enabling a large number of owners to entrust it to a small number of expert managers.

From the practical point of view, since the promoters of a business may be unable to find fifty or more persons willing and able to provide finance for a project, it is now customary for a company wishing to raise money from the public to enlist the aid of the financial houses (i.e. Issuing Houses) in Nigeria specializing in public issues. Like other countries, the new issues market is now virtually monopolized by a small number of firms who are experts in this type of transaction. After they devote themselves entirely to public issues or combine the activity with merchant banking, company registrar duties, etc.

B. Listed or Quoted Companies

In the case of a public issue by a company, it is often necessary for the securities to be listed on the Nigerian Stock Exchange. Otherwise they will not be freely marketable and that liquidity is one of the main attractions of shares and debentures as investments. Therefore, the Issuing Houses will normally insist on the company taking the necessary steps to comply with the exacting requirements of the Exchange. In consequence, these rules are as important in practice as those laid down in the Companies Act of 1968.

The basic principle underlying these requirements is to ensure that full disclosure is made of all information needed to enable a potential investor to assess the worth of the securities offered. The Stock Exchange scrutinizes the documents before they are finalized and does its best to see that no false or misleading statement is included.

In order to obtain quotation, it is necessary, amongst other things, that the company wishing to raise funds should have a paid-up share capital of more than ₦1,000,000 and the amount intended to be raised should not be less than ₦250,000. In addition, on closure of the Application List, allotment must be made to not less than five hundred subscribers and upon allotment, these shares must be fully paid-up.

Application for listing is entertained by the Stock Exchange only if sponsored by any of the dealing members of the Stock Exchange.

A prospectus complying with certain requirements as to its contents must be published normally in two leading newspapers. When the company's securities are first listed it enters into a Listing Agreement regarding its future conduct towards its security holders and towards the Exchange. These stringent requirements are mainly to safeguard the interests of investors and are not to be seen as an attempt to assess the financial merits of the offer. This safeguard is a continuing one and the covenants under the Listing Agreement help to keep an eye on the company.

IV. EQUIPMENT LEASES (OR QUASI-LOANS)

A. General Principles

An investor, more often than not, is faced with the problems of financing large expensive, but essential machinery and equipment for his industry. An alternative, or an addition to other means of raising money, is the concept of 'leasing' such equipment from a financial institution and thus indirectly obtain what is in actual fact a loan or quasi-loan. As Nigerians shall endeavour to explain, the advantages of equipment lease are obvious — it simplifies budgeting, improves liquidity, frees working capital, and leaves other credit lines unimpaired.

Most financial institutions, especially banks, have a limit on the extent of credit facilities that may be given to an investor. They, therefore, see equipment leasing as a convenient alternative or addition to direct term loans or overdraft facilities — much to the mutual benefit of both the lessor and the lessee. The equipment is chosen by the lessee but purchased by the lessor who retains legal ownership of it at all times. However, contrary to the concept of leasing in some other countries, the trend in Nigeria has been to grant the lessee an option to purchase the equipment after the primary or basic lease period.

In a typical equipment lease arrangement the lessee has the exclusive right to use the equipment during the whole period of the lease, subject to the payment of rentals and compliance with the other terms of the lease. There is a non-cancellable clause in the lease during which period the financial or leasing institution is able to recover the whole or major part of its capital expenditure together with its outgoings and a profit margin.

Besides the main characteristics outlined above, there are several others that have with practice become normal features of most equipment leases. Leases are usually with well established commercial or industrial customers for the provision of equipment required for their business and about which the lessee has proper working knowledge. In other words, the responsibility for the suitability of an equipment rests with the lessee since it is purchased by the lessor at his request, but happily the financial or leasing institutions are often also competent to offer or have access to expert advice on the most suitable type of equipment for various businesses. In most cases, the lessee is also responsible for the maintenance and insurance of the equipment and, as stated earlier on, at the end of the obligatory lease period the lessee has an option either to buy the equipment or to continue the lease at a reduced rental.

The concept of lease-purchasing being greatly promoted as a new financing technique is in many respects similar to but nevertheless different from the time-worn concepts of hire-purchase and installment credit. It is, therefore, not an alternative to them, but rather for the investor, an advantage to be used in conjunction with those other methods.

There are almost as many types of equipment leasing as there are types of equipment that can be leased. The type of leasing is more often than not determined by the type of assets involved, the type of facility available, and the market. Most leasing is domestic, but cross-border and export leasing though not yet significant in Nigeria, is of great interest in some parts of the world.

While it is true that there is such a wide range of equipment that can be leased, in practice, financial lessors do tend to prefer to lease separately identifiable equipment rather than a part of a larger item of plant of machinery. These types of equipment range from aircraft to buses, from drilling rigs to ships, from office equipment and computers to tractors and agricultural equipment, from juggernauts and other commercial vehicles to quarrying and mining equipment. The list goes on and on.

B. The Advantages of an Equipment Lease

The merits of leasing from an investor's or potential lessee's point of view are many. Leasing may be the cheapest or only means of obtaining the use of the most sophisticated and up-to-date equipment because of import to export controls or the existence of patent rights or of other forms of monopolistic restriction on the free supply of the equipment by way of sale. Properly understood, leasing is not only an alternative source of finance but an extension of the range of methods of financing the acquisition of capital equipment. The use of equipment is obtained without capital outlay. As an additional source of finance, it enables an entity to increase its overall debt-raising capacity. The lessor's security is the asset financed and a leasing facility does not adversely affect a company's ability to arrange other general credit lines.

The certainty of the terms of a leasing contract is a major advantage to both lessor and lessee. For example, a lease, a medium-term facility unlike a loan repayable on demand, cannot be withdrawn or curtailed in the event of a credit squeeze or a change in economic conditions. And except in case of a default on the part of the lessee the lessor cannot accelerate the payment of rentals during the primary lease period. Furthermore, leasing may be the only suitable form of outside finance available to a company at times when it is not possible for it to arrange a comparable loan for a five-year or longer period either at a fixed interest rate or on any terms.

Put differently, while the ownership of an asset may be thought to be prestigious, the truth is that the ownership of a fully depreciated asset sometimes delays the replacement of outdated equipment by preventing a clear appreciation of the considerations relevant to a replacement decision.

To the extent that rentals fixed in relation to change in money costs are available, the lessee is able to hedge against inflation as payments are made in fixed money terms out of future earnings which will rise with inflation. This, of course, is an advantage of this kind of transaction.

As already mentioned, leasing is a simple and convenient method of financing the acquisition of capital equipment. Bookkeeping, for example, is streamlined and the regular nature of rental payments assist expense budgeting and cash flow forecasting. Leases can be arranged in tailor-made terms to reflect the particular needs of individuals. Rentals may also be related to the earning power of the leased equipment and the opportunity to match cash flows over the expected life of an asset provides an element of financial stability.

Other advantages of an equipment lease can be appreciated considering that rentals for leased assets are frequently treated differently from interest and depreciation charges for purchased equipment in profit and loss accounts. Thus, by leasing, lower costs may be shown in the first few years of the useful life of equipment and a higher return on total assets achieved if the equipment is not capitalized on the lessee's balance sheet. On the other hand, a more rapid write-off of leased assets may also be used as a means of reducing reported profits or increasing allowable costs.

C. Possible Disadvantages

The advantages of leasing over other forms of medium-term finance must be weighed against the possible disadvantages.

In practice, a commercial concern that purchases its own equipment avoids any of the restrictions found in an equipment leasing agreement, albeit that these restrictions are not often unduly onerous.

One possible disadvantage of an equipment lease is the fact that a lessee gives up some or all of the benefit of the residual value of the equipment at the end of the lease period. For certain types of assets, this may be significant and it is suggested that, in preparing the lease, the current value of this foregone future benefit should be compared with the possible cost savings during the primary lease period.

Equipment leasing may not be appropriate if a company requires an asset for only a short-term and as already mentioned if a lease is cancelled early in the primary lease period, there are usually additional costs to reflect the reduction in the period.

From the lessee's point of view an equipment lease may be a disadvantage, if he is unable to include the leased equipment in a pool of assets available as security for general borrowing. Bankers and trade creditors may consider a company leasing a significant proportion of the plant and equipment used in its business to have a weaker financial position than a company owning the assets. Certainly, the right to use equipment for a major part of its useful life is an intangible asset not shown on the lessee's balance sheet unless the leased assets are capitalized at economic values. A firm leasing equipment may thus be understating its assets. In consequence, shareholders and other users of the firm's accounts, including a possible bidder for its shares or assets, may undervalue the business.

The financial complexities of equipment leasing are outside the scope of this booklet but for the investor or businessman who requires the use of capital equipment that he can ill-afford, the advantages of equipment leasing outweigh its disadvantages and would appear to offer a better solution to his problems than other medium-term financing methods.

Appendix 5.C Companies, their major industries and organizational charts

Companies:	Ntiki Group of Cos.	Nwoke & Sons Ltd.	Francis Group of Cos.
Industries:			
Service:			
Construction	++	++	—
Engineering Services	—	—	—
Merchandising	+	+	++
Transportation	+	—	—
Manufacturing	+	+	++
Brewers, Soft Drink Bottling	+	+	—
Agriculture/Agro Allied	—	—	+
Health Care/ Pharmaceutical	—	—	+
Electrical/Electronics	—	—	+
Container	—	+	—
Food/Beverage	—	—	+
Chemical/Petro Chemical	—	—	—
Steel/Tin/Aluminum	—	—	+
Lumber/Mill	—	—	—

Legend:
++ Organization's major industries
+ Organization operates in this industry
− Organization has little or no activity in this industry

Oko Holdings Limited	Onyeukwu & Sons Limited	Amadi & Sons Limited	Ginano Holdings Limited	Standard Enterprises Limited
+	+	++	+	++
+	−	−	+	−
+	+	+	++	−
−	++	+	+	−
+	+	−	+	+
+	−	−	+	+
++	+	−	+	−
−	−	−	−	++
+	−	−	+	−
−	−	−	+	−
+	−	−	++	−
−	++	−	−	−
−	−	−	+	−
+	+	++	−	−

Organizational Chart

Ntiki Group of Companies

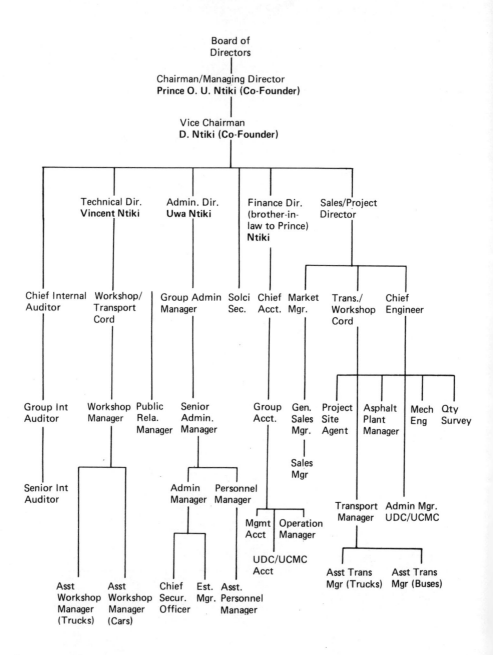

Organizational Chart

Nwoke Group of Companies

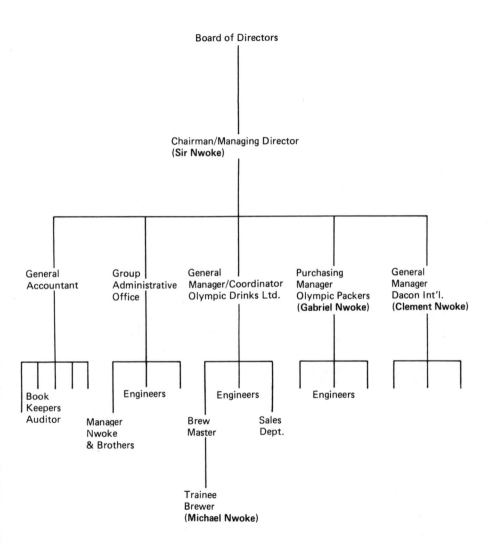

Board of Directors

Chairman/Managing Director
(Sir Nwoke)

General Accountant

Group Administrative Office

General Manager/Coordinator Olympic Drinks Ltd.

Purchasing Manager Olympic Packers (Gabriel Nwoke)

General Manager Dacon Int'l. (Clement Nwoke)

Book Keepers Auditor

Engineers

Manager Nwoke & Brothers

Engineers

Brew Master

Sales Dept.

Engineers

Engineers

Trainee Brewer (Michael Nwoke)

Founder's sons.
Drawn by writer per description.

Organizational Chart

Francis Group of Companies

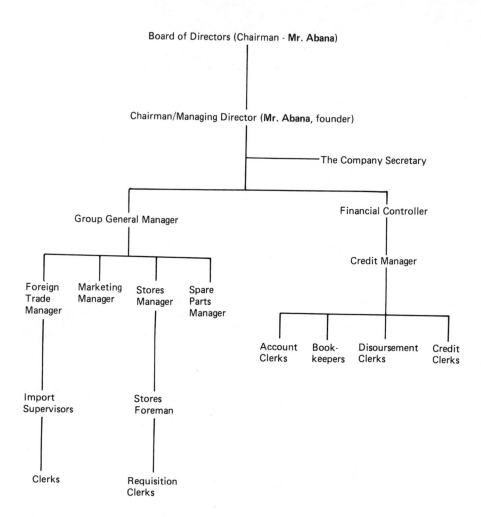

Board of Directors (Chairman - **Mr. Abana**)

Chairman/Managing Director (**Mr. Abana**, founder)

The Company Secretary

Group General Manager

Financial Controller

Foreign Trade Manager

Marketing Manager

Stores Manager

Spare Parts Manager

Credit Manager

Import Supervisors

Stores Foreman

Account Clerks

Book-keepers

Disoursement Clerks

Credit Clerks

Clerks

Requisition Clerks

1983, as rendered by writer.

Organizational Chart

Okome Organization

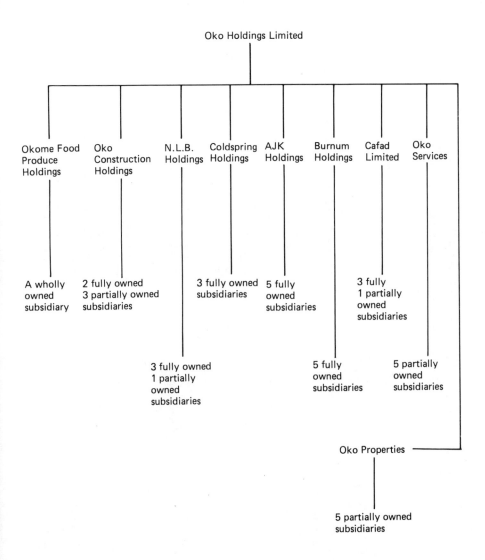

Oko Holdings Limited
List of Member Companies

Name of Group & Activity		Name of Company	Nature of Activity	Degree of Control	Year Estab.
Okome Food Produce Holdings Frozen food distributing supply and servicing of cold stores and refrigeration equipment. Distribution of frozen meat and poultry.	i.	Delta Freeze Limited	Supply, installation and maintenance cold stores	100%	
	ii.	Granimac Foods Limited	Meat and poultry production and distribution	100%	
	iii.	Okome Merchandise 33 Ltd.	General trading, import and distribution	100%	
	iv.	Okome Sea Foods Limited	Importers and distributors of frozen fish	100%	1963
Oko Construction Civil engineering and construction, general building and contracting.	i.	ACE Jimona Limited	General building and construction	100%	
	ii.	Mermaid Swimpool Ltd.	Swimming pool contractors	100%	
	iii.	Bos Kalis Nigeria Ltd.	Civil engineering and building contractors	60%	
	iv.	Spie-Batignolles Nigeria Ltd.	Civil engineering and building contractors	60%	
	v.	George Cohen (Nigeria)	Importers and stockists of steel sections	40%	
AJK Holdings Sales and services of agricultural and construction machinery, cars and commercial vehicles.	i.	AJK Motors Limited	Long distance haulage, drilling and irrigation supplies	100%	
	ii.	Camplant Engineering	Sales, maintenance, spare parts and hire services for Komatsu heavy earth moving equipment	100%	

194

Drilling and irrigation supplies and contracting. Bulk road haulage.		including sales and services of generating sets	
iii.	Lilleshall (Nigeria) Ltd.	Distributors of industrial fasteners, nuts, bolts and other supplies	100%	1959 (acquired by Okome 1972)
iv.	Nigeria Truck & Equipment Company Limited	Sales and service of commercial and private vehicles, agents for Volkswagen products	100%	1971
v.	Nigeria Marine & Trading Company Limited	Marine supplies	90%	
Coldspring Holdings	i.	L & K Fine Foods Ltd.	Soft drinks bottling	100%
Brewing, bottling and distribution of beer.	ii.	Rainbow Limited	Bottling, distribution and sales of Pepsi Cola	100%
Bottling and distribution of soft drinks.	iii.	Superbru Limited	Brewers, bottlers and distributors of beer	100%
CAFAD (Corporation for Agricultural Finance and Development Limited	i.	Aden River Estates Ltd.	Oil palm plantations with milling facilities	100%
	ii.	Food and Commodities Production Group Limited	Production of poultry products under the name "Mitchell Farms"	100%
	iii.	Nigerian Hardwood Co. Ltd.	Logging, milling, and timber processing and finishing operation. Manufacture of building components and furniture	100%
	iv.	Agbarha Farms	Citrus and pineapple plantations	100%
	v.	Osdjere Fishing Co. Ltd.	Fisheries operation dealing mainly with catching, processing and export of shrimp and prawns	70%

Name of Group & Activity	Name of Company	Nature of Activity	Degree of Control	Year Estab.
Burnum Holdings				
Assembly and distribution of electronic equipment, clocks, watches. Supply and service of survey equipment and air conditioning. Distribution of various food stuffs, wines, spirits, domestic goods, and jewelry.	i. Flowershop Limited	Sale of silver and glassware and other gift items	100%	
	ii. Jewelers Company of Nigeria Limited	Sale of jewelry	100%	
	iii. F. Steiner & Company Ltd.	Sales and local assembly of Omega watches. Also sale of precision instruments for surveying	100%	1949 (1973)
	iv. W.F. Clarke (Nigeria) Ltd.	General trading, import and distribution of fast moving consumer goods	100%	1949 (1973)
	v. Zabadne & Company Ltd.	Assembly, sales and servicing of electrical and electronics goods (audio and video equipment)	100%	1960 (1972)
NLB Holdings				
Marine engineering and construction	i. Blue Water Marines Supplies & Services Ltd.	Sales and servicing of power boats, marine engines, etc.	100%	
	ii. SYBUD Limited	Structural engineers and boat builders, prefabricated buildings	100%	
	iii. Sepcol-Sanqui (Nigeria) Limited		100%	
Oko Properties and Investments	i. Aero Contractors Co. of Nigeria Limited	Fixed and rotary wing aircraft operations. General charter and oil industry support services	60%	

	Company	Activity	%	
Property investment and development and investment in joint venture companies.	ii. IBACHEM (Ibafon Chemical) Limited	Industrial and agricultural chemicals operation, active in bulk storage and distribution, as well as formulation and manufacturing facilities	60%	
	iii. Stim (Nigeria) Properties Limited	Property development	60%	
	iv. Minet Nigeria	Insurance brokerage	60%	
	v. Rutam Holdings Limited	Sales and distribution of Peugeot and Mercedes brands of vehicles	30%	1981
Oko Services	i. Agfics Limited	Provision of group central services	100%	
	ii. Boardroom Services Ltd.	Company secretarial and administrative services	100%	
Mangement and secretarial services, security services, ships agency, clearing and forwarding.	iii. Emsee Shipping Ltd.	Terminal operations shipping, clearing and forwarding services	100%	
	iv. Feprisa Limited	Security services	100%	
	v. Okome Limited	Business and management consultants, providing project research/development and services	100%	
	vi. The Guardian (Publ.) Co.	Daily newspaper publishing		

Organizational Chart
Onyeukwu and Sons Limited

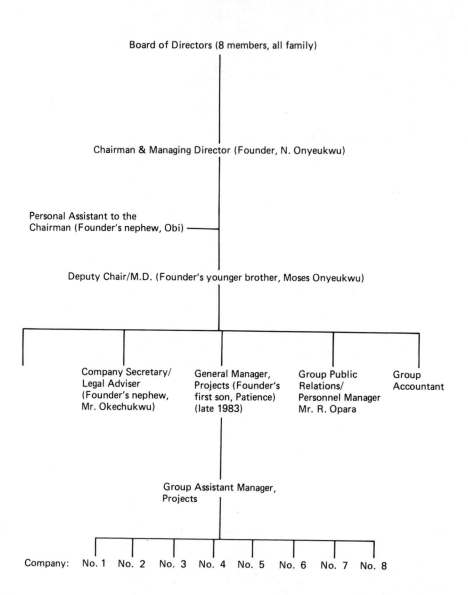

Board of Directors (8 members, all family)

Chairman & Managing Director (Founder, N. Onyeukwu)

Personal Assistant to the
Chairman (Founder's nephew, Obi)

Deputy Chair/M.D. (Founder's younger brother, Moses Onyeukwu)

Company Secretary/
Legal Adviser
(Founder's nephew,
Mr. Okechukwu)

General Manager,
Projects (Founder's
first son, Patience)
(late 1983)

Group Public
Relations/
Personnel Manager
Mr. R. Opara

Group
Accountant

Group Assistant Manager,
Projects

Company: No. 1   No. 2   No. 3   No. 4   No. 5   No. 6   No. 7   No. 8

Organization Structure of Amadi and Sons

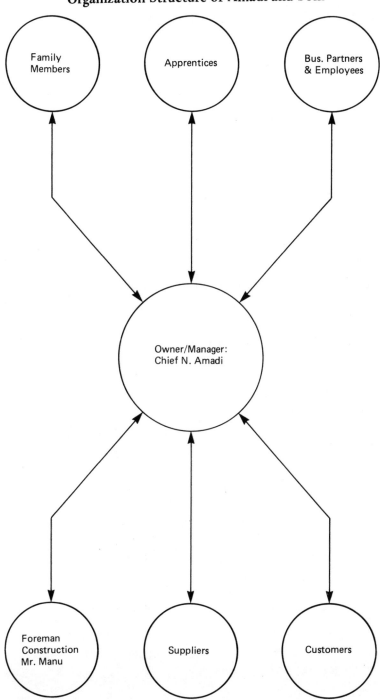

Organizational Chart
Ginano Holdings Limited

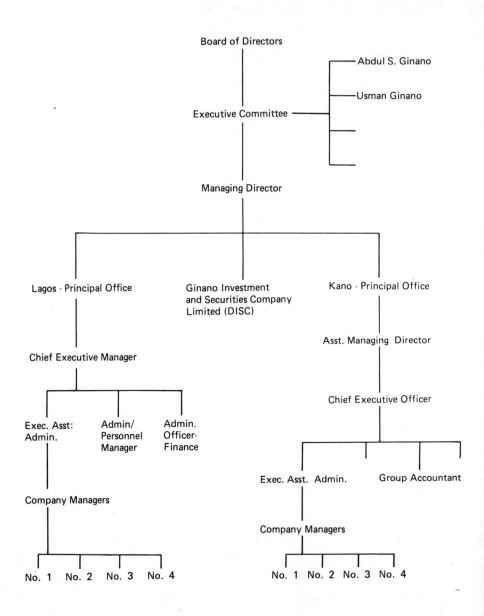

Board of Directors

Executive Committee ── Abdul S. Ginano

Usman Ginano

Managing Director

Lagos - Principal Office

Ginano Investment
and Securities Company
Limited (DISC)

Kano - Principal Office

Chief Executive Manager

Asst. Managing Director

Exec. Asst:
Admin.

Admin/
Personnel
Manager

Admin.
Officer-
Finance

Chief Executive Officer

Company Managers

Exec. Asst. Admin.

Group Accountant

No. 1   No. 2   No. 3   No. 4

Company Managers

No. 1   No. 2   No. 3   No. 4

Organizational Structure
Standard Enterprises Limited (1983)

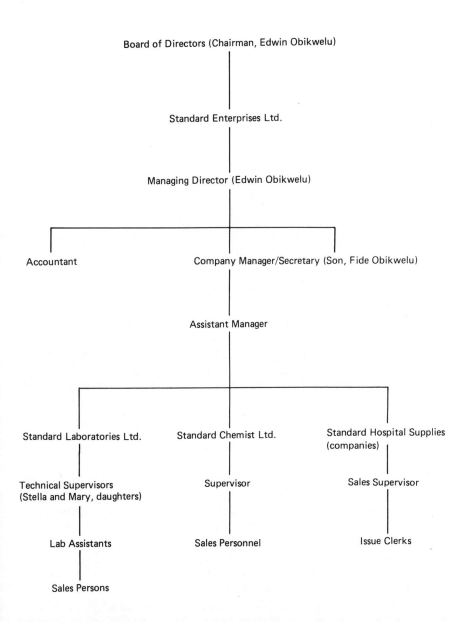

Board of Directors (Chairman, Edwin Obikwelu)

Standard Enterprises Ltd.

Managing Director (Edwin Obikwelu)

Accountant

Company Manager/Secretary (Son, Fide Obikwelu)

Assistant Manager

Standard Laboratories Ltd.

Standard Chemist Ltd.

Standard Hospital Supplies (companies)

Technical Supervisors (Stella and Mary, daughters)

Supervisor

Sales Supervisor

Lab Assistants

Sales Personnel

Issue Clerks

Sales Persons

6 Management in Nigeria

Introduction

The political instability in the country makes it almost impossible for entrepreneurs to plan and develop a solid management style. Nevertheless, several management practices are evident and these include entrepreneurship/opportunistic, adaptive/adoptive, family focus interface/conflict management and retail practices among women entrepreneurs. These management practices are discussed relative to the macro-environment of the country and those of the large companies examined.

Entrepreneurship/opportunity management

Major traits of the Nigerian entrepreneurs include low education level (90 per cent of original founders have primary six or less level of education), an average age of 35 when they become successful (the majority started out as trade apprentices at the age of 16 or earlier), married, risk-takers/adventurers and innovative relative to marketing.

Opportunistic management is the key to survival and growth in Nigeria, and entrepreneurs recognize and practice this style of management. This practice was evident in companies such as Oko Holdings, Nwoke Group of Companies, Ntiki Group, Ginano and Onyeukwu and Sons. The successes of these companies relative to Amadi and Sons whose chairman is not only near retirement but is also having financial problems as he refuses to venture outside his locality are very obvious.

The growing and successful companies have seized such opportunities as the government's indigenization programmes, the Pioneer Industries Programme, the industrial development financing programmes and other tax incentive opportunities. On a smaller scale, both men and women traders have sought and travelled to new markets in order to sell to the highest bidder. This venture often involves high risks and has developed into the popular 'black market' operations. Further evidence of the entrepreneurs' marketing innovativeness and opportunistic practices is the development of an indirect foreign exchange outlet after the government put an embargo on the issuance of foreign exchange. Businessmen developed a system whereby indigenes outside the country paid their foreign partners in international currency while the naira (N) equivalent is deposited in a respective Nigerian account. The SFEM, which came into effect in October 1986, is designed not only to help devalue the naira for an IMF loan but also to make it possible for business and foreign investors to obtain the much needed foreign exchange. The full impact of the SFEM is yet to be known. However, excerpts from the official guidelines on the SFEM issued by the Nigerian Central Bank are available in Appendix 6.A.

Adaptive/adoptive practices

Evidence of adaptive management practices is rare. Adoptive practices, especially in management education and training have dominated. Businesses have tended to adopt developed countries' reward and control systems — a selective management practice which has not worked well within the predominant family focus interface.

Family focus interface/conflict management

Many people assume that conflict is necessarily dysfunctional and therefore should be avoided or eliminated. But conflict can be highly functional in some cases. For example, conflict may lead to decisions that either hasten an organization's decline or delay failure by serving to rejuvenate the firm. It can lead to a search for new ideas and mechanisms for solutions to organizational problems. Conflict can stimulate innovation and change, as well as possibly facilitate employee motivation in cases where employees need to excel and, as a result, cooperate and push themselves to meet performance objectives.

However, conflict can also have negative consequences for both individuals and the organization. These dysfunctional consequences occur when conflict causes people to divert energies away from performance and goal attainment while continuing to deal with conflict. Continued and excessive conflict contributes to stress and the psychological consequences of stress. It also affects the social climate of the group and inhibits group cohesiveness, as can be seen in some of the cases described in this chapter.

Conflict exists at various levels, but in this study conflict was identified and discussed at two levels — family and organization. Factors leading to conflict in the family and organizations, as well as mechanisms for reducing these conflicts, are discussed in this chapter. Although the factors affecting conflict at both levels are not mutually exclusive, the issues are examined separately at each level to bring out the implications associated with each. At the family level, the factors in their functional mode were present at the Ntiki Group of Companies, and Standard Enterprises Limited. In their dysfunctional mode, the factors were present at Amadi and Sons Limited only. At the other four companies (Oko Holdings Limited, Onyeukwu and Sons Limited, Nwoke Group of Companies, and Ginano Group of Companies) the implications of the factors at family level were not clearly observed. However, implications at the organizational and family levels were developing at the Ginano Company and Onyeukwu and Sons, respectively.

- Conflictual factors include:
- Ownership status
- Company's future
- Succession issues
- Profit-sharing system
- Status/promotion inconsistencies
- Societal/ethnic differences

- Reduction processes/mechanisms include:
- Avoidance
- Limited interaction
- Using mediators
- Accommodating
- Competing

Tables 6.1 and 6.2 summarize the status of the factors and the reduction processes at the eight firms, while Figure 6.1 specifically presents the process of conflict episodes at Ntiki Group of Companies. The factors and mechanisms are described in the following paragraphs.

Table 6.1 Conflicting factors

Companies: / Factors:	Ntiki Group of Cos.	Nwoke & Sons Ltd.	Francis Group of Cos.	Oko Holdings Limited	Onyeukwu & Sons Limited	Amadi & Sons Limited	Ginano Holdings Limited	Standard Entprs. Limited
Ownership status	+	N	+	N	−	+	−	−
Company's future	+	−	−	N	+	−	−	+
Succession issues	+	N	+	N	+	+	−	−
Profit-sharing	+	N	+	N	N	+	−	−
Status/promotion inconsistencies	−	N	−	+	N	−	+	+
Social/ethnic differences	+	N	−	−	+	−	+	N

Legend:
+ Factor contributed to conflict
− Factor not contributory to conflict
N Not observed

Conflicting factors

Ownership status: The issue of ownership among the firms appeared to be a major factor promoting conflict among members of the family. This factor of conflict was clearly identified in Ntiki Group of Companies, Francis Group of Companies, and Amadi and Sons Limited. In Ntiki Company, as evidenced by data included, three brothers, Chief A. Ntiki, Prince Ntiki and the younger brother, Damian, inherited a palm produce business from their father in the early 1940s. There was no oral or written agreement as to the percentage of ownership among the brothers. Rather, according to culture, the oldest, Chief A, became the head of the family and thus assumed responsibilities for its younger members. By 1945, the company was registered with the three brothers actively involved in company operations.

The business and family relationships proceeded satisfactorily until around 1968 when the two younger brothers requested some re-organization and a clear definition of the ownership structure. At that point in the history of the organization, the two younger brothers were paid salaries and the Chief's first son was about to join the business. Specifically, the Prince and Damian wanted 'a little less than one-third each in ownership'.

In a similar manner, ownership status was the basis for conflict between older and younger brothers in the Francis Group and Amadi and Sons. This ownership issue appeared to be more problematic, as there was more than one brother inheriting capital or business from the father, and the brothers had worked together from the early history of the company without ownership specification.

The outcome in Ntiki presents an example of the functional aspect of conflict, considering what happened to the original firm, while the results in Amadi and Francis were yet to be determined.

Company's future: This factor is closely tied to ownership status. Sometimes family members and owners of business present differing desires as to the future state of an enterprise. Some may want the firm liquidated and capital shared while others see a brighter, profitable future and want the business expanded. Examples of divergent views of a company's future occurred in Standard Enterprises Limited, where the younger brother, Fidelis Obikwelu, wanted the company liquidated to finance his education and the older brother was determined to rejuvenate the failing pharmacy business. Also, in the Ntiki Company, the two younger brothers demanded and offered plans for expansion of the business. Nevertheless, this suggestion was seen by the older brother as an example of overzealous behaviour showing signs of immaturity and lack of experience. According to Prince Ntiki,

We presented the plans for expansion to him even before we demanded for ownership clarification, and in response to our ideas he said, '. . . I have carried this company so far without losing money, also the families are okay. Why don't you continue selling and let me do the planning instead of getting too wise?' But the above statement was not unusual in a society where children raised in the early nineteenth century speak only when spoken to and wisdom was almost synonymous with old age.

Succession: Onyeukwu and Sons presents a good example of the type of conflict caused by approach to the selection of successors with the sudden death of the founder's oldest son, who, according to cultural norms, would have succeeded the father.

However, unlike the above two cases where the company's future is in question, in Onyeukwu and Sons Limited the major concern is selection of a successor from the large number of possible candidates.[1] According to the group secretary:

> There is a growing concern over who gets to be on the founder's seat when he retires in a few years. Each of the wives would want a new business created or part of the older organization carved out for her children.

Death of the natural and accepted heir has led to some strife among the wives, their children and the founder's nephew as to who will take over the organization. The first wife, mother of the deceased, also had the next oldest child, but a daughter. But according to the social norms, women were not considered for succession where there was a son, no matter how young. The next oldest son belonged to the second wife. She may not want to see the 'chair' passed to the founder's nephew. However, the nephew has been with the company since its formation.

The group secretary described the relationship between the founder and the nephew thus: 'Although officially he [the nephew] is the personal assistant to the Chairman, I will say with confidence that he is more than that. He [the nephew] can read the Chief's mind, and is always able to predict his moves.' Explaining further, the group secretary said, 'Let me put it this way, they can communicate with signs, that is he [the nephew] can understand his "eye blink" which is a lot more than I can say for his children.'

In the other three companies studied (Amadi, Ntiki and Francis), the succession issue led to the question of ownership status among the three sets of brothers. In each case the younger brothers saw the possibility of their immediate family being disinherited as a result of the older brother's children or wife getting involved in the operations of the family business. The succession issue has often created major conflicts in family firms, especially when written agreements have never existed to determine relationships among apparent owners.

In Nigeria, the traditional norms of succession have contributed immensely to intense conflict between the old and the young, especially with the influence of Western culture which was gradually reducing the 'sanctity' of the 'age and wisdom' myths.[2]

The above factors (ownership, company's future and succession) could be easily identified as causing conflict in the family, while the next three, starting with profit-sharing, may occur at either family and/or organizational levels.

Profit-sharing: Among the firms studied, there were three cases of conflict based on profit-sharing issues. The Ntiki brothers wanted an adequate percentage share of profit rather than salaries. In Francis Enterprises and Amadi and Sons Limited, the younger brothers wanted equal shares of the companies' assets which they claimed they helped to build. There also exists the potentiality that non-family employees might raise the issue of profit-sharing as a bonus and recognition of their contribution to the organization. However, there was no indication of this type of conflict in any of the other companies studied.

Status/promotion inconsistencies: Although outside employees usually recognize and acknowledge the fact that 'family firms belong to members of family',[3] they sometimes challenge some promotions or the status of some relatives of the founder. For example, in the Oko Holding Company, Mr Obi,[4] director of one of the companies, concluded an interview session with the following remarks:

> In the past, it had been easy working with the founders, because there was nothing to remind you that you are working in a private/family company. However, things are beginning to change as a result of the family's need to provide jobs for its members . . . . Recently I have had two members of the family who were high school drop-outs dumped into my operations and I tell you, they are beginning to get not only on my nerves, but on those of other conscientious employees. For one thing, these boys cannot do one satisfactory job, yet we have to keep them.

Similar situations in Standard Enterprises Limited and Ginano Group had outside employees complaining about special treatment of relatives or certain groups. In Standard, the issue arose in Fidesco's Construction Company,[5] as to the efficiency and economics of making two of his sons who dropped out of college, 'site managers' of building projects. The supervisors directly over them have complained that they never did a full hour's job in a day and 'yet we had to go to them for clearance or authority for actions'.

In Ginano Group the issue was more about privileges granted to members of the Muslim[6] employees who were regarded as being closer to the family than the Christian employees. The Christians were demanding extra pay for hours worked Friday afternoons while the Muslims worshipped.

Although conflict based on status or promotion inconsistencies was witnessed in this study mostly at the organizational level, such conflictual factors are also often present at the family levels. In Nigeria, for example, where there are brothers as founders, tradition demanded higher position/status allocation to the oldest. However, with the permeation of Western culture and education into the society a few second- and third-generation members were beginning to question the economic value of traditional norms.

Societal/ethnic differences: It is rather difficult for companies to survive and grow without cognizance and adaptation to their environmental factors. In Nigeria, where diversity of the ethnic groups, cultures and languages is almost as numerous as its 83-million people, companies have often been affected by conflict originating outside their premises and among different ethnic or religious groups represented among the employees. The Ginano Group is experiencing religious strife.

Both the Ntiki and Onyeukwu cases represent examples of conflicts originating from ethnic differences. At the end of 1983, Onyeukwu and Ntiki each had abandoned plants located in the Rivers State of the country. Because both founders were from different states,[7] their employees from Rivers State and others from Anambra and Cross Rivers had differing opinions about the Civil War in Nigeria (1967—70). The strife resulted in the destruction of some properties of the companies by the Rivers State indigenes. These employees demanded closure and confiscation of the mills (plants) since their owners were originally from Anambra and Cross Rivers States and these were regarded as major capitalist groups in Nigeria. Some of the slogans read 'Go make your money elsewhere and leave our state alone'.[8]

For several years after the Civil War, many ethnic groups (especially the Ibos) were hesitant to relocate, expand or do business outside their state of origin. However, with the war wounds slowly healing, interstate business began to flourish everywhere. At the time of this study Ntiki was making decisions on whether to liquidate or sell the plant in Rivers while Onyeukwu relocated the business at Anambra after salvaging some assets and selling the facility.

There were evidences in the above for both functional and dysfunctional conflict. The implications of the processes or mechanisms for their reduction/resolution on the firms' transitions are the subject of the following section.

Does conflict affect an organization's performance or family relationships? If yes, as some incidents in the above section suggested, how then do the processes of conflict resolution influence the firm's ability to move from one state of development to another? The answer to the latter question will be answered by describing the five processes identified in this study and by showing the implications for the organizations which have applied them as presented in Table 6.2.

Five processes of conflict resolution were identified among the firms which have been involved in one or both levels of conflict as described above. Some firms (families) evidenced use of only one kind of conflict reduction process; others used two or more in combination. The outcomes of the processes in relation to their functional or dysfunctional implications for the firms' performance are also presented. These processes include the following.

Avoidance: Avoidance occurred in five of the cases studied with the individuals trying to ignore the issue and doing things such as travelling out of the company headquarters/out of the city or being occupied with other activities to avoid discussion of, or confrontation with, the issues. Oko Holdings and Ginano Group were the only two companies which had applied this process in isolation. The Oko management and family had simply ignored and will not accommodate any discussions regarding employment of family members. And the Ginano family also refuses to seek resolution of the conflict over religious worship which has been gradually developing between the Muslim and Christian employees.

Management at both companies has forbidden employees to discuss the particular area of conflict and, thus, these employees could only mention the inequity but not discuss it with the author. According to a personnel officer/public relations officer, 'Some of us will like to push for the resolution of the issue, but this is definitely the wrong time [mid-1984, with economic depression and retrenchment of the workforce].' Explaining, he said that there were a lot of qualified but unemployed workers ready to fill someone else's position if fired, and that he and many others were not willing to risk their jobs for just a little extra cash or Friday afternoons off.

The implications at both companies appeared to be neutral as at the end of 1984. There have been no employee strikes at either of the companies.

Limited interaction: This process, which was easy to apply, was evident at Ntiki Group, Francis Group, Amadi and Sons and the

Table 6.2 Reduction processes

Companies:	Ntiki Group of Cos.	Nwoke & Sons Ltd.	Francis Group of Cos.	Oko Holdings Limited	Onyeukwu & Sons Limited	Amadi & Sons Limited	Ginano Holdings Limited	Standard Entprs. Limited
Factors:								
Avoiding	−	N	+	+	N	+	+	+
Limiting interaction	+	N	+	N	N	+	N	+
Using mediators	+	N	+	N	−	+	N	−
Accommodation	−	N	+	N	+	+	−	−
Competing	+	N	+	N	N	−	−	+

Legend:

+   Process applied in reducing/resolving conflict
−   Process not applied in reducing conflict
N   Not observed

Standard Enterprise but was used in combination with other processes which included using mediators, accommodation and competing. The impact of these methods on the process is discussed by company in order to bring out their implications on the company's development.

Ntiki Group of Companies is an example of a functional (considering what happened to the original firm) outcome of conflict. The Ntikis, immediately after confrontation among the brothers, applied limited interaction technique, thereby cutting down the number of interactions between the opposing brothers (see Figure 6.1). The two younger brothers immediately started making plans to find a separate operation while waiting on the decision of the selected elders of the 'clan' as to the ownership status of the firm. However, upon receiving the verdict that tradition allowed their oldest brother, Chief Ntiki to be responsible for their activities and therefore to decide on the issue, they immediately set up a business that was directly in competition with the oldest brother's or the old family business.

By the end of 1973, the old company failed and was liquidated following the death of the founder. By 1983, the new firm, founded by the two younger brothers, had diversified and was operating with over five companies in its group. Prince Ntiki, co-founder of the new company, claimed that the oldest brother's action was the main motivation for the zeal with which he and his younger brother pursued their new venture. 'We wanted to show him that our plans for expansion and need for some control were reasonable and we can only do that by succeeding,' concluded the Prince.

It could be said that the processes used in this company were both functional and dysfunctional, considering the negative effects on the family relationships which were still precarious as of 1983. On a positive note, the decision to break up has resulted in the development of a larger firm, thereby preserving the family name in the business sector.

Francis Group of Companies is the only firm which has combined the five processes identified. Although the conflict was yet to be resolved at the end of 1984, the company has at one time or another tried each of the five resolution techniques. At the start of the conflict, the older brother, Francis, would not discuss the issue with the younger brother. 'I told him he must be joking,' said Francis, 'when he first told me that we need to restructure the company, profits and all to reflect ownership.'

After several months of Francis's refusal to discuss the issue, the younger brother withdrew himself from the services of the organization and the temporary mediators who were invited suggested that Hygenius move to a new (another branch) office and control the operations located around the new city. This temporary separation brought about

212

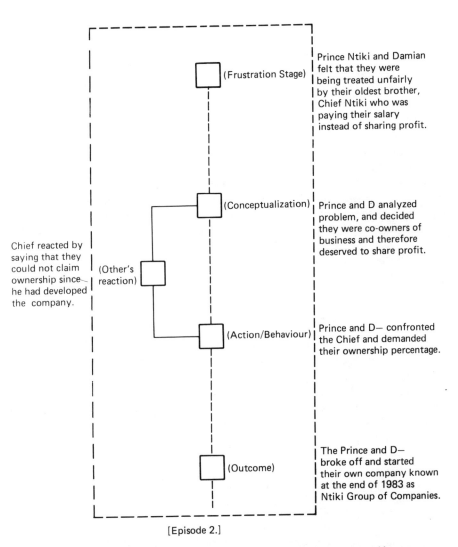

(Frustration Stage) — Prince Ntiki and Damian felt that they were being treated unfairly by their oldest brother, Chief Ntiki who was paying their salary instead of sharing profit.

(Conceptualization) — Prince and D analyzed problem, and decided they were co-owners of business and therefore deserved to share profit.

Chief reacted by saying that they could not claim ownership since he had developed the company.

(Other's reaction)

(Action/Behaviour) — Prince and D— confronted the Chief and demanded their ownership percentage.

(Outcome) — The Prince and D— broke off and started their own company known at the end of 1983 as Ntiki Group of Companies.

[Episode 2.]

Source: Model adapted from Kenneth Thomas, 'Conflict and conflict Management' in M. Dunnette (ed.) *Handbook of Industrial and Educational Psychology*, Chicago, 1976.

Fig. 6.1 Process of conflict: Ntiki Group of Companies

some limited interaction, but lasted only a few more months. In the next step, Francis was obliged to accommodate his brother and to offer some money to him. The younger brother immediately set up a business similar to his brother's and opened his two main offices in the same cities as Francis. By the end of 1983, the two were still competing actively in several merchandising businesses, while the final decision by a committee of related elders, which included their father and other clan members, was awaited.

So far, this conflict had not interrupted activities of Francis Group in any dysfunctional manner. If for some reason, the assets were to be shared in the final outcome, the process might reduce the net worth of the Group. However, if the elders were to succeed in reconciling the brothers' differences, then the result would be further growth in the family business since the continued market growth in the country has made intensive competition almost negligible.

The Amadi and Sons Limited situation is somewhat similar to Francis's in that the issues between the brothers are yet to be resolved. So far, the older brother, Noah, has tried avoiding the issue with the hope that the younger brother will see things differently. As Noah Amadi described the development of the conflict,

> I believe it was my decision to discontinue the transportation business and thereby not be involved in his unprofitable operation that triggered this issue. For over fifty years I have helped him with the care of his family. He has continued to personally thank me for my assistance but never questioned the ownership status of my business. But then, six months after I told him he was on his own with the transportation business, he came up with the idea of being part owner of all the real estate property. I am hoping that when he settles down and that with time he will come to his senses.

Meanwhile, Nwofar, the younger brother, had been sending a delegation to elderly relatives and 'clansmen' to persuade his brother to negotiate. But Noah maintained that he had done what he felt was his responsibility and beyond for a younger brother.

> I arranged and financed the purchase of a used vehicle for him before asking him to start taking care of himself. I am planning to retire and probably liquidate the timber business. I refuse to borrow money from others to support my younger brother and his family.

It appears that Amadi and Sons business operations had started to decline prior to this conflict. From the data collected, Chief Amadi will soon retire, either leaving the timber business to one of the sons or liquidating it. Thus, implications for the outcome of the conflict resolution process can only affect the value of assets retained by Noah, and on a lesser note, the firm's ability to grow. As it is, Nwofar did not want to be involved in any other form of business except transportation.

There was little or no conflict identified in the other companies. However, as can be seen from the above description, the outcome of conflict resolution processes in Nigeria was strongly influenced by cultural norms, which included respect for the elders, for the wisdom of the elders and responsibility of the older sibling to direct and care for the welfare of the younger ones.

Women entrepreneurs and retail activities

Historical background

African women, and particularly Nigerians, are culturally very enterprising. They are basically responsible through marketing activities for bringing the much needed food items to the masses. Traditionally, Nigerian women have less formal education than the men. In the late 1930s only one out of eight females attended formal school. This situation was the result of the cultural value attached to the continuity of family name and the belief that formal education opens the door to government jobs.[9] Since women usually adopt their husband's name when they get married, to the Nigerian and most African parents, a family name will eventually be forgotten without a progressive male child to perpetuate it. On this basis, families were more willing to offer a male child an opportunity for a better career than the females.

Nonetheless, and typically in Southern Nigeria, women became actively involved with the retail business soon after maturity or marriage, both of which usually occur concurrently. About one or two years after marriage, as according to custom, the wife receives some capital from the husband or some piece of land[10] depending on her husband's status and/or where they have settled after marriage. Statistics indicate that two out of every three women become traders while the remaining one-third are usually small-scale farmers.

This small business activity was solely at the discretion of the woman who kept the profits and received funds from her husband for housekeeping. Traditionally, society frowned at men who demanded money from their wives or depended on their wives for livelihood. However, there are some parts of society where women have become so dominant in their enterprising activities and more industrious than the men that society is gradually 'looking the other way' while these women are becoming the family 'breadwinners'.

To date (1980s), women's apparent success in this small retail

215

activity has been the only factor which has ever turned the government's (colonial and independent) attention on them. In 1929, there was a record demonstration by over 5,000 women traders (market women) in the Aba, South-eastern Nigeria, to protest against the colonial government's regulation and continued insistence that women traders should pay tax. Because there were no data or formalized procedure for determining the revenues and profits made by the women, a flat tax levy was imposed. This unsystematic tax collection method contributed to the 1929 riot.[11] There have been other minor conflicts between the governments and the associations of Nigerian Business Women[12] since 1929 but recently, in 1984 there was another major uprising of over 8,000 women traders[13] in Ibadan, protesting against the military governor's imposition of a flat tax on every woman independently conducting business in Ibadan city and/or growing and marketing crops in the whole of Oyo State.

Currently, women comprise 75 per cent of the small-scale retail industry. The businesses are not incorporated nor registered making it rather difficult to establish a database on their performance. Basically these activities comprise owning and controlling the retail of produce (food items — fresh or processed), provision stores, tailoring centres, and currently the women are rising to become subcontractors to major civil construction companies and the government. Women's average share capital has remained between N1,000—5,000 (equivalent to $1,150—5,750)[14] in the above traditional business sectors.

Profile of women entrepreneurs

Table 6.3 summarizes the status of women entrepreneurs based on a sample review of 1,000 businesses. The result indicates that out of 1,000 incorporated businesses, six (0.6 per cent) were owned and directed by women. Fifty-nine (5.9 per cent), which are mostly family-owned and/or controlled, had the founders' wives listed as members of the board of directors. There were no data to indicate whether these women were in any way involved with the management of the business. However, 38 (3.8 per cent) of the businesses had women listed as major shareholders — again without any involvement in the management. Furthermore, 41 (4.1 per cent) businesses listed women as professional members of the board of directors, although they own no shares in any of these businesses.

The above statistics indicate that women entrepreneurs consist of only 0.6 per cent in every 1,000 established businesses where the definition proposed by US SBA is applied. However, the percentage may be a lot higher if a survey of all the non-incorporated (registered) women-controlled businesses was conducted and included.

Table 6.3 Summary statistics of number of women entrepreneurs in 1,000 Nigerian registered businesses

	No. of Businesses	Percentage
Owned and controlled by a woman	6*	.6
Family business with wife as member of Board of Directors	59	5.9
With a woman elected officially to the board	41	4.1
With a woman listed as a major shareholder	38	3.8

Note:
* Each of six businesses was listed as 40 per cent owned by foreign investors. Dominant industries include two consultancies, one pharmaceutical wholesale, two retails and one food processing and packaging.

Table 6.4 summarizes the survey with industry types, average share capital in the businesses and employee size. Data in this area indicate more extensive involvement of women in the general service industry with 39 businesses compared with the 27 in manufacturing. However, in relation to the 1,000 surveyed, 39 becomes less impressive when compared to the over 307 service companies. Building construction, insurance and consultancy services had more women directors than other service areas. There are two consultancy firms owned and controlled by women out of a total of six. Average share capital for the 92 businesses (out of the 1,000 surveyed) involving women as outside directors and/or part-owners was approximately $759,000. Average share capital in the six businesses owned and controlled by women was $24,000 and each of these businesses was 40 per cent owned by a foreign investor.

It is difficult to determine performance of these businesses without data on volume of sales over a period of at least five to ten years. Also lack of information on other factors such as profits, total assets, liabilities and other financial data make it difficult to determine the strengths and weaknesses of these women entrepreneurs and therefore areas of types of assistance.

There is a need to establish a broader and larger database on women entrepreneurs. This task will be very costly in both time and money because currently there is no form of data bank and an exploratory survey method is necessary for the development of a good database.

Table 6.4 Summary statistics of women entrepreneurs by industry type and size

Industry Type	No. of Businesses in the Industry Observed	No. with Women as Directors	Range of Employees[1]	Average Share Capital[2] ($000)
General merchandise and trading companies (wholesale and retail)	260	51	3–52	750
Wholesale		25		
Retail		24		
General services	307	39	43–101	24
Insurance		7		
Consultancy		6		
Banking		2		
Printing		2		
Other		22		
Manufacturing	108	27	10–1,219	1,800
Agriculture	79	1	8–	30
Construction and Engineering	282	11	16–1,000	2,700
Total	1,036[3]			

Notes:
1 Range of employees included only those companies with women involved.
2 Share capital average also includes only companies with women owners or directors.
3 Some of the companies are involved in more than one industry.

The limitations in this area are obvious and have hindered the determination of the problems, accomplishment and contributions of women entrepreneurs to the society. Establishment of an appropriate database or bases is important for the better understanding of the impact of women entrepreneurs on the society. Studies based on the data can yield important information for policy-makers, consultants and any future programme designers. While this pilot survey can serve as a ground-breaker for future research, it is also believed that the involvement of women as professionals reflects trends towards more women-owned and -controlled formal/registered businesses compared to the traditional retail and informal businesses of the past. A good database will also make it possible to plan more joint ventures and investment opportunities, possibly with other women entrepreneurs in the USA and other countries. The data bank will also serve as a base for better comparative studies of women entrepreneurs among different cultures.

Summary

Available data presented evidence for the predominance of conflict management. A typical example from the study was shown by the outcome of Ntiki Group of Companies, where the 'offshoot' company resulting from the conflict prospered and diversified while the original company failed and was finally liquidated.

Factors affecting conflict among the cases included ownership status, the company's continuity, succession, profit-sharing, status or promotion inconsistencies, and societal or ethnic differences. Ownership status was most common among the firms.

Six out of the eight companies studied showed evidence of conflict, but only three of them (Ntiki, Francis and Amadi) had reached the stage of action and possible outcomes (see Figure 6.1, page 213). Considering the level of cultural influence on the process of conflict resolution, it is almost possible to predict the decisions for the Amadi and Francis cases.

Processes identified in the study include avoidance, limited interaction, mediation, accommodation and competing. Data show that the process of mediation was common among the cases and that the members of this mediating group consisted mainly of immediate family members and older relatives. Also, in all the cases, the basic goal for resolving conflict had been that of keeping the family united.

Accommodation and competition were two other processes common among the cases. These two processes, where applied (Francis, Amadi, Standard and Ntiki), had resulted in some kind of a motivational

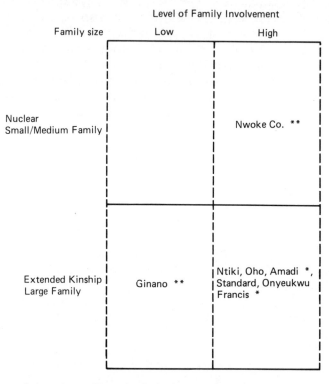

Fig. 6.2 Level of family involvement and conflict in organizations

process for the 'apparent underdog'. They have invariably been applied to show that the 'underdogs' were capable of succeeding. The results had been expansion of the 'family' assets and net worth. For example, in Standard Enterprises, Fidelis's determination to show his brother, Edwin, that he could be successful even though he had not finished high school, resulted in three major companies of his own. If they succeed in merging the two firms, the Obikwelu family will then have a larger organization of six companies. The same outcome may be realized in the Francis Group of Companies.

Avoidance and limited interaction processes appeared to be temporary techniques of conflict resolution. The above two, in the same order, were applied by companies in this study prior to the most popular process — mediation.

All the families in the study were categorized as being large and of the extended kinship type. However, analysis of data shows that the families with high level of member involvement in the organization have more serious conflict, with major factors arising on the family level (see the matrix in Figure 6.2). On the other hand, the family with a lesser member involvement in operation and a moderately large family seem to have conflict arising more at the organizational level.

Opportunistic, adoptive and adaptive practices will continue to flourish as long as the instability in the government and economic environment exists.

Notes

1 Chief Onyeukwu had four wives and over 22 children who are half-brothers and sisters.

2 Traditionally, no one questions the fact that the oldest son succeeds the father as the head of the family. It is against the norms for the younger children to rise up or challenge the older.

3 Mr Etinem of the Ntiki Group of Companies, in describing the involvement of the Utuks family in the organization, said, 'Of course the company belongs to them [the children]. Their parents founded the company and we all expect them to join the company at the management level.' Then he added, 'After all, they are all directors of all the companies in the group.'

4 Mr Obi holds a PhD in Administration from a US university. At the end of 1983, he had been with the company for eight years.

5 Fidesco Group of Companies belonged to the younger brother of Standard's founders. These two brothers (Edwin, founder of Standard, and Fidelis, the younger brother) have been considering a merger of their operations since 1980.

6 The Ginano family are strong adherents to the Muslim faith and acknowledged the right of Muslim employees to worship on Friday afternoons without loss in pay. Christian employees are expected to work those same hours with no difference in compensation.

7 The Ntiki Companies' family were from Cross Rivers state while the Onyeukwu's were from Anambra state.

8 Interviews with Prince Ntiki of Ntiki Group and the General Secretary of Onyeukwu and Sons Limited.

9 With Nigeria under the British colonial government, men who went to school and therefore worked for the government were respected and believed to make more money, considering that the introduction of British currency was replacing the barter system.

10 When a husband is educated and has a government position or is working for one of the few private companies in the cities, the wife usually receives capital for retail business. However, wives of farmers locating in rural areas, receive small pieces of land to grow vegetables and then minor crops, which they usually retail after harvesting.

11 The riot, which is popularly known as the 'Women's Revolt of 1929', started brewing when colonial government agents were sent into houses to attempt to take account of women's property in order to assess appropriate tax on each household.

12 The Association of Nigerian Women was formed in the early 1940s to cater for the interests of women in business. Its headquarters are in Lagos with branches all over the country's 19 states.

13 In September 1984, the military governor's office in Ibadan was besieged by over 8,000 businesswomen demanding to have a discussion with the governor. Several women representatives camped out on the governor's office grounds for two days until the governor gave them audience. A major demand, among others, was that the government establish a systematic method of levying tax on the non-incorporated retail business run by the women as well as a procedure for more effective collection leading to loan assistance for the women.

14 Naira (₦) is the Nigerian currency and ₦1 = $1.25 in September 1984. In February 1986 ₦1 = $1.07.

Appendix 6.A Guide to Second-tier Foreign Exchange Market (SFEM)

Excerpts from the official 'Guidelines on the Second-tier Foreign Exchange Market' issued by the Central Bank, *West Africa Magazine*, October 1986.

Spatial coverage of the SFEM

The market will operate in every part of the country.

Participants

The SFEM is a free market where anyone can buy or sell foreign exchange. However, transactions in the market will be executed through authorised dealers appointed by the minister. For the purpose of the SFEM, an 'Authorized Dealer' or 'Appointed Foreign Exchange Dealer' is a corporate organisation which has been appointed by the government to deal in the SFEM. Such authorisation will be liberally granted to organisations that show evidence of adequate resources and intentions of operating in accordance with their guidelines.

Mode of transactions

Dealing in the SFEM will be by way of spot and forward contracts. Spot transaction means the purchase/sale of foreign exchange for immediate delivery, or within a period of three working days of the transaction. Forward transaction means the purchase/sale of foreign exchange for delivery at a fixed date in the future not earlier than four days after the transaction.

Domiciliary accounts and SFEM

Funds acquired from SFEM are to be used for the purpose they were applied for and for which they have been granted. It is also emphasised that domiciliary accounts are to be funded with foreign exchange derived from external sources.

Although funds deposited in domiciliary accounts may be sold in SFEM, funding of such accounts with foreign exchange acquired from SFEM is illegal and inconsistent with the objectives both of the domiciliary accounts scheme and of SFEM.

Hours of business

The hours of business will be the normal banking hours, viz 8.00am to 3.00pm on Mondays, and 8.00am to 1.30pm on Tuesday through Fridays. However, authorised dealers may provide services on a 24-hour basis at the various entry and exit points to and from the country.

Hotels appointed as authorised buyers of foreign exchange may buy foreign exchange from visitors to Nigeria and may convert the unspent naira balances of such visitors into foreign exchange any time, provided evidence of previous conversion to naira is provided and attached at the underlying documentation. However, reconversion of unspent naira balances in hotels is limited to US$100, or equivalent, per visitor for the duration of stay. The above transactions may be done by a hotel only for visitors who are actually lodged in that hotel. However, authorised buyers cannot sell foreign exchange as they are not authorised foreign exchange dealers.

Mode of operation

All authorised dealers will display in a conspicuous public place in their offices their quotations of buying and selling rates for various foreign currencies.

These same rates will be communicated to the Central Bank of Nigeria on a daily basis and to the press. These rates will apply to all transactions up to $5,000 or its equivalent. Rates for amounts above $5,000 or equivalent will be subject to negotiation with customers but within the maximum spread of one percent allowed to dealers. Anyone who wishes to buy or sell foreign exchange for any of the eligible transactions may apply to any authorised dealer of his choice.

The applicant is required to furnish documentary evidence of the underlying commercial or service transaction. The rate at which each transaction is finally executed will be the rate that is mutually agreed between the applicant and the authorised dealer but subject to the maximum spread of one per cent allowed to dealers. All banks and other dealers are required to satisfy themselves that the relevant documents as per the processing guidelines, are furnished and that payment is due. All foreign exchange dealers are required to maintain a file or files for each applicant and ensure that documents in support of each transaction are properly filed and produced for verification by Central Bank of Nigeria inspectors.

Bidding/fixing sessions

Once a week, on Thursday, beginning at 10.00am a price-fixing session will be conducted by the Central Bank with the participation of the authorised foreign exchange dealers held by them in excess of the specified working balances and foreign exchange supplied by the Central Bank. Observers including the Federal Ministry of Finance and Department of Customs and Excise, may attend the price-fixing sessions. The exchange rate by this bidding process will be used as the reference or base rate by the authorised dealers for the subsequent week and the authorised dealers are required to maintain a maximum spread of one per cent on this base rate. The same base rate shall be used in the subsequent week to value imports and exports, payment of the relevant duties and taxes and for adjustment of prices set or administered by the government. The fixing session also provides an opportunity for discussion of broad developments influencing the foreign exchange market. A 0.5 per cent exchange levy on foreign exchange transactions at the weekly fixing session will be payable to the Central Bank and kept in an Exchange Equalisation Account under the control of the Ministry of Finance.

Measures for ensuring an efficient and competitive market

To reduce monopolistic or oligopolistic tendencies and to ensure an efficient and competitive market, SFEM has been designed to include the following features:

i)   Number of dealers

There will be a large number of dealers appointed by the govern-ment after having met certain minimum requirements, all of whom will participate.

ii)   Access to the market

Anyone who wishes to buy or sell foreign exchange can approach an authorised dealer of his choice and such a dealer may not refuse to deal with the person merely because the person is not an account holder.

Also, an authorised dealer may not refuse the sale of foreign exchange on the basis of unavailability. The SFEM is designed such that a dealer can purchase from other dealers as soon as his supply runs below the specified minimum limit of his holdings. There is no restriction on funds that may be brought to the market from external sources. However, every applicant who wishes to buy foreign exchange from SFEM must satisfy the minimum requirement of proof of underlying commercial or service transaction or approved capital transaction and furnish the relevant documents.

iii) Information on the market

In order to ensure free access to information in the market, rates which emerge at the weekly price-fixing session will be published in the national dailies, evening papers and broadcast on radio and television not later than 12 hours after the price-fixing session. Moreover, all authorised dealers are required to display in their offices the selling and buying rates for the major currencies.

iv) Specification of limits

Upper and lower limits for working balances and purchase will be specified for authorised dealers in order to forestall market cornering or collusion by some dealers or group of dealers and to prevent their over-exposure to foreign exchange risks.

v) Prescription and monitoring of margins spreads

Spreads between buying and selling rates of individual authorised dealers will be monitored periodically by the Central Bank to ensure that they do not indicate any collusive practices. The spread allowed is a maximum of one per cent between buying and selling rates. It should be noted that this excludes the 0.5 per cent exchange levy on certain foreign exchange transactions payable to the Central Bank of Nigeria . . .

vii) Appointment of commercial banks and merchant banks as authorised dealers

Commercial banks and merchant banks that have been appointed authorised foreign exchange dealers under the Exchange Control Act of 1962 remain authorised foreign exchange dealers under the SFEM provided the dealership appointment has not been suspended or revoked by the Federal Minister of Finance.

viii) Appointment of non-bank institutions as foreign exchange dealers

Non-bank corporate organisations may be appointed foreign exchange dealers by government subject to such organisations meeting the prescribed requirements. Such requirements include relevant experience and expertise, integrity, capital adequacy level and spread of infrastructural facilities, good credit rating or bank reference.

Non-bank corporate organisations appointed by government will only act as brokers and deal for their customers' accounts. They will also not be involved in import and export transactions and limits will be set in respect of the value of individual and global transactions that they may execute . . .

xii)   The Comprehensive Import Supervision Scheme (CISS)

The CISS will be retained under SFEM.

The pre-shipment inspection of goods on a comprehensive basis is to ensure that the country gets value for money and facilitate the implementation of the new tariff policy.

Consequently, all imports value $5,000 and above (except those specifically exempted by Government) shall be subject to pre-shipment inspection. Banks are required to be vigilant and to advise reception.

xiii)   Role of the Central Bank and the Federal Finance Ministry

The Central Bank and the Federal Ministry of Finance will supervise and monitor operations in SFEM on an on-going basis through returns and field examinations and spot checks.

Transitional arrangements

i)   All outstanding transactions for which the related documents have been submitted to the Central Bank for cover not later than December 31, 1983 are subject to refinancing and will therefore be treated within the framework of the refinancing scheme.

ii) The transactions listed under subsection (iii) below will be treated in the official first-tier foreign exchange market at the exchange rate prevailing as at the date when all the following conditions were completed.

   a.   All documentation prescribed by the Central Bank to be relevant to the transaction concerned was submitted to the Central Bank.

   b.   The obligation to which the documentation relates has, having regard to the nature of such transaction, become due and payable, and

c. The corresponding naira component of the transaction has been deposited with the Central Bank.

Whichever last happens, with the additional condition that no such transaction shall be regarded as due and payable unless the provisions of paragraphs (a) to (c) above have been complied with.

iii) The transactions referred in subsection (ii) above are as follows:

a. Any transaction covered by a specified important licence listed in 1985 or 1986 for which a confirmed and irrevocable letter of credit was established on or before the last day immediately preceding the commencement of the market.

b. Capital transfers, profits, dividends, and other invisible payments for which approval has been granted by the Federal Ministry of Finance or the Central Bank on or before the last day immediately preceding the commencement of the market.

c. Public and private sector transactions relating to debt service obligations that are due and payable, official contributions and grants to international organisations and remittance to Nigerian missions abroad.

d. Net proceeds of air tickets sold by foreign airlines up to and including the last day immediately preceding the commencement of the market, provided that the first leg of the journey out of Nigeria had begun before the date of commencement of the market.

e. Any transaction valid for foreign exchange in respect of which advance import duty or form C 188A had been paid, a clean report of findings issued by the inspection agent, and documents, submitted to the Central Bank of Nigeria for the issue of cover not later than the last day immediately preceding the commencement of the market.

iv) All outstanding obligations to surrender foreign exchange or submit documents evidencing receipt of goods for which the Central Bank had provided foreign exchange on the basis of confirmed claims are not extinguished of SFEM.

Non-resident visitors

Non-resident visitors shall continue to pay their hotel bills in foreign currency.

228

Exportation/importation of notes

The exportation and importation of naira is still prohibited except for the maximum of ₦55.00 allowance for residents for settlement of expenses immediately on their return to Nigeria.

Declaration of foreign currency imports

For statistical purposes only, declaration of foreign currency imports of the equivalent of $5,000 and above, is required. However, where the traveller may wish to re-export part or all the foreign currency brought in by way of bank notes and travellers' cheques he should declare the total amount brought in whether it is less than $5,000 or not.

Abolition of mandatory surrender of foreign currency

The requirement of mandatory surrender of foreign currency imports by residents of Nigeria has been abolished. Exporters are however, expected to open foreign currency accounts domiciled with banks in Nigeria to which export proceeds shall be fully credited.

Status of certain transactions

Although there is a separate manual giving comprehensive processing guidelines for the benefit of all foreign exchange dealers it is desirable to give here the status of certain transactions for the information of the general public.

International air tickets

Payments for international air tickets may be made in naira or foreign exchange at the option of the traveller. Travellers will be required to pay the equivalent in naira or equivalent foreign exchange at the operating SFEM exchange rates.

Capital transactions

To facilitate the inflow of direct capital investment, the industrial development and coordinating committee (IDCC) will deal promptly and under one roof, with all matters relating to approval for direct capital investment, subject to the provisions of the Nigerian Enterprises Promotions Decree, 1977.

Applications for the remittance of profits, dividends etc in respect of capital investment made through SFEM will be considered by the Federal Ministry of Finance and approved subject to the usual documentation requirements. Any funds so approved would be repatriated through SFEM.

Expatriate home remittances

Transfers of up to 50 per cent of net salary after tax may be considered by authorised dealers subject to the usual documentation requirements. However, final balance applications involving the transfer of accumulated savings should be considered subject to the approved guidelines and confirmation by the Central Bank in each case, that the expatriate concerned had not previously been granted his final balance entitlement.

To give further guidance to the banks in this respect the Central Bank will compile a list of expatriates who had received their final balances and up-date the first list from time to time by way of circulars.

Unmatched refinancing items (pre-1984 transactions)

The status of such transactions is being determined. Until a decision is taken on such transactions, the funds are not eligible for transfer through SFEM.

Blacklisted companies and persons

All companies and individuals who had been placed on foreign exchange embargo and duly notified to the banks are not allowed to engage in any transaction in SFEM until the embargo is lifted and duly advised by the competent authority.

Cash transactions

Transactions involving the sale of foreign bank notes and travellers' cheques by foreign exchange dealers are to be kept within the reasonable limits relative to amounts allowed for travel.

Basic Travel Allowance (BTA)

A sum of $2,500 per trip per person subject to two trips per annum based on presentation of adequate documentation.

Disallow split orders which are undertaken to avoid pre-shipment inspection, clean reports of findings issued in respect of inspection goods are mandatory documents for the computation of duty payable and clearance of the goods on arrival in Nigeria.

Clean reports of findings are also required documentation in support of applications for payment of goods subject to pre-shipment inspection and imported on the basis of bills for collection usance bill and open accounts prepayment of import duties is still mandatory. In this regard pre-shipment inspection agents will now in addition, verify that the correct foreign currency equivalent of import duties has been paid with respect to tariff and value of goods. Inspection agents will issue a clean report of findings if duty paid falls within tolerance limits (five per cent of inspection agents will issue a discrepancy report with which the importer will pay the excess import duty or get a refund as the case may be from the Board of Customs and Excise).

Returns

Banks and other foreign exchange dealers are required to render the following returns to the Central Bank of Nigeria on the format given in the attached appendices: *Weekly report on net foreign exchange position*, to be submitted not later than 12 noon every Wednesday. *Weekly analysis of form 'A' and form 'M' approvals and disbursements — Schedules I to IV*, to be submitted to the Central Bank not later than 12 noon every Wednesday.

Sanctions

All authorised foreign exchange dealers are required to scrutinise documents submitted to them by their customers in support of their foreign exchange applications and satisfy themselves that such documents are in order.

They should also ensure that they follow the laid down processing guidelines and procedures. Sanctions will be imposed on dealers who release funds on the basis of forged documents or for fradulent transactions.

Any foreign exchange dealer whose performance is unsatisfactory will be fined or will have his dealership permit suspended or withdrawn depending on the degree of default or offence. Other sanctions and penalties have been specified in the decree establishing the SFEM.

Application for additional amounts of foreign exchange under paragraphs (C), (G), (H) and (I) above shall be approved by the

minister, if he is satisfied that they are not for the purpose of transferring capital abroad.

7 Comparative management practices

Introduction

What are the major issues in this study? What further research can be carried out to learn more about these issues? How do the management practices identified compare with the Western European models? The answers to the above questions are the theme of this chapter.

Chapter 8 will discuss the framework for developing appropriate management education and also the future of management practices.

Findings and related theories

Major findings drawn from the data (cases) included:

1 The economic and industrial environment of Nigeria was more trade and service oriented than manufacturing.
2 There were more family firms in the society than public and other forms of organizations.
3 Companies evolved through stages, growing from expansion (volume and market) to diversification (see Figure 7.1).
4 The companies are largely diversified horizontally; nonetheless, backward integration was identified.
5 Family 'constellations' largely influenced the pattern of structural (interaction patterns) evolution while other ecological factors and government actions influenced strategic choices (see Figure 7.2).

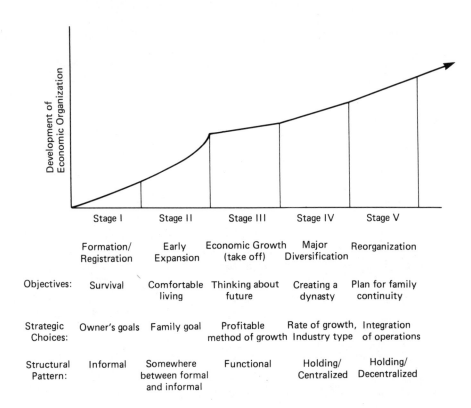

Fig. 7.1 Stages in evolution (with objectives, strategies and structure)

234

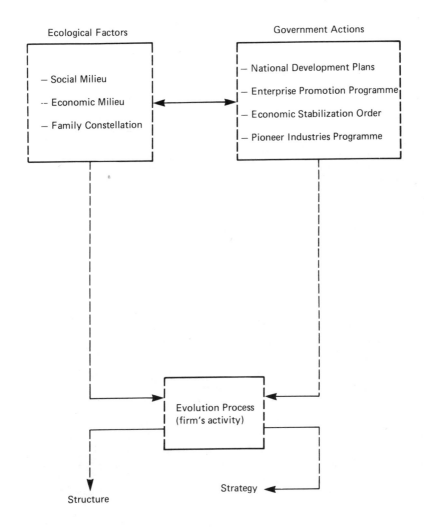

Fig. 7.2 Relationships among the factors affecting evolution patterns

235

6   Several factors affected the interpersonal and intergroup conflict at both family and organization levels.

7   Conflict resolution mechanisms/processes were influenced by culture and traditional norms in the society.

8   The mechanisms employed to resolve or reduce conflict influenced the firms' evolution in a more functional than dysfunctional way.

Saiyadan and Nambudiri (1981) have suggested that 'all nations are development-minded, but that the only difference was the level and nature of development that the nation has been able to achieve'.[1] These authors have further suggested that all processes of economic development start with 'attempt for mastery over economic and political institutions, the attitudes of the people, their predispositions and values'.[2] The above factors usually play a significant role in the nature of development. Lawrence and Lorsch (1969), Woodward (1965), and Burns and Stalker (1966), in their contingency theory orientation also suggested that attributes of environment play a major role in the economic structure of organizations. Findings in this study tend to lend towards the above suggestions, although none of these studies has empirically studied the impact of ecology. Considering the fact that firm-type economic development in Nigeria was initiated by the colonial government, which brought with it Western European traders and merchants, it is no surprise then that, up to the end of 1983, trading and service organizations still dominated the industries. Among the firms studied, trading companies with which they all started remained a significant and viable subsidiary of each of the organizations.

Data collected on the description of the main research setting (Nigeria) also relate to several theories of social change. Specific among these theories are those proposed by Hagen (1962), McClelland (1976), and Lauer (1982). Hagen argued that economic development, which may be defined in terms of continuing increase in per capita income through technological advances, depends on creative personality. He then described personality in terms of 'needs, values, and cognitive elements of world view, together with intelligence and energy level'.[3] Needs were illustrated as needs for autonomy, self-understanding and nurture which the author describes as major characteristics of innovational personalities needed for the work of economic development.

McClelland argued that

> it is the entrepreneurial spirit that impels development, and the task of the theorist is to account for the emergence of that spirit . . . . This spirit is exemplified in the businessmen, who contrary to popular image, are not driven by profit motive *per se*, but rather by a strong desire for achievement.[4]

236

The profit aspect is presently a major motive for entrepreneurism in Nigeria.

Both authors agree that this personality may exist among a group in a society and that economic development often starts from this group. In this study, the Ibo tribe, as research data indicate, showed the highest signs of entrepreneurial characteristics and fits into the above description. In the Saiyadan and Nambudiri (1981) study, the Ibo group was also found to possess the highest need achievement rate. This study did not go into detailed analysis of social dynamics of family relations but evidence exists to show the diverse dispositions and characteristics of the tribes. Lauer's (1982) and Rostow's (1960) theories on structural patterns and stages of economic development, respectively, also reflect the socio-economic conditions in Nigeria. Lauer's conclusion that 'different kinds of leaders may be required for different kinds of changes and different types of situation',[5] describes the Nigerian political situation; where military leadership has often been popularly associated with better economic growth and improved standards of living. The natural resources in Nigeria, especially oil, provide the country with the necessary base for development (Rostow's preconditions for take-off). What the country really needs is a stable political and social infrastructure to manage and capitalize on its natural wealth.

In summary, the findings of this study have significant implications for development planning in Nigeria and other similar societies. It is apparent that the Nigerian government had no complete knowledge of its actions on the growth and performance of its enterprises. It is therefore left to the governments to clearly identify the entrepreneurial spirit in the society and continue to encourage their activities through the incentive plans designed to meet more realistic developments.

Data also indicated the prevalence of private family controlled firms in Nigeria. This finding is consistent with the reports on the prevalence of family controlled and family owned businesses in the United States and other countries. In the USA, it is reported that 95 per cent of all companies are either family owned or family controlled (Donnelly, 1964; Beckhard, 1969; Barnes and Hershon, 1976; and Hollander (1984). In Nigeria, over 60 per cent of the established firms are family owned or family controlled while over 90 per cent of the small-scale, 'unestablished' trading businesses also remain family owned. These data support the prevalence and growing influence of family firms in the economies of nations.

Major studies in stages of evolution (Chandler, 1962; Scott, 1971; Greiner, 1972) suggest that the evolution of firms was a function of the external environment in which 'structure follows strategy'. Chandler also maintained that strategy was an intervening variable between environment and the organizational structure. However, Chandler's model has been based on geographic expansion, virtually disregarding the influence of ecology. Data from this study indicate that structural changes have been initiated after a significant growth through expansion or diversification in the organization or mostly when there is a need to make adjustments to accommodate a member of the family in the organization. However, this expansion and diversification are both strategies of growth and control, which were largely influenced by ecological factors that were not considered by Chandler.

Scott, in his studies which were built on Chandler's work, developed three stages of development which were based on the increasing pressure of environmental and organizational complexity. Although Scott's stages and other findings were broadly supported by the four studies carried out in Western European nations (France, England, Italy and Germany), the findings in this study appear to differ from the Scott model. As shown in Figure 7.1, five stages of evolution were determined, from the formation phase to the reorganization after major diversification. The growth pattern of expanding trade activities through expansion of product lines in a horizontal integration differs from Scott's single product development, as well as the vertical integration strategies. Although the strategy of diversification as a growth method appears to be common to both findings, Nigerian companies appeared to have diversified much more than the US companies studied by Scott, Chandler, Wrigley or Rumelt. All the companies studied have developed from the mastery of the market and sales strategies to entry into manufacturing of products. Most diversifications have also been made through establishment of new companies, rather than acquisition of an ongoing one. This finding appears to be similar to the findings of Suziki in Japan.

In addition, the informal functional, holding/centralized and holding/decentralized structural pattern appear to differ somewhat from Scott's functional, departmentational and divisionalization. Although both structural patterns appear to move from simple to more complex structures, and the observed pattern in this study appears to support Scott's model that the stages of development emerge under increasing pressure of complexities; however, Scott and his associates have virtually taken ecology for granted thereby leaving one to wonder about these models. This pattern also reflects the value systems of the founders (Figure 7.1) which range from survival and comfortable living to economic growth and plans for continuity of the organization. Many factors appear to be responsible for the major differences identified above and implications of these factors are summarized in the following paragraphs.

Of all the studies on organizational forms, Ouchi's (1981) research came closest to the understanding of the types of strategies and structures found in this study. Ouchi argued that leading Japanese firms rely on informal control systems extending lifetime employment to significant numbers of employees. This human resource practice which Ouchi terms 'clan' support tends to explain the family focus interface management practices which rely more on family values, beliefs and the culture of the people. This study found that the traditional value of unquestionable respect for elders significantly influenced the outcome of conflict resolution processes.

The clan mechanism also explains the ability of family firms to survive and grow on private funds since it tends to obviate the need to consider the equity of every transaction between and within groups.

Several factors have been determined to have effect on the evolution patterns of organizations in Nigeria. As shown in Figure 7.2, these factors include ecological factors and government actions. The ecological factors include the social and economic milieu which has greatly affected the status of the third factor, the family 'constellation'. The nature of the development of the society and firm-type economy (trade orientation, multiple product ventures, etc.) was largely influenced by the colonization of the country and the activities of the colonial government. The heterogeneity of both population and culture in Nigeria also contributed to the development of the predominant 'extended kinship' relationships within the country. This form of family serves both as the provider of job opportunities (to many, and relatives in particular) and a source of economic development for the community. The ecological factors in general, according to data in this study, have implications for development of both strategies and structures, while the family constellation in particular influences structural development.

Factors under government actions include:

1 Four National Development Plans which formulated the objectives and thereby formed the basis for the development of other specific programmes in this group of actions (1962–68, 1970–74, 1975–80, and 1980–85);
2 Enterprises Promotion Act or what is popularly known as 'indigenization' programme;
3 Economic Stabilization Order (temporary order); and
4 Pioneer Industries Programmes.

The above programmes were, in the order listed, designed to place most of the established enterprises in the hands of Nigerian citizens, while the Stabilization Order controlled the import and export activities in the society. The Pioneer Industries Programme with its several benefits was intended to steer the entrepreneurs into manufacturing and processing industries that would utilize the raw materials abundant in Nigeria.

This study has determined that the above programmes played significant roles in steering the pattern of evolution, especially with the strategies of diversification. The indigenization programme had implications for the few diversifications through acquisition, while the Pioneer Industries Programme affected the diversification strategy through establishment of new manufacturing companies.

Six factors were determined to be affecting conflict and five reduction mechanisms were applied by the firms in the study. Factors affecting interpersonal or intergroup conflict included:

— Ownership status
— Succession issues
— Company's future
— Social/ethnic differences
— Profit-sharing system
— Status/promotion inconsistencies.

This study has also developed evidence to support the findings by Barnes and Hershon which suggest that family firms inherit some unique problems which may not be associated with non-family firms. Six of the eight firms in the study have either been through major family conflict or were going through a process of reducing or resolving a conflict. Barnes and Hershon (1976) also identified family rifts (succession, continuity of investment and involvement, building a dynasty, income-sharing, etc.) which were similar to the factors identified in this study. According to these authors, 'family and company transitions were more productive when they were simultaneous';[6] Levinson (1971) suggested that it was often a better strategy to establish a trust for family members or hire professional managers to run the family enterprise. But data from this study suggest that a lot of conflict may be reduced where ownership and profit-sharing plans were drawn up at the start of the business although this was not the case. Levinson's recommendation was intended to save organizations from failing as a result of the internal family rifts. Although this study was designed to explore the process and support Levinson on the existence of the never-ending rifts, conflicts are not always destructive. There is evidence from this study to show that conflicts could be functional as well as dysfunctional, and according to the data set in this study, the conflicts identified have been more functional in generating new business, but dysfunctional to the family unity and harmony.

Perhaps the finding that the processes used to resolve conflict are strongly influenced by the Nigerian culture had something to do with this outcome. Another author on family business, Beckhard (1983) has suggested that conflict or rifts were not solely responsible for firms' stagnation. In the paper, 'Conversation with Beckhard', Dr Beckhard said:

> Typically I think you will find that family firms, particularly in the developing countries, tend to be very significantly intertwined with the traditional life of the community in which they operate. Thus, characteristically, the consequences of the family firm's fate go beyond its own economic consequences.[7]

This statement is true of the findings of this study where traditional family rulers who had intervened in the mediation did all they could to save or prevent the firm from failing. Dr Beckhard also identified the succession issue as the most significant factor affecting conflict. He also maintained that 'unless structures and mechanisms are developed to manage these succession issues, the probabilities of survival of the firms are sharply curtailed'.[8]

This issue of succession is closely tied to the ownership percentage — another major issue. Prior to the fieldwork in this study, I had an opportunity for an interview with Dr Harry Levinson on issues of family firms, especially succession. In essence Dr Levinson analyzed the varying phases of conflict development in the family firm. He maintained that family cohesion often became fragmented and is lost 'by the third generation unless there is a social structure which defines what the roles and responsibilities are'.[9] Further, Dr Levinson wondered about what the findings would be in Nigerian society, and after hearing a brief description of the cultural background, he added:

> Well, it will be fascinating to see what has happened with the underlying psychological issues of family rivalry, and my guess is that what you are finding there in the first generation is what you'd find here in the second or third generation.[10]

The findings here, as mentioned earlier, appear to have supported Dr Levinson's contentions. The conflict resolution process was predominantly controlled by the social order, which places the older members of the family in strict control.

Of the five processes used by the firms to resolve conflict, the mediation process was most frequently used and appeared to be most appropriate and productive, relative to 'confrontation' and dialogue mechanisms. This finding also supports those of Barnes and Hershon. Also gaining experience outside the family firm (designed to build the son's confidence in himself and the father's confidence in the son, as suggested by Dr Levinson) appeared to be working for the Ntiki Group of Companies in Nigeria, where the second- and third-generation members were working in harmony.

Management problems in developing countries

Management problems abound for the developing nations as evidenced by the Nigerian situation. Private firms are becoming very sensitive to new markets and are eager to shift from one market/industry to another as opportunities develop. Nonetheless, these moves are not always driven by market forces but rather by public policies.

Major problems include: inclination by government to over-regulate the economic industries. Even in the industrialized West — for example, France — this inclination appears to be interfering with the natural direction of corporate evolution, which has been unfortunate for all concerned. It would do the society better if government would find ways to work with and encourage private enterprise activities rather than stifling them through regulations and inadequate subsidies.

In an attempt to control the economy, governments often invest heavily in prestigious projects in basic industries such as cement products. These industries are noted for yielding the lowest returns not only in profitability but also in employment per dollar investment. It may be argued that these projects are valuable economically since they serve as a necessary backbone for a modern industrial country. Nonetheless, this validity lies on the production side of economy and ignores the context of the modern industrial state — competition and free enterprise.

Another major management problem lies with the status of the management education sector. Safavi (1981) concludes that despite abundant natural resources, Africa faces a bleak economic future, owing in large part to its inability to effectively train capable managers. Most of the management education programmes are developed and taught by educators from Western industrialized nations who know little or nothing about the African cultures. It was indicated in the early chapters of the book that societal factors have impact on the structural and strategic evolutions of the enterprise. Efforts to develop appropriate management programmes and education would help train indigenous African managers to be more effective. Short-term professional seminars and courses (using materials and cases from the country) will also help to improve current practices.

Other management problems are consequences of technological environment, educational factors, socio-cultural norms. The tendency to centralize and avoid delegation is predominant. Delegation is equated with indecisiveness. Among the problems facing senior managers are adaptability, reliance on subordinates and productivity.

The problem of adaptability was mentioned in Chapter 6. Nigerian businessmen may be described as individualists with few cases of unrelated partnership (the proportion of corporate and sole proprietorship in company registration in the 1980s still stands at 7.6 per cent corporate and 92.4 per cent sole proprietorship). Leadership tends to seek trade, technology and management from a large number of developed countries rather than develop internal programmes. All these management problems may be resolved when the society learns to develop a systematic framework for a management education programme based on its own needs.

Notes

1 M.S. Saiyadan and C.N.S. Nambudiri, *Attitudes and Values of Upcoming Nigerian Professionals: a question of concern*, Business Publishing Division, College of Business Administration, Georgia State University, Atlanta GA, 1981, pp.62–70.
2 Ibid., p.63.
3 E.E. Hagen, *On the Theory of Social Change*, The Dorsey Press Inc., Homewood Il, 1962, p.133.
4 D.C. McClelland, *The Achieving Society*, Halstead Press, Irvington Publishers Inc., 1976, p.26.
5 R.H. Lauer, *Perspectives on Social Change*, 3rd edn, Allyn and Bacon Inc., 1982, pp.16–21.
6 L.B. Barnes and S.A. Hershon, 'Transferring power in the family business', *Harvard Business Review*, July–August 1976, pp.105–14, number 76401.
7 R. Beckhard and W.G. Dyer Jr, 'SMR Forum: Managing change in the family firm – issues and strategies', *Sloan Management Review*, Spring 1983, p.59–65.
8 Ibid., pp.31–2.
9 14 August 1984, Belmont Mass., Boston.
10 Ibid.

8 Towards a developing country-oriented management theory: Nigerian case

The indigenization decree and its amendment started the Nigerian corporate ownership revolution and industrialization. Nevertheless, the programme never included a local management revolution which is necessary for effective implementation and success of the programme. Foreign management theories still dominate the industries.

Introduction

Indigenization is a household word which started a local ownership revolution among Nigerians. With the institution of the Enterprises Promotion Decree in 1972, the Nigerian government took a giant step towards indigenizing ownership of many firms operating in the country. Briefly, the decree and its Amendment Act (1977) attempted to make it possible for Nigerians to own and be involved in the management of such firms. The Act categorized enterprises into three schedules. Enterprises under Schedule I are reserved exclusively for indigenous exploitation. Schedule II allows for 40 per cent foreign ownership and 60 per cent Nigerian, while Schedule III enterprises allow for 60 per cent foreign participation and 40 per cent Nigerian. Furthermore, to facilitate this indigenization programme, industrial and investment banks were established to provide Nigerians with the necessary capital.

However, ownership transfer notwithstanding, management and decision-making strategies remained and still rely on foreign consultants. *There was no effective step taken to indigenize management theories and practices.* One of the weaknesses often identified by studies on management education and training in Africa is that there are very high percentages of foreign management educators and consultants who are mostly responsible for the development of the educational and training programmes (Sarpong and Rawls, 1976; Gilmore, 1978; Rake, 1979). Further, when the programmes are developed by indigenous educators or trainers, they also use texts and studies based on Western, industrialized cultures and assumptions, thereby leaving room for doubt about their effectiveness in a setting such as Nigeria.

This chapter is concerned with the lack of appropriate effort to indigenize management models theories; whether there are needs for them; problems hindering their development and strategies for development of appropriate management theories. It specifically reviews existing management styles, the framework for theory building and, in summary, factors limiting and facilitating development of Nigerian management theories.

Management styles

Management is business performance, achievement rather than knowledge and in other words, it is practice rather than a 'science or a profession'. How then can one understand this *practice* without close observation of the activities of the practitioner.

> No greater damage could be done to a society or economy than to attempt not to understand and apply the corporate cultures of the society.

Major authors in management (Lawrence and Lorsch, 1967; Kretner, 1977; Mintzberg, 1973; Ouchi, 1981) acknowledge and concern their studies with cultural differences among enterprises and countries. Many consultants make fortunes advising investors on the business or corporate cultures of future host countries while many international corporations have failed abroad for failure to acknowledge the cultural differences in methods of doing business. These authors identified such factors as social/tribal norms and socio-economic environment as influencing outcomes for effective and efficient management.

How then does Nigeria expect an effective indigenization programme with foreign management theories?

Today, there are such 'hot' terms as American and Japanese management styles. The Chinese and the Indian styles are yet to be acknowledged. An examination of the characteristics of these management styles indicates culture-bound practices designed to accommodate social norms. A summary of the styles given in Table 8.1 compares the American and Japanese which are currently the most popular.

The characteristics are a blend of social/cultural and economic environment, making management practices congruent with social and economic norms. A basic argument for the Japanese management style rests on the unparalleled growth witnessed recently in the Japanese economy. Many feel that a primary reason for this success is the rather unique way in which Japanese companies are organized and run. The Japanese holistic and paternalistic approach and the American individualistic and businesslike approach to management are the results of years of studies, later forming a basis for development of such theories as motivation, employee satisfaction and performance, leadership effectiveness and the like. The theories then form a basis for models such as that shown in a recent model created to summarize Japanese management style in a manner that should be helpful to students of management (Hatvany and Pucik, 1981). The model captures the essence of the basic Japanese approach to management and consists of three parts, the *Focus, General Strategies* and *Specific Techniques.*

Similar studies and developments are springing up in China and other developing countries in their attempt at effective industrialization and economic development.

Developing a management theory

Figure 8.1 below presents a framework for the development of a management theory.

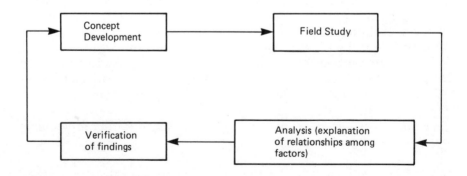

Fig. 8.1   A framework for developing theories

Table 8.1 Comparison of traditional North American and Japanese management styles

Characteristics	Traditional North American Management Style	Japanese Management Style
Employment	Employment contracts last only as long as individual contributes.	Employment is for life.
Promotion	Rapid promotion and feedback.	Slower rates of promotion.
Control System	Explicit formal control system.	Somewhat more implicit less formal control system.
Concern for Employees	Little concern for the total person.	More concern for the total person.
Specialization	Specialization of function with rotation only for people on a general management track.	More cross-functional rotation and emphasis on becoming a generalist.
Decision-making	Individual, top-down decision-making.	Relatively high level of participation and consensual decision-making.
Responsibility Emphasis	Emphasis on individual responsibility.	Emphasis on group responsibility.

Source: W. Ouchi, *Theory Z*, 1981.

Theory building is time-consuming, very expensive in planning and needs to be channelled to the goals of the corporation as well as the country. For an example, the essence of management in major Japanese corporations is the maximum development of employee talents and skills so that they may be used in attaining organizational goals. The framework is a cyclical process designed to discover and create a steady pattern and trend in any management practices.

Field studies should be designed to capture the essence of management

The steps in the framework are summarized below.

1 *Concept.* This conceptual stage deals with development of ideas. It includes determination or listing of concepts to be investigated. Examples include motivational programmes, worker satisfaction and productivity, job design, decision-making processes and others. It is not necessary to develop any hypothesis about the concept so as to allow the ideas to develop further in the research process.
2 *Field study.* Field study involves both qualitative and quantitative methods. This step includes selection of sites, data gathering methods and more. A qualitative research with its major advantage of versatility and process-orientation makes it possible to pull out a good theory. A good theory should have:

    (a) internal consistency,
    (b) external consistency,
    (c) scientific parsimony,
    (d) generalizability, and
    (e) be verifiable.

The third and fourth steps of analysis and verification cover explanation of relationship between facts and tests and re-tests until a good theory is developed.

We know what a good theory should be, but how do we define a theory, what are the uses of a theory and is there a need for a Nigerian-oriented management theory? The responses to the above questions will be presented in such a way as to bring out the factors influencing the management styles in the society.

Briefly stated, a theory is a set of statements that serve to amplify the manner in which certain concepts or variables are interrelated. These statements develop out of the concepts or variables leading to logical propositions. In short, theory is simply a technique or model that permits people to better understand how different variables fit together (Dubin, 1976). Uses of theories in research and management are invaluable and three major uses are worth mentioning (Hamner and Organ, 1978).

1 Theories help organize knowledge about a given subject in a pattern of relationships that lends meaning to a series of observed events.
2 Theories help summarize diverse findings so that one can focus on major relationships and not get bogged down in details.
3 Theories point the way to future research efforts. They raise new questions and suggest answers. As Curt Lewin said, 'There is nothing so practical as a good theory.'[1]

Nigeria is a developing country with distinct cultural and behavioural characteristics. To benefit from good theories, she needs to gather facts about events in her society and develop a pattern of relationships between the events. Nigeria cannot grow effectively on relationships developed on facts from a different society. There has to be some consistency between goals and strategies for achieving those goals. The society has the human and material resources to find and develop her management theories or style. However, there are some hindering factors to this much needed project. These limiting factors include the poor relationship between institutions of higher learning and firms. This lack of understanding and cooperation between these two institutions is responsible for fewer or no field studies among the academics. Another cause of fewer field studies, and also a limiting factor, is the high cost in time and money for field research. Because a successful academic career depends on the number of articles or books published, theoretical papers are often preferred to intensive fieldwork. Foreign theories are then easier to adapt and even adopt than developing appropriate ones.

An improvement of the relationship between institutions of higher learning and firms is recommended

Firms and institutions of higher learning should be able to work together for mutual benefits. Internships, student group projects and case studies on specific issues or variables should be arranged between Nigerian firms and management students. This arrangement should lead to more studies and management education development. Theory building is only a starting-point. Based on theory, researchers and managers can proceed to design studies aimed at verifying and refining the theories themselves. The time is ripe for Nigeria to utilize her resources for a holistic economic development. The development of a Nigerian-oriented management theory is a good place to start.

Future of management practices and implications

This study has suggested several issues worthy of future research. These issues are theoretical in nature and may be examined qualitatively, quantitatively or both. The following discussion describes issues that merit attention.

First is the issue of factors affecting the evolution pattern. This study has discussed the natural or ecological factors and planned government actions. The data show that the planned government actions had strong effects in directing the strategies ultimately implemented. However, it is obvious that not all the developing countries have the resources of Nigeria (i.e., oil) so that such nations are not likely to be able to plan for economic development in the same way. It will therefore be important to design more studies that will determine the patterns of evolution based on the influence of the existing factors only. This study may be explored in another developing country relatively similar in size and level of development to Nigeria and will help resolve the issue of whether the pattern of evolution observed from this study is common to all developing countries or is specific to Nigeria.

The second research question is related to the first and deals with the finding that family constellations influenced the evolution of the structural patterns. Data from this study show that, because of the social and economic milieu, family form has been more of the large, extended kinship type rather than nuclear. Although one of the firms (Nwoke) behaved more like a nuclear family, it was, by nature and definition, an extended kinship. The study, therefore, did not offer any insight into the pattern of influence on firms by a nuclear family. However with the Western influence in the society, some nuclear forms of family are developing. By 1984, the nuclear families in the society had not begun to engage in or develop their own family firms, and it will be fascinating to investigate whether there is any difference in the structural evolution pattern in firms directed by these families. One thing is certain though. If a nuclear family inherited a family firm founded by a large, extended kinship, there is bound to be major conflict developing between the other relatives and the new form. Investigation of these kinds of situations will help develop appropriate intervention mechanisms for conflict resolution.

The next research area deals with family business *per se*. To date, studies in family businesses are few and, yet, their contributions to the economic development of both industrialized and non-industrialized nations are tremendous. An important research area will be one that determines and develops mechanisms for understanding the issues of human resources management in the firm. The issue of human resources is problematic in all its forms, but even more severe in the family firm where human resources are centred around the family, especially at the managerial level. A major objective is to retain control in the hands of family members. This practice has resulted in the selection for management positions on the basis of blood relation rather than qualification and this, in turn, has resulted in some inefficiency and unsatisfactory performance. Development of a system of maintaining control in the family without compromising efficiency is needed to ensure continuity of the organization. As Beckhard (1981) put it, the consequences of the family firm's fate go beyond its own economic consequences. Family firms provide more than 50 per cent of the employment in Nigeria and substantial employment in other nations (42 per cent in the USA); therefore, it is important that appropriate techniques be developed for successful management. The findings in this study on human resources practice are closely related to Ouchi's model of the clan mechanism and a study designed with this mechanism as a base may prove to be a good explanation.

A comparative study of family firms is another interesting area of research. Considering that the prevalence of family firms is common to both industrialized and developing countries, a comparative study designed to compare the influence of environment and technology on their development will go a long way towards developing theories about these unique types of organizations. This study could also test other related variables to see how the firms compare. This research may lead to the discussion of what may be called 'the American/Nigerian corporate clan or tribe'.

Another area of research interest is decision-making in family firms. In all the cases of this study, the chairman and majority members of the board of directors have been members of the family. The directors were responsible for all policy decisions. This structure definitely implies all symptoms of group-think. Research that could examine the implications of this possible group-think effect on the effectiveness of the decisions is in order for better understanding of and consultation with family firms.

To understand the operations of these firms, especially the highly diversified firms in Nigeria, there is a need to study the selection and implementation of strategies and structures as the organization evolves. This study did not go into this issue of implementation in detail and there is a need for this understanding to facilitate the determination of issues and thus make appropriate recommendations for their resolution. In general, there is a need for a wide variety of studies on family firms, mostly to determine ways of reducing some of the problems facing firms and families and also to retain and improve their growing economic contribution to the societies.

Conclusions

The findings in this study are the results of an exploratory research which has little or no precedent in Nigeria and few precedents in the USA and other industrialized nations of Western Europe. For example, in the evolution patterns, the findings partially (process) support the model by Scott and others who have studied stages of organizational development, but differ in their significant findings, taking into account that these authors took ecology for granted. In the issues of conflict and conflict resolution processes among family firms, the findings were also consistent with the factors and some processes developed by Barnes and Hershon, and Levinson and Beckhard. However, no studies have examined the issue of the influence of family constellations and other ecological factors on the evolution patterns in the West and this study is the first of its kind in Nigeria. Three methodological issues will be addressed here.

1   Generalizability of the findings to other family firms. This study briefly examined over 78 firms and studied eight in detail. This sample is small. However, the selected firms represented the heterogeneous nature of the society. The findings at specific firms appear to represent the ethnic background of each group in the society. It is generally expected that further study will show the same trend in evolution patterns. Slight modification or differences may be developed as a result of the growing tendency for the younger generation to shed some of the rigid traditional norms for some modern practices. This development will have most implications for the conflict resolution mechanisms, though the outcome is not expected to be radically different. In addition, industrialization and modernization will also influence stages observed as Nigeria's economic growth plans are implemented and competition becomes more intense.

2   Generalizability to non-family controlled firms in the country. There are about 20,000 (all indigenous) established firms in Nigeria. The characteristics of less than 80 firms were briefly examined in order to determine their status for classification. The data from the firms involved in this study showed that, in terms of strategic patterns of development, no differences may be found while some moderation in the structural determination may exist. Evidence from the Ginano Company, which is family owned but has little family involvement in the operations, indicates that private firms develop structures based on existing strategies rather than family structure. Contrasting the existence of conflict originating at the family level, the researcher would expect to see more conflict at

the organizational level just as the findings in the Ginano Group in this study demonstrate.

3 Generalizability to other developing countries. Whether the findings here are generalizable to other developing nations is questionable. However, as mentioned earlier, it would be interesting to explore this phenomenon in other nations to determine whether the findings are unique to Nigeria or are generalizable to other non-industrialized nations. I would expect some differences considering that:

   (a) Nigeria is blessed with at least one rather unique means of development (oil). Not many developing nations have that resource.

   (b) There are cultural and environmental factors which have been determined to have major influences on the findings of this study.

But, like the findings in Nigeria and in the USA on stages of development and factors affecting conflict, I expect the organizations to go through phases of development and for the families' or firms' conflicts to be a function of similar or related factors. African countries as a whole, and West African nations in particular, stand to benefit from this study, primarily because the cultures of these Third World nations are more similar to Nigerian cultures than other Third World nations such as Indonesia, Bangladesh, Kampuchea, Vietnam, Malaysia and Sri Lanka.

These findings are dependent on several factors — therefore generalizability in the above three levels should be undertaken with caution. In effect, it is expected that the findings of this study will have a broad impact on the management field in general, and on management in Third World countries in particular, because:

1 The findings will provide the basis for the development of appropriate techniques in Third World countries through better understanding of their respective organizational characteristics. This step is based on the findings that there are some differences in the evolution patterns compared to Scott's and other models which did not consider ecological factors.

2 The finding that social anthropological or ecological factors, such as the family relationships, influence the firms' structure should spur further research into family firms. This understanding again will lead towards better management of family businesses all over the world. This finding is important, considering the impact of family/private firms on the economy, especially in the rural community development of the Third World countries.

3   The Nigerian government actions, designed to achieve economic development objectives, were observed to have substantial influence on the growth strategies of organizations, thus providing evidence for organizations in Third World countries to consider strategically most government development plans.

Notes

1   W.C. Hamner and D. Organ, *Organizational Behavior: An Applied Psychological Approach*, Business Publications, Dallas, 1978, p.124.

Bibliography

Akarele, A., Olufune, D. and Adebayo, O. (1978), 'Need achievement, self-concept and academic achievement of children from polygamous and monogamous homes', *The Nigerian Journal of Economic and Social Studies*, vol.20, no.1, March.

Aluko, S. (1984), 'The progress of industrialization in Nigeria since independence', *Daily Times of Nigeria*, 1 October, p.3.

Anyansi-Archibong, Chi. B. (1986), 'Strategy and structure of enterprise: implications of family constellations for family business', *Proceedings of the Small Business Institute Directors' Conference*, Washington DC, February.

Anyansi-Archibong, Chi. B. (1986), 'Profile of women entrepreneurs', *Proceedings of the 31st World Conference of the International Council of Small Business*, Denver, June.

Anyansi-Archibong, Chi. B. (1987), 'Small business and entrepreneurship research: beyond characteristic identification', *Proceedings of SBDA*, February.

Barnes, L.B. and Hershon, S.A. (1976), 'Transferring power in the family business', *Harvard Business Review*, July–August.

Bassell, J.E. and Roberts, R.A.J. (1963), 'Income and expenditure in relation to age of cultivator and education of the family', *Unzalpi*, Report no.5, University of Nottingham.

Becker, B.M. and Tillman, F. (1981), 'Management checklist for a family business', *Management Aids*, no.3,002, US Small Business Administration Support Services Division.

Becker, H.S. (1958), 'Problems of inference and proof in participant observation', *American Sociological Review*, vol.23, December.

Becker, H.S. (1970), *Sociological Work: Methods and Substance*, Aldine, Chicago.

Beckhard, R. (1969), *Organization Development: Strategies and Models*, Addison Wesley, Reading, MA.

Beckhard, R. and Dyer, W.G.Jr. (1983), 'SMR Forum: managing change in the family firm — issues and strategies', *Sloan ManagementReview*, Spring, pp.59—65.

Beckhard, R. and Dyer, W.G.Jr. (1983), 'Managing continuity in family firms', *Organizational Dynamics*, Summer.

Beparta, P.C. (1964), 'Familial structure and fertility', *Proceedings of the Fifty-first and Fifty-second Sessions of the Indian Science Congress, Part III*, Indian Schoence Congress, Calcutta.

Burch, T.K. and Gendell, M. (1971), 'Extended family structure and fertility: some conceptual and methodological issues', *Journal of Marriage and Family*, vol.32, pp.277—86.

Burns, T. and Stalker, G.M. (1966), *The Management of Innovation*, 2nd edn, Tavistock, London.

Calder, G.H. (1961), 'The peculiar problems of family business', *Business Horizon*, vol.4, June, pp.96—7.

Carr, M. (1979), 'Economically appropriate technology for developing countries: an annotated bibliography', *IT Developing Group (ITDG)*, Sections on Agriculture and Manufacturing.

Chandler, A.D. (1962), *Strategy and Structure*, MIT Press, Cambridge MA.

Chandler, A.D. (1977), *The Visible Hand*, The Belknop Press of Harvard University Press, Cambridge MA.

Channon, D.F. (1971), *The Strategy and Structure of British Enterprise*, unpublished doctoral dissertation, Harvard Business School, Division of Research, Boston.

Channon, D.F. (1979), 'Leadership and corporate performance in the service industry', *Journal of Management Studies*, vol.16, pp.185—201.

Churchill, N.C. and Lewis, V.L. (1983), 'Growing concerns. . .', *Harvard Business Review*, May—June, p.30.

Cohn, T. and Lindberg, R.A. (1974), 'Survival and growth: management strategies for small firms', *AMACOM*, New York.

Coser, L. (1956), *The Functions of Social Conflict*, The Free Press, New York.

Davis, P. (1982), *The Influence of Life Style on Father-Son Work Relationships in Family Companies*, unpublished doctoral dissertation, Harvard Business School.

Davis, P. (1983), 'Realizing the potential of the family business', *Organizational Dynamics*, Summer.

Davis, P. (1984), 'Family business: perspectives on change', *The Wharton Annual*.

Donnelley, R.G. (1964), 'The family business', *Harvard Business Review*, vol.42, July—August.

Downey, H. Kirk and Ireland, R.D. (1979), 'Quantitative versus qualitative: environmental assessment in organizational studies', *Administrative Science Quarterly*, vol.24, December.

Druker, P. (1973), *Management: Tasks, Responsibilities, Practices*, Harper and Row, New York.

Dubin, R. (1976), *Theory Building*, The Free Press, New York.

Dyas, G.P. (1972), *The Strategy and Structure of French Industrial Enterprise*, unpublished doctoral disseration, Harvard Business School.

Emery, F.E. and Trist, E.L. (1975), *Towards Social Ecology*, Pelnum Publishing Co.

Epstein, T.S. (1975), *Economics and Social Aspects of Labor Utilization in the Tropics*, International Crops Research Institute, Hyderabad, India.

Ervenlong, J. and Parsons, H.K. (1950), 'How family labor affects Wisconsin farming', *Research Bulletin*, vol.167, University of Wisconsin, Madison.

Evered, R. and Louis, M.R. (1981), 'Alternative perspectives in the organizational science: "Inquiry from the Inside" and "Inquiry from the Outside"', *Academy of Management Review*, vol.6, no.3, pp.385—95.

Filley, A.C. and Aldage, J.R. (1978), 'Characteristics and measurement of an organizational typology', *Academy and Management Journal*, vol.21, no.4.

Filley, A.C. and House, R.J. (1976), *Managerial Processes and Organizational Behavior*, 2nd edn, Scott, Foresman, Glenview Il.

Freedman, R. and Takeshita, J.Y. (1969), *Family Planning in Taiwan: An Experiment in Social Change*, Princeton University Press, Princeton. (A follow-up to 1964 study.)

Friedlander, I. and Pickle, H. (1967), 'Seven societal criteria of organizational success', *Personal Psychology*, no.2, pp.165—78.

Galbraith, J.R. and Nathason, D.A. (1979), 'The role of organizational structure and processes', *Strategy Implementation*, Little Brown, Boston, pp.249—83.

Gerth, H. and Mills, C.W. (eds) (1958), *From Max Weber: Essays in Sociology*, Oxford University Press, New York.

Gilmore, H.L. (1978), 'Mining in a developing nation: a quality systems design application', *Quality Progress*, vol.11, pp.14—15.

Glaser, B.G. and Strauss, A.L. (1965), 'Discovery of substantive theory: a basic strategy underlying qualitative research', *American Behavioral Scientist*, vol.8, February, pp.5—12.

257

Glaser, B.G. and Strauss, A.L. (1967), *The Discovery of Grounded Theory: Strategies for Qualitative Research*, AVC, Chicago.

Glick, P.C. (1947), 'The family cycle', *American Sociological Review*, vol.12, April, pp.164—74.

Glick, P.C. (1955), 'The life cycle of the family', *Marriage and Family Living*, vol.18, February, pp.3—9.

Glueck, W.F. and Willis, R. (1979), 'Documentary sources and strategic management research', *Academy of Management Review*, vol.4, pp.95—102.

Graves, J.P. (1978), 'Successful management and organizational mugging' in J.Paap (ed.), *New Directions in Human Resources Management*, Prentice Hall, Englewood Cliffs, NJ.

Greiner, L.E. (1972), 'Evolution and revolution as organizations grow', *Harvard Business Review*, July—August, p.37.

Hagen, E.E. (1962), *On the Theory of Social Change*, The Dorsey Press, Inc., Homewood, Il.

Hall, D.T. (1972), 'A model of coping with role conflict: the role behavior of college educated women', *Administrative Science Quarterly*, December, pp.471—85.

Hamner, W.C. and Organ, D. (1978), *Organizational Behavior: An Applied Psychological Approach*, Business Publications Inc., Dallas.

Handwerker, W.P. (1970), 'Kinship, friendship and business failure among market sellers in Monrovia, Liberia', *Africa*, vol.42, pp.228—301.

Harrell-Bond, B. (1977), 'Studying élites: some special problems' in Michael A. Rynkiewich and James P. Spradley (eds), *Ethics and Anthropology: Dilemmas in Fieldwork*, Wiley, New York, pp.110—22.

Harrison, A. (1965), 'Some features of farm business structures', *Journal of Agricultural Economics*, vol.XVI, no.3.

Hatvany, N. and Pucik, V. (1981), 'An integrated management system: lessons from the Japanese experience', *Academy of Management Review*, vol.6.

Hershon, S.A. (1975), *The Problem of Management Succession in Family Businesses*, unpublished doctoral dissertation, Harvard Business School, Boston MA.

Hill, P. (1972), *Rural Hausa*, Cambridge University Press.

Hofstede, G. (1980a), *Cultures Consequences*, Sage Publications, Beverly Hills, CA.

Hofstede, G. (1980b), 'Motivation, leadership and organization: do American theories apply abroad?', *Organizational Dynamics*, Summer, pp.42—62.

Hollander, B. (1984), *The Family Business as a System*, a paper presented at the Academy of Management Meeting, Boston MA.

Holsti, O.R. (1969), *Content Analysis for the Social Sciences and Humanities*, Addison-Wesley, Reading, MA.

Jaeger, Alfred M. (1984), *An Examination of the Appropriateness of Organization Development Overseas*, paper presented at Academy of Management 44th Annual Meeting, International Management Division, Boston MA.

Kanter, R.M. (1977), *Work and Family in the United States: A Critical Review and Agenda for Research and Policy*, Russell Saga Publication, New York.

Kaplan, A. and Golden, B. (1964), *The Conduct of Inquiry*, Chandler, San Francisco.

Katz, D. and Kahn, R.L. (1978), *The Social Psychology of Organizations*, 2nd edn, John Wiley and Sons, New York.

Keesing, R. (1974), 'Theories of culture', *Annual Review of Anthropology*, pp.73–9.

Kepner, E. (1983), *The Family and the Firm: A Coevolutionary Perspective*.

Kilman, R.H. and Herden, R.P. (1976), 'Towards a systematic methodology for evaluating the impact of interventions on organizational effectiveness', *Academy of Management Review*, July, pp.87–98.

Kindleberger, C. (1965), *Economic Development*, 2nd edn, McGraw-Hill Book Company, New York.

Kurian, G.T. (1983), *Nigeria: Encyclopedia of the Third-World* (rev. edn), vol.2.

Landsberg, I. (1983), 'Managing human resources in family firms: the problem of institutional overlap', *Organizational Dynamics*, Summer.

Lasswell, H.D. (1968), 'The future of comparative method', *Comparative Politics*, vol.1, pp.3–18.

Lauer, R.H. (1982), *Perspectives on Social Change*, 3rd edn, Allyn and Bacon Inc., Boston.

Lawrence, P.R. and Lorsch, J.W. (1965), *Organization and Environment: Managing Differentiation and Integration*, Irwin, Homewood Il.

Lawrence, P.R. and Lorsch, J.W. (1967), *Organization and Environment*, Irwin, Homewood Il.

Lawrence, P.R. and Lorsch, J.W. (1969), *Developing Organizations: Diagnosis and Actions*, Addison-Wesley, Reading, MA.

Levinson, H. (1971), 'Conflicts that plague family business', *Harvard Business Review*, March–April, p.90.

Levinson, H. (1983), 'Consulting with family business: what to look for', *Organizational Dynamics*, Summer.

Levinson, R.E. (1975), 'Making your family business more profitable', *University of Michigan Business Review*, May, pp.24–9.

Levinson, R.E. (1981), 'Problems in managing a family owned business', *Management Aids*, no.2.004, US Small Business Administration Support Service Division, Washington DC.

Lewin, L. (1955), *A Dynamic Theory of Personality*, McGraw-Hill, New York.

Lewis, A.W. (1970), *Theory of Economic Development*, George Allen and Unwin Limited, London.

Lofland, J. (1971), *Analyzing Social Settings*, Wardsworth, Belmont CA.

Longnecker, J.G. and Shoen, J.E. (1978), 'Management succession in the family business', *Small Business Management*, vol.16, July.

Lopata, H.Z. (1966), 'The life cycle of the house-wife', *Sociology and Social Research*, vol.51, pp.5–22.

McClelland, D.C. and Winler, X. (1969), *Motivating Economic Achievement*, Free Press, New York.

McClelland, D.C. (1976), *The Achieving Society*, Irvington Publishers Inc., New York.

Mead, M. (1977), *Letters from the Field 1925–1975*, Harper and Row, New York.

Meyers, D. (1973), *Personal Administration: A Point of View and a Method*, 7th edn, McGraw-Hill Inc., New York.

Miles, M.B. (1979), 'Qualitative data as an attractive nuisance: the problem of analysis', *Administrative Science Quarterly*, vol.24, December, pp.590–61.

Miles, R.H. (1980), *Macro Organizational Behavior*, Scott Foresman, Glenview Il.

Miles, R. and Snow, C. (1978), *Organizational Strategy, Structure and Process*, McGraw-Hill, New York.

Merton, R. (1972), 'Insiders and outsiders: a chapter in the sociology of knowledge' in *Varieties of Political Expression in Sociology*, University of Chicago Press, Chicago.

Mintzberg, H. (1983), *The Structuring of Organization*, Prentice-Hall, Englewood Cliffs, NJ.

Mintzberg, H. (1984), 'Power and organization life cycles', *Academy of Management Review*, vol.9, no.2, pp.207–24.

Mitroff, I. (1974), *The Subjective Side of Science*, Elsevier, Amsterdam.

Morgan, G. and Smircich, L. (1980), 'The case for qualitative research', *Academy of Management Review*, vol.5, no.4, pp.491–500.

Nafzinger, E.W. (1977), *African Capitalism: A Case Study of Nigerian Entrepreneurship*, Stanford, California.

Narayanan, V.K. (1975), *The Middle Class: Family, Work and their Interrelationship*, unpublished manuscript.

Neilsen, E.H. (1976), 'Understanding and managing intergroup conflict' in P. Lawrence, L. Barnes and J. Lorsch (eds), *Readings: Organizational Behavior and Administration*, Richard D. Irwin Inc., Homewood Il.

'Nigeria. Detailed Survey of Progress: Focus on Trade, Banking, Industry and Agriculture', *Financial Times*, 3 November 1981.

'Nigeria. Government Shifts Focus of Agricultural Policy from Large to Smaller Scale Producers', *West African Magazine*, 26 October 1981, p.2492.

'Nigeria. National Government Expenditure for Industry Development by Type', *African Business*, December 1981.

Okali, *et al.* (1974), 'Report on the socio-economic characteristics of the Ashanti Cocoa Rehabilitation Project', *ISSER*, University of Ghana, Legon.

Olakoku, F.A. (1979), *The Structure of the Nigerian Economy*, New York.

Onyemelukwe, C.C. (1967), 'Problems of industrial planning and management in Nigeria', *World Bank Encyclopedia of Nations*, University Press.

Oppong, C. (1978), 'Marriage, fertility and parentage', *Journal of Economic and Social Research*, vol.7, no.2.

Ouchi, W. (1981), *Theory Z*, Addison-Wesley, Reading MA.

Patton, M.Q. (1980), *Qualitative Evaluation Methods*, Sage Publications, Beverly Hills CA.

Pavan, R.J. (1972), *The Strategy and Structure of Italian Enterprise*, unpublished doctoral dissertation, Harvard Business School, June.

Pfeffer, J. (1978), *Power in Organizations*, Harper and Row, Marsfield MA.

Piore, M.J. (1979), 'Qualitative research techniques in economics', *Administrative Science Quarterly*, vol.24, December.

Pondy, L.R. (1967), 'Organizational conflict: concepts and models', *Administrative Science Quarterly*, vol.12, pp.296—320.

Rake, A. (1979), 'Drive for higher education', *New African Development*, February, pp.83—6.

Reichardt, C.S. and Cook, T.D. (1979), *Qualitative and Quantitative Methods in Evaluation Research*, Sage Publications, Beverly Hills CA.

Riley, M. (1963), *Sociological Research*, Harcourt, Brace, Jovanovich, New York.

Rostow, W.W. (1960), *The Stages of Economic Growth*, Cambridge University Press, Cambridge.

Rowe, J.D. 'Qualitative research methodology in the social sciences: issues, methods and applications', *Vance Bibliography*, Public Administration Series: Bibliography #P1146, ISBN: 0-88066-396-0.

Rumelt, R.P. (1972), *Strategy, Structure and Financial Performance of the Fortune '500', 1950–1970*, unpublished DBA dissertation, Harvard Business School.

Rumelt, R.P. (1974), *Strategy, Structure and Economic Performance*, Division of Research, Graduate School of Business Administration, Harvard University, Boston MA.

Safavi, F. (1981), 'A model of management education in Africa', *Academy of Management Review*, vol.6, no.2, pp.319–31.

Saiyadan, M.S. and Nambudiri, C.N.S. (1981), 'Attitudes and values of upcoming Nigerian professionals: a question of concern', *Business Publishing Division*, College of Business Administration, Georgia State University, Atlanta GA.

Sarpong, K. and Rawls, R. (1976), 'A study of the transfer of training from developed to less developed countries: the case of Ghana', *Journal of Management Studies*, vol.13, no.1, pp.16–31.

Schendel, D. and Hafer, C.W. (1978), *Strategy Formulation: Analytical Concepts*, West Publishing Company, St. Paul, Minn.

Schien, Edgar H. (1981), 'SMR Forum: does Japanese management style have a message for American managers?', *Sloan Management Review*, Autumn, pp.55–68.

Scott, B.R. (1971), *Stages of Corporate Development*, Report no. 9-371-274 BP 998, Harvard University Intercollegiate Case Clearing House, Boston MA.

Selznick, P. (1948), 'Foundations of the theory of organization', *American Sociological Review*, vol.13, pp.25–35.

Selznick, P. (1957), *Leadership in Administration*, Harper and Row, New York.

Siegel, S. (1956), *Non-Parametric Statistics for the Behavioral Sciences*, McGraw-Hill Book Company, New York.

Starbuck, W.H. (1965), 'Organizational growth and development' in M.J.G. March (ed.), *Handbook of Organizations*, Rand-McNally, Chicago Il.

Steimetz, L.L. (1969), 'Critical stages of small business growth', *Business Horizon*, February, p.29.

Suzuki, Y. (1980), 'The strategy and structure of the top 100 Japanese industrial enterprises 1950–1970', *Strategic Management Journal*, vol.1, pp.265–91, John Wiley and Sons Ltd.

Tashakori, M. (1977), *Management Succession: From the Owner-Founder to the Professional President*, unpublished doctoral dissertation, Harvard Business School, Boston MA.

Thanheiser, Heinz T. (1972), *Strategy and Structure of German Industrial Enterprise*, unpublished doctoral dissertation, Harvard Business School.

Thomas, K.W. (1976), 'Conflict and conflict management' in M. Dunnette (ed.), *Handbook of Industrial and Organizational Psychology*, Chicago.

Thompson, J.D. (1967), *Organizations in Action*, McGraw-Hill, New York.

Trow, D.B. (1961), 'Executive succession in small companies', *Administrative Science Quarterly*, vol.24, December, pp.520—6.

Udy, S. (1959), *Organization of Work*, Human Relations Area Files Press, New Haven CT.

Van Maanan, J. (1979), 'Reclaiming qualitative methods for organizational research: a preface', *Administrative Science Quarterly*, vol.24, December, pp.520—6.

Walton, R. (1969), *Interpersonal Peacemaking: Confrontations and Third-Party Consultations*, Addison-Wesley, Reading MA.

Webb, E., Donald, T., Campbell, R., Schwartz, I. and Sechrest, L. (1966), *Unobtrusive Measures: Nonreactive Research in the Social Sciences*, Rand McNally College Publishing Company, Chicago Il.

Williams, J. (1976), *Nigeria: Economy and Society*, Totowa Publishers, Totowa NJ.

Williamson, O. (1975), *Markets and Hierarchies: Analysis and Antitrust Implications*, Free Press, New York.

Woodward, J. (1965), *Industrial Organization: Theory and Practice*, Oxford University Press, London.

Wrigley, L. (1970), *Divisional Autonomy and Diversification*, unpublished doctoral dissertation, Harvard Business School, Cambridge MA.

Yin, R. and Herald, K. (1975), 'Using the case survey method to analyze policy studies', *Administrative Science Quarterly*, vol.20, pp.271—81.

Zelditch, Morris Jr. (1962), 'Some methodological problems of field studies', *Journal of Sociology*, vol.67, pp.566—76.

Zukermann, P.S. (1978), 'Growth cycle, income stream and decision-making: a case study of Yoruba smallholders', *The Nigerian Journal of Economic and Social Studies*, Lagos.

Index

industries (cont.)
  small-scale, to be developed 21
inefficiency 251
inflation 88, 90
  quasi-loans as hedge against 186
innovation 13
integration
  backward 5, 143, 147, 153, 172, 233
  forward 5, 143, 169, 172
  of related firms 154
  vertical and horizontal 143, 238
interaction pattern 5
International Labor Organization (ILO) Report 1969 18
International Monetary Fund (IMF), no loan 90
interviews 38
investment in basic industries 242
iron and steel complex 86

Japan, organizational development 59—61
joint venture agreement 172

labour, skilled and unskilled 81
language 2
language diversity, and rivalry 78
lease-purchasing, concept of 185
limited interaction 221
  conflict reduction processes 210—15
liquid assets 147
liquidity 183
living standards, improving 173
loans, external 130—1
local borrowing 131

majority control, founder or family 64
management
  influences on effectiveness of 2—3

management (cont.)
  low quality of 18
  in Nigeria 202—21
  opportunistic 202—3
  poor 88
management practices
  comparative 233—43
  congruent with social/economic norms 246
  and implications, future of 249—50
management problems, developing countries 242—3
management programmes
  need for appropriate programmes 242
  need for better quality and co-ordination 18
management research 24
management styles 245—6, 247
management techniques 5
management theory, development of 246, 248—51
  concept of 248
  field study 248—51
management theory and practice, not indigenized 244—5
management training and education 9, 12, 18, 242
manager, ascendency of 52
marketing activities 215
markets 141
mediation 219, 241
mineral deposits 81, 82, 83
mining/extraction 84
multidivisional structure, Europe and Japan 56
Muslims (Islam) 80

National Development Plan (1962—68) 86—7
National Development Plan (1970—74) 18—19